The Art of Faulkner's Novels

THE ART OF FAULKNER'S NOVELS

By Peter Swiggart

UNIVERSITY OF TEXAS PRESS · AUSTIN

Library of Congress Catalog Card Number 62–14504

Copyright © 1962 by Peter Swiggart
All Rights Reserved
Manufactured in the United States of America

International Standard Book Number 0-292-73166-3
Fourth Printing, 1970

*This book is published with the assistance of a grant
from the University Research Institute of The University of Texas*

TO MARY

Acknowledgments of Permissions

The editor of the *Sewanee Review* has granted permission to include in this critical study various sections which had been previously published in that journal.

Liveright Publishing Corporation has granted permission to use quotations as follows:

From *Mosquitoes,* by William Faulkner. Copyright 1955 by William Faulkner. Reprinted by permission of Liveright Publishing Corporation.

From *Soldiers' Pay,* by William Faulkner. Copyright 1954 by William Faulkner. Reprinted by permission of Liveright Publishing Corporation.

Random House has granted permission to use quotations as follows:

From *The Sound and the Fury,* by William Faulkner. Copyright 1929 and renewed 1956 by William Faulkner. Reprinted by permission of Random House, Inc.

From *The Hamlet,* by William Faulkner. Copyright 1940 by William Faulkner. Reprinted by permission of Random House, Inc.

From *As I Lay Dying,* by William Faulkner. Copyright 1930 and renewed 1957 by William Faulkner. Reprinted by permission of Random House, Inc.

From *Requiem for a Nun,* by William Faulkner. Copyright 1950, 1951 by William Faulkner. Reprinted by permission of Random House, Inc.

From *Absalom, Absalom!* by William Faulkner. Copyright 1936 by William Faulkner. Reprinted by permission of Random House, Inc.

From *The Mansion,* by William Faulkner. © Copyright 1955, 1959 by William Faulkner. Reprinted by permission of Random House, Inc.

From *Sanctuary,* by William Faulkner. Copyright 1931 and renewed 1958 by William Faulkner. Reprinted by permission of Random House, Inc.

From *The Town,* by William Faulkner. © Copyright 1957 by William Faulkner. Reprinted by permission of Random House, Inc.

From "All the Dead Pilots" in *Collected Stories of William Faulkner.* Copyright 1931 and renewed 1959 by William Faulkner. Reprinted by permission of Random House, Inc.

From *Go Down, Moses,* by William Faulkner. Copyright 1941 by William Faulkner. Reprinted by permission of Random House, Inc.

From *Sartoris,* by William Faulkner. Copyright 1929 and renewed 1956 by William Faulkner. Reprinted by permission of Random House, Inc.

From *Pylon,* by William Faulkner. Copyright 1935 and renewed 1962 by William Faulkner. Reprinted by permission of Random House, Inc.

From *Light in August,* by William Faulkner. Copyright 1932 and renewed 1959 by William Faulkner. Reprinted by permission of Random House, Inc.

From *A Fable,* by William Faulkner. Copyright 1950, 1954 by William Faulkner. Reprinted by permission of Random House, Inc.

From *Intruder in the Dust,* by William Faulkner. Copyright 1948 by William Faulkner. Reprinted by permission of Random House, Inc.

From *The Wild Palms,* by William Faulkner. Copyright 1939 by William Faulkner. Reprinted by permission of Random House, Inc.

From *The Reivers,* by William Faulkner. © Copyright 1962 by William Faulkner. Reprinted by permission of Random House, Inc.

Chatto and Windus, Ltd., has given permission for these quotations to appear in publications within the British Commonwealth.

CONTENTS

PREFACE

In this study I discuss Faulkner's narrative techniques as a whole and provide close readings of four major novels, *The Sound and the Fury, As I Lay Dying, Light in August,* and *Absalom, Absalom!* The organization of chapters indicates my effort both to explore elements of Faulkner's artistry in all his novels and story collections and to treat individual novels as distinct works of art in which these elements are successfully fused. In the first two chapters of Part One I examine Faulkner's stylized characterization and isolate various techniques by which he establishes moral and social themes without sacrificing crucial elements of narrative realism. The next two chapters concern Faulkner's use of social mythology and the presence in his work of extreme contrasts between figures representing rational or "puritan" man and figures suggesting primitive or natural forces. In the final chapter of Part One I discuss Faulkner's use of the interior monologue and other devices by which point-of-view problems are both created and solved. Part Two consists of detailed analyses of the four novels, with an emphasis upon elements of language structure and theme, as well as characterization. Part Three is devoted to publications subsequent to *The Hamlet* (1940), and compares these later works to more successful earlier ones.

The original version of this study, very different in emphasis and scope, was submitted as a graduate thesis at Yale University. I am deeply indebted to Norman Holmes Pearson, who directed the thesis, and to other members of the Yale graduate faculty, in particular Cleanth Brooks, Frederick A. Pottle, and Louis Martz. A number of friends have read portions of the final manuscript and offered helpful criticism, among them Joseph J. Moldenhauer, Julian Moynahan, and Jay Halio. I remember with great pleasure the lectures given by John Hite and Lawrance Thompson at Princeton in 1948 and 1949, which first introduced me to the delight of studying Faulkner's novels.

Preface

The page numbers appended to quotations from Faulkner publications are drawn whenever possible from easily obtainable Modern Library editions. Otherwise the references are to first editions. In the case of *Absalom, Absalom!*, *Go Down, Moses,* and *Sanctuary* the pagination in the Modern Library text is the same as in the first edition. In an appendix I have provided a list of the Faulkner works referred to, plus publication dates. There is no general discussion of Faulkner criticism in this study, and I have included relatively few references to such criticism. An excellent bibliography of Faulkner criticism is provided in *William Faulkner: Three Decades of Criticism,* edited by Frederick J. Hoffman and Olga W. Vickery (East Lansing: Michigan State University Press, 1960).

PETER SWIGGART

The University of Texas
Austin

PART ONE

Faulkner's Narrative World

Chapter One

FAULKNER AS ROMANCER

$\mathcal{I}$N RESTATING the old distinction between the novel and the romance, Northrop Frye isolates two conceptions of characterization. "The romancer does not attempt to create 'real people' so much as stylized figures which expand into psychological archetypes." This is why the romance "so often radiates a glow of subjective intensity that the novel lacks, and why a suggestion of allegory is constantly creeping in around its fringes." [1] One may agree with Henry James that the novel-romance distinction is an unnecessary concession to the "occasional queer predicaments" of critics and general readers. [2] Nevertheless, Mr. Frye's description of prose-

[1] Northrop Frye, *Anatomy of Criticism* (Princeton, Princeton University Press, 1957), p. 304.
[2] "The Art of Fiction," originally published in *Longman's Magazine* (September, 1884) and reprinted in *Partial Portraits* (1888) and *The Art of Fiction and Other Essays by Henry James* (New York, Oxford University Press, 1948), p. 14.

3

romance characterization is a useful means of isolating William Faulkner's work from that of contemporary realists and of relating his novels to the nineteenth-century romance tradition associated with Hawthorne and Melville. Faulkner is a twentieth-century novelist, deeply influenced by modern experiments in narrative point of view and the creation of realistic effects; but his use of characterization as a direct means of expressing moral and social concerns associates him with earlier American writers.

According to Mr. Frye the characters of a novel are placed in a relatively stable environment and given conventional social *personae*. But a prose romance is concerned with human individuality, and something "nihilistic and untamable" threatens to break from its pages.[3] The novel tends to expand into a fictional approach to history, whereas most "historical novels" are romances. According to Hawthorne the author of a romance must be faithful to the truth of the human heart, but he may present that truth "under circumstances, to a great extent, of the writer's own choosing or creation." [4] The romancer's emphasis upon man's unchanging moral nature, in contrast to changing environments, frees him from the obligation to give a realistic account of social appearances. Faulkner seems to echo Hawthorne's words by insisting, in his Nobel Prize speech, that the writer concern himself with "the old verities and truths of the heart, the old universal truths lacking which any story is ephemeral and doomed." [5] Both authors explore the moral and psychological truths of the heart, and both employ stylized characters placed in situations designed primarily to illustrate their symbolic or allegorical function.

It might be added to Mr. Frye's description of the novel as a kind of history that the writer of the prose romance has the obligation not to create history but to organize a fantastical world in such a way that it takes the place of history in the reader's imagination. This

[3] Northrop Frye, *op. cit.*, p. 305.

[4] Preface to *The House of the Seven Gables*, in *The Complete Novels and Selected Tales of Nathaniel Hawthorne*, edited by Norman Holmes Pearson (New York, Modern Library, 1937), p. 243.

[5] "The Stockholm Address," in *William Faulkner: Three Decades of Criticism*, edited by Frederick J. Hoffman and Olga W. Vickery (East Lansing, Michigan State University Press, 1960), p. 348.

task of creating believable incidents within an unbelievable world is made difficult by the use of two-dimensional characters. If the romancer wishes to induce in his reader the illusion of a realistic action he must act to conceal the fact of stylization in his work and yet emphasize the patterns of symbolism made possible by the stylization. This can best be achieved by narrative devices that dissuade the reader from comparing the characters to real people or the narrative situations to actual events. The romancer may create intense and vivid narrative action, as in melodrama, or he may rely instead upon a skilful use of symbolism and upon other devices of narrative craft.

Faulkner's narrative achievements may be explained in terms of his ability to express abstract themes by means of stylized characters without detracting from the dramatic force, and the apparent realism, of his narrative situations. Arbitrary stylization is compensated for in his work by the creation of characters who have explicit symbolic functions, yet live in the reader's imagination as if they were real people. The desire both to humanize his characters and to magnify their symbolic importance is responsible for Faulkner's numerous experiments with the interior monologue and other devices involving point of view of narration. His favorite technique is to conceal the stylized function of a major character until the reader has become familiar with what is assumed to be a realistic social atmosphere. Meanwhile an atmosphere of mystery surrounds the important figures, who often remain in the dramatic background. Faulkner both uses and parodies the devices of realistic narration by giving the reader a wealth of unrelated details and unreconciled meanings. But when the complexities of style and symbolism are penetrated, the reader discovers that each item is part of an artistic whole. At this point the reader is usually too absorbed in the symbolism and in the complexity of narrative relationships to be much disturbed by the two-dimensional characterization. The Gothic individuality of Joe Christmas and Thomas Sutpen would be a discordant element in realistic fiction. But in *Light in August* and *Absalom, Absalom!* their stylization supports and is supported by Faulkner's thematic analysis of the guilt-ridden puritan South. Similar techniques are used in Hawthorne's stories, where mysterious character traits are openly allegorical, and in *Moby Dick,* where Captain Ahab's personality is inseparable from the symbolism of the white whale.

Another device in Faulkner's work for maintaining the illusion of a representative social world is the use of minor figures who function either as outright narrators or as observers with a point of view that is mirrored by the semiomniscient narrator. Such witness-figures tend to be less stylized than the characters about whom they speculate. In this way a bridge is established between the reader's social world and the fantastic action of a prose romance.

The clearest example of this technique is the narration of *Absalom, Absalom!* where the actions of Thomas Sutpen and his family are filtered through the conflicting reactions of a number of partially informed witness-narrators. A related technique is used in *The Sound and the Fury* and *As I Lay Dying* in that the secrets of characterization are at first kept hidden by the complexities of interior-monologue narration. In these novels and in others Faulkner gives the reader a wealth of factual information which cannot be properly interpreted until the obsessions and motivations to action of the principal figures have been understood. The reader cannot correlate the details that flicker through Quentin Compson's neurotic mind until the youth's suicidal obsessions, and what they signify about the Southern aristocracy, have been grasped. There is very little if any social allegory in *As I Lay Dying,* but a similar use is made of the interior-monologue narration. Here it is the complexity of family relationships, in particular the role played by the living as well as the dead Addie Bundren, that the reader must comprehend.

André Malraux's statement that *Sanctuary* combines the form of the detective novel with the themes of Greek tragedy [6] can be applied in a general sense to all of Faulkner's novels. Faulkner interests the reader simultaneously in problems of narrative fact and in questions involving moral and psychological concerns, the truths of the human heart "in conflict with itself." He establishes intriguing and often violent dramatic situations in which the reader is encouraged to work out for himself complex problems of motivation

[6] André Malraux, "Préface à 'Sanctuaire' de William Faulkner," *La Nouvelle Revue Française,* 41 (November, 1933), translated and reprinted in *Yale French Studies,* No. 10 (Fall, 1952).

and moral theme. The reader is often aided in this task by tne presence of witness-figures who are themselves psychological and sociological investigators. In "The Bear" (*Go Down, Moses*) the reader looks over Ike McCaslin's shoulder as this scion of aristocrats discovers in family records the source of family guilt and works out a means for expiation. It is significant that Faulkner has published an orthodox detective novel, *Intruder in the Dust,* as well as a collection of detective stories, *Knight's Gambit.* But whether a real detective is supplied or not, the reader of Faulkner's novels is encouraged to correlate significant details and to uncover underlying themes and patterns of symbolism.

Hawthorne says of the prose romance that impaling the story with a moral is like "sticking a pin through a butterfly"; the work is deprived of life and stiffens in an ungainly *rigor mortis.*[7] When a romance fails to capture the reader's imagination the stylized characters are likely to prove far more disturbing than the equivalent characters of a bad novel. It would be foolish to claim that the artistry of a Faulkner novel is always successful, that the weaknesses of characterization are always compensated for by narrative skill and rhetorical brilliance. But Faulkner has written more excellent novels than any other American novelist, with the possible exception of Henry James, and he has demonstrated an extraordinary diversity in his literary career. His present importance in the history of the twentieth-century novel is unlikely ever to be seriously questioned.

[7] Hawthorne, *op. cit.,* p. 244.

7

Chapter Two

THEMES AND TECHNIQUES

THREE ASPECTS of Faulkner's work seem to me of special importance. One is the novelist's interest in Southern history and culture, and the presence of an imaginary Mississippi county as a setting for most of his published novels and stories. A second feature is Faulkner's psychology of characterization, in particular his creation of "puritan" figures who are dominated by obsessive desires to impose rational categories upon the rebellious facts of human experience. Finally there is the technical mastery by which stylized characters are made vehicles of moral and social analysis. Psychological descriptions in Faulkner's work are unrealistic in the sense that they could not be applied to actual human individuals without obvious distortion. Nevertheless the reader often senses in Faulkner's work a profundity of insight and observation that seems derived from and yet is independent of the characterization. In a similar

8

way, Faulkner's experimental techniques lack a theoretical rationale and are not employed consistently. All the same, Faulkner is an experimental craftsman of the highest order, and his use of the interior monologue and related forms deserves an honored place in the history of the psychological novel. A pragmatist in matters of craft, Faulkner is more anxious to create forceful narrative effects than to achieve the greatest possible degree of realism or to speak philosophically about man and his social world. Occasionally his plot situations are melodramatic, his style is florid, and his characterization is sentimental. But in Faulkner's best work these weaknesses are avoided or adequately compensated for by dramatic power and by strength of characterization and theme.

THE FUNCTION of Yoknapatawpha County, Faulkner's private narrative universe, can be described in various ways. From one point of view it is the aggregate of the characters, events, and social themes found in isolated County novels. By establishing a common environment, and by using elaborate cross references, Faulkner persuades the reader that each separate work deals with only one feature of a unified imaginative world. On the one hand Yoknapatawpha is a clear analogue or microcosm of the Deep South, sharing that region's history and traditions. On the other hand it serves as a vehicle for moral and social commentary, enabling Faulkner to explain the South's tragic failure. In this way underlying atmospheres both of social realism and of social allegory are supplied to novels where characterization is stylized and moral problems unrealistically defined. Thus the County novels may be said to comprise a single prose epic, in which the opposition between history and allegory is effectively resolved.

Yet it cannot be assumed that Faulkner deliberately created his fictional world in order to unify a number of scattered and otherwise heterogeneous works. The development of Yoknapatawpha County may be traced to Faulkner's early tendency to favor the short story or episodic mode of narration. Prior to World War II a large proportion of his work consisted of groups of short stories closely related in subject matter and theme. One important novel, *The Hamlet*, is based almost wholly upon previously published stories, and its sequel, *The Town*, incorporates two such stories into its structure. Yoknapatawpha County bears much the same relation to Faulkner's Mississippi novels that an individual novel or story collection bears to the stories and episodes that compose it. Whether writing a story or a novel, Faulkner often gives the impression that not all the relevant events have been narrated, or that not everything pertinent to an action has been revealed. Even though his stylized characters do not belong to the ordinary world, they seem to have a permanent place in Faulkner's mythological universe.

Faulkner's technique of grouping works together is best illustrated by novels not usually regarded as his most successful or most unified creations. The earliest Yoknapatawpha publication, *Sartoris* (1929), is in this respect a seminal work. It is closely related to *The Unvanquished* (1938), a collection of Civil War stories, and many of its characters reappear in *Sanctuary* (1931). In both *Sartoris* and *The Unvanquished* use is made of the Snopes family, the center of focus in *The Hamlet* (1940) and its sequels, *The Town* (1957) and *The Mansion* (1959). The Sartoris bank plays an important role in the symbolism of each of these last three novels, and many of the *Sartoris* situations are echoed in *The Town*, where the despicable Horace Benbow of the early work becomes metamorphosed into the not altogether admirable Gavin Stevens. Other connections are established by Gavin Stevens's multiple appearances, for example in *Intruder in the Dust* (1948), *Requiem for a Nun* (1951), *The Town*, and *The Mansion*, and in the detective stories of *Knight's Gambit* (1949). Similar connections of plot and character exist between *Sanctuary* and *Requiem for a Nun*, and between the stories of *Go Down, Moses* (1942) and the detective novel, *Intruder in the Dust*.

On the other hand Faulkner's best novels are not those with the most intimate Yoknapatawpha connections. *As I Lay Dying* (1930) and *Light in August* (1932) have a County setting and include one or two characters that reappear in other works. But each novel seems an entirely distinct artistic creation. The Compsons of *The Sound and the Fury* (1929) are indeed the principal narrators of *Absalom, Absalom!* (1936), but Faulkner makes only minor references in the latter novel to the situation of the former. Although the Compson and Sutpen families have a significant role in the history of the Jefferson aristocracy, they appear less often in Yoknapatawpha works than do the Sartoris family or the McCaslins of *Go Down, Moses* and *Intruder in the Dust*. Other works may lay claim to the category of Faulkner's major novels, for example *Sanctuary*, *The Hamlet*, *Go Down, Moses*, and *The Wild Palms*. But the first two of these are uneven in quality and imperfect in structure: for example, the conclusion to *Sanctuary* is awkward and many of *The Hamlet* episodes are inferior. The same can be said of *Go Down, Moses*, if it is regarded as a novel and not as a collection of related stories. *The Wild Palms* (1939) is more difficult to classify, since it is composed of two distinct though thematically related novellas, "Old Man" and "Wild Palms," published with interlaced chapters. Both novellas include Mississippi references, but they do not otherwise fit into the Yoknapatawpha canon.

The reader will unquestionably miss the full significance of *Intruder in the Dust* and *Requiem for a Nun* if he is not already acquainted with earlier works. In a similar way Faulkner's references in *Sanctuary* and *The Hamlet* to the events of *Sartoris* provide a level of social symbolism that would otherwise be lacking. However, in *The Sound and the Fury*, *Light in August*, and *Absalom, Absalom!* the allegorical atmosphere is relatively independent of other Yoknapatawpha novels. A comprehension of one novel naturally facilitates an understanding of others, but the reader does not require the sense of an underlying imaginative world. It is significant that *As I Lay Dying* is the most obviously self-sufficient of the four major works; as a comic work it neither generates nor requires an atmosphere of Yoknapatawpha allegory.

Faulkner novels entirely removed from a Mississippi setting tend to lack allegorical themes that involve the aristocratic South. *Soldiers' Pay* (1926), *Mosquitoes* (1927), and *Pylon* (1935) are concerned with loneliness and despair in general, and not with the special problems of archetypal Southerners. *A Fable* (1954) is Faulkner's most direct expression of the abstract moral themes that may be said to underlie all his fiction. But in *A Fable* these themes are not applied to believable characters or associated with sharply conceived dramatic situations. Such non-Yoknapatawpha works suffer not from a lack of relation to other novels, but from the absence of the detailed psychological analysis that characterizes Faulkner novels with a distinct regional setting.

The relative isolation of such Yoknapatawpha novels as *Absalom, Absalom!* and *As I Lay Dying* can be explained in terms of the greater stylization of central characters. Bizarre and obsessed figures like Thomas Sutpen and Darl Bundren seem rooted to the unique fictional world in which they first appear. Characters that are transported from novel to novel tend to be minor figures or semi-detached witnesses of the novel's main action. Such characters usually seem more realistic, if only because of their ability to control the reader's interpretation of the central action. They function as connecting links between the reader and characters with stylized roles and allegorical functions. The difference is illustrated by what happens to Quentin Compson when he becomes a narrator of *Absalom, Absalom!* His intelligent awareness of the South's moral failure is retained, but his stylized puritan obsession with his sister's promiscuity is more or less abandoned. When Flem Snopes and Eula Varner are transferred from the rural world of *The Hamlet* to the urban milieu of *The Town* and *The Mansion* their original characterization undergoes a disastrous change, in that elements of extreme stylization, retained from the earlier work, are in conflict with their realistic functions. Faulkner makes excellent use of his witness or narrator-figures in novels where they are not the center of focus. But when such free-moving characters as Gavin Stevens and V. K. Ratliff dominate a novel or episode, the results are unsatisfactory. It is no accident that Yoknapatawpha County allusions seem more important in novels where such a figure is given a strong dramatic role in addition to his function as a witness-figure.

Finally, Yoknapatawpha County relationships may be viewed in terms of the help they provide the reader in comprehending particular novels. In his best work Faulkner places extreme demands upon the understanding as well as the sympathy of the average reader. More than other great novelists, except perhaps James Joyce, Faulkner writes to the reader who has adjusted himself to a special kind of narrative reality, and who in effect knows what and what not to look for. It is a well-known aesthetic fact that the qualities a person expects to find in a work of art deeply influence what he actually discovers there. In the case of Faulkner's novels the extreme stylizations of character and event make it advantageous that the reader's adjustment be controlled as much as possible. Yoknapatawpha County relationships make explicit the reader's need to recognize and accept Faulkner's unique characterization and rhetorical style.

Although Faulkner's County novels by no means share a sharply defined "mythology," the term may be loosely applied to the stylization of Southern history and culture in novels and story collections from *Sartoris* (1929) to *Go Down, Moses* (1940). In these works the Southern aristocracy has suffered a moral and social collapse traceable both to the Civil War and to the presence of a destructive psychological flaw. The social vacuum thus created is partially filled by the rise of two formerly exploited groups—one is a class of backwoods farmers, who achieve bourgeois respectability, and the other is a new and proud generation of mulatto Negroes. In his early noncomic work Faulkner deals almost solely with themes involving the moral corruption of the Southern aristocracy, as revealed by its inhuman treatment of both poor-whites and Negroes. Negro characters either symbolize a moral stability which corrupted white Southerners are incapable of achieving or they represent a future South in which racial conflict will no longer exist. Faulkner's comic treatment of the ambitious poor-whites, mainly represented by the Snopes family, may be distinguished from his serious analysis of traditional white society. Flem Snopes's social triumph in Jefferson, as described in *The Town,* is only awkwardly related to the discussion of rural Snopesism in the more successful *The Hamlet.* Faulkner uses Yoknapatawpha mythology mainly as a device for enhancing the symbolic roles of characters that represent in some way the South's tragic moral flaw.

Faulkner's Yoknapatawpha mythology corresponds very closely to the South's romantic legend of a proud society compelled to endure humiliating defeat by an external force. However, Faulkner protects his work from the charge of romanticism by keeping such themes in the background of particular novels. Moreover, he insists that the aristocratic South is responsible for its own degeneration, and that the ravages of war only symbolize the consequences of inward decay. At the same time it is implied in his work that past social ideals, however corrupt they might have been, are superior to the debased values of modern life, whether represented by the amoral Snopeses or by decadent aristocrats like Jason Compson and Horace Benbow.

In particular novels Faulkner locates the source of aristocratic decay within the personalities of individual characters, who are treated as archetypal representatives of Southern puritanism. General references to the collapse of the South's aristocracy have the primary function, as in *Absalom, Absalom!* of establishing an atmosphere of social allegory, which is then focussed upon the psychological obsessions of individual characters.

FAULKNER'S ABILITY to combine social theme with psychological analysis reaches its fullest expression in *Light in August* and *Absalom, Absalom!* In the former novel Joe Christmas, the adopted son of a white farmer, becomes convinced that he has a Negro ancestor. His hatred of himself and his effort to expiate his real or imagined sin are symbolic, albeit ironically, of the white Southerner's latent sense of responsibility for inhuman treatment of the Negro race. Unlike Joe Christmas, Thomas Sutpen never directs his moral and social pride against himself, except in the sense that his inhuman moral code proves just as self-destructive. But Joe Christmas and the archetypal aristocrat both represent the dark puritan vein simultaneously strengthening and weakening the South. By the end of the novel Sutpen's characterization has blended with his role as representative of the South's inability to reconcile successfully democratic idealism and aristocratic society.

Faulkner describes the self-destructive moral rationality of Joe Christmas, Thomas Sutpen, and other archetypal white Southerners as essentially "puritan" in composition. The concept of puritanism plays an important role in Faulkner's characterization, and the term is applied not only to religious and sexual obsessions, but to habits of thought residual from the South's long Protestant tradition. Virtually every white male in Faulkner's novels, from educated lawyers to escaped convicts, can be described, either directly or indirectly, as puritan. Such figures are committed to the rationalization of experience, or the effort to fit the ebb and flow of events into logical categories, usually but not necessarily moral. Characters insisting upon organizing and controlling human experience by rational means act in a puritan manner and are potential victims of the inadequacy of human reason.

Direct references to puritanism as a psychological flaw appear most frequently in novels openly critical of the aristocratic South. In *The Sound and the Fury* Quentin Compson's suicide is traced to his puritan rage at the promiscuity of his sister, specifically to his effort to conquer, through exertion of rational will, the ravages both of nature and of time. In an explanatory appendix [1] Faulkner traces Quentin's obsession to a destructive "presbyterian concept." In trying to convince himself that he has committed incest with Caddy, Quentin seeks an eternal punishment for them both, so that "he could guard her forever and keep her forevermore intact amid the eternal fires" (9). In *Absalom, Absalom!* Thomas Sutpen's inhuman treatment of other characters, in particular his first wife, his poor-white retainer, and his part-Negro son, is traced to his puritan "innocence" or the belief "that the ingredients of morality were like the ingredients of pie or cake and once you had measured them and balanced them and mixed them and put them into the oven it was all finished and nothing but pie or cake could come out" (263). The tragic consequences of Southern puritanism also dominate the action of *Light in August,* where Joe Christmas's destiny is molded by his response to a strict Presbyterian background. Throughout Faulkner's work puritan figures are described as able to deceive themselves by placing a dogmatic religion and an equally dogmatic social morality into separate compartments. Thus a Protestant church service in *Light in August* can be described by Gail Hightower as an ironic "declaration and dedication" of the lynching of Joe Christmas on the following day (322).

Even when he is not criticizing Southern habits of mind, Faulkner makes use of characters whose thoughts are dominated by puritanism. However, such characters are less likely to be destroyed by their excess of moral rationality. In *The Wild Palms,* puritan attitudes control the behavior not only of Harry Wilbourne of "Wild Palms," whose sense of moral guilt is responsible for the death of his mistress, but also of the convict of "Old Man," who resists the temptations of freedom and returns to his prison sanctuary. Both characters seek to impose rational categories upon the forces of

[1] This appendix appears in *The Portable Faulkner,* edited by Malcolm Cowley (New York, The Viking Press, 1946) and in the Modern Library edition of *The Sound and the Fury.* Page references are to the Modern Library edition.

nature, but the convict seems to realize that only by escaping nature can he avoid the penalty imposed on those who try to control it. Male characters in *The Hamlet,* with the exception of Flem Snopes and one or two of his cousins, dissipate their energy in puritan outrage at the uncontrollable sensuality around them. In this novel, as in "Old Man," the emphasis falls upon comic contrasts between archetypal puritans and individuals who represent forces of nature beyond rational control. Eula Varner's animal sexuality is opposed to the futile puritan efforts of Jody Varner and the local schoolmaster, the one to preserve her virginity and the other to overcome it. In other chapters the farmers of the region are presented as utterly helpless before natural forces, whether represented by Eula Varner, by an idiot's love for a cow, or by the wild ponies Flem Snopes brings from Texas.

Throughout his work Faulkner tends to create sharp distinctions between characters who function in the world as rational agents and those who do not. This psychological demarcation, with its consequences for style and narration, is related to an equally sharp distinction between adult puritans and representatives of primitive nature: Negroes, idiots, women, and sometimes children. The structure of an individual novel usually depends upon a contrast between figures involved in social activity, or representative of social forces, and figures who symbolize a nonsocial primitivism or a moral awareness that cannot be translated into effective social action. Thus Quentin and Jason Compson, as representatives of aristocratic decay, are contrasted to Benjy, their idiot brother, and to Dilsey, the Negro servant. In *Light in August* Joe Christmas's tragedy is placed in psychological perspective by the presence of the primitive Lena Grove, who accepts the flow of experience and is not destroyed by puritan self-consciousness. Throughout his work Faulkner dramatizes his treatment of puritanism by establishing such extreme contrasts, or by creating situations in which rational characters are conspicuously unable to control or even understand the forces of nature.

An important consequence of Faulkner's stylized characterization is the tendency for any social activity, inasmuch as it is rationally directed, to be inherently self-defeating. Faulkner's puritan figures are often motivated by socially-oriented ideals which have become corrupted by personal will and thus prove disastrous, both for the would-be moral agent and for those around him. Even when the moral agent is not initially characterized as a puritan, his very involvement in the lives of others brings destruction. Thus the reporter of *Pylon* tries to help Roger Shumann and his barnstorming friends, but the effort only leads to the aviator's death and the reporter's own despair. Horace Benbow tries to save Lee Goodwin in *Sanctuary* by bringing Temple Drake to the witness stand, but this only sets the stage for her act of betrayal. The Bundrens of *As I Lay Dying* seem exceptions to the rule that social behavior must prove corrupting. But the incentives behind their gesture of carrying out the mother's wish to be buried in Jefferson are ultimately revealed as selfish and personal. Although their social action is apparently successful, the individual Bundrens undergo a series of personal tragedies. The character least burdened by initiative, the father, is the only one who remains free of misfortune and who achieves his private aim. The absurdity of the family's social achievement, contrasted to the personal failures that accompany it, creates the comic or mock-epic tone which distinguishes the novel.

In *Light in August* Faulkner attempts the difficult task of establishing the violent death of Joe Christmas as a Christ-like sacrificial act, while still treating Joe's racial obsession as essentially demonic. He achieves this by depicting Joe's drive toward moral expiation as self-conscious without being deliberately rational. Joe is able to exorcise the puritan fury and violence in his nature only by committing murder and thus forcing society to punish him. At the same time Joe is described as martyring himself to the South's self-destructive social traditions. The crux of the paradox is that Joe cannot fully understand the significance of his martyrdom, even though his role depends upon his calm acceptance of an inexorable fate. Joe Christmas may be contrasted to Thomas Sutpen of *Absalom, Absalom!*, who functions as the symbolic architect of a morally tormented society and not as its sacrificial victim. Sutpen never consciously grapples with his destiny, and his inevitable death has allegorical meaning only for the reader and the narrators.

Just as Faulkner makes social action destructive and in this sense demonic, he locates human value in primitive characters who are generally free of social involvement as well as puritan rationality.

17

The moral function given to Benjy and Dilsey in *The Sound and the Fury* is in direct proportion to their dramatic and psychological removal from the puritan Compsons. The childbearers of *Light in August* and *The Hamlet,* Lena Grove and Eula Varner, have a similar role, although its moral aspect is much less pronounced. In "The Bear" Faulkner makes a determined effort to create a rational character who functions as a genuine moral agent. Ike McCaslin is permitted to make a social gesture that reflects his moral awareness, but the repudiation of his inheritance, the McCaslin plantation, suggests his social ineffectuality as well as his repudiation of a tainted heritage.

A difficulty arising from Faulkner's treatment of human reason as corrupt or ineffectual is the absence of characters with whom the reader can identify. In his search for such characters Irving Howe sees Faulkner as trying to place rational observers within each novel as intellectual guideposts to the reader. He sees Quentin Compson as an intended Hamlet figure, "a center of intelligence, an ethical agent and critic." [2] He also assumes that Gail Hightower is supposed to be an intellectual "reverberator," a witness-figure capable of appreciating the full meaning of Joe Christmas's tragedy. Mr. Howe criticizes Faulkner for the failure of these characters to measure up to such a role. However, these characters are not intended as the author's spokesmen; their corrupt rationality is related symbolically to the general Protestant *hubris* of the aristocratic South.

In later works Faulkner tries to create both uncorrupted rational witnesses and effective moral agents. But his task is made difficult by his concept of the moral inadequacy of reason. When Faulkner fashions a true spokesman-character, such as Gavin Stevens, the frequent result is a conflict of tone between the dramatic action and the moral commentary. In *Intruder in the Dust* and *Requiem for a Nun* Stevens is allowed to discuss at length redeeming actions that, as a rational adult, he is incapable of performing. These actions are performed instead by characters normally removed from social involvement who act intuitively, in a manner comparable to that of Faulkner's primitive figures. It takes a youth and an old woman, in

[2] Irving Howe, *William Faulkner: A Critical Study* (New York, Random House, 1951), p. 121.

Intruder in the Dust, to disregard logical evidence of guilt and help to free the innocent Lucas Beauchamp. Nancy Mannigoe preserves the marriage of her white employers in *Requiem for a Nun* by murdering their infant son and thus preventing its mother from abandoning the rest of her family. In both cases the redeeming action is described as in some way intuitive, even though the motivation seems to be largely rational. The fact that Nancy Mannigoe must die for the crime of murder suggests a comparison between her role and Joe Christmas's situation in *Light in August.* But in *Requiem* there is too great a disparity between Nancy's action and the moral glamour by which it is described.

A similar conflict of tone is present in *A Fable.* Here the equation of puritanism with social leadership is reflected in the characterization of the old Marshal, who symbolizes not only French society but all of Western civilization. The Marshal, a figure in many ways like Sutpen, is given insight into his own corruption, and he shapes his consequent pessimism into a philosophical system presented as idealistic. Since evil and sin are just as much a part of man as goodness, they must be accepted or "believed." Man will endure and prevail not merely because he is good but because he is also evil. Man's inherent corruption, his infinite "rapacity," is described, paradoxically, as adequate justification for a philosophical "belief" in man.

The Marshal's reconciliation of faith and despair is at thematic odds with the role of a traditional Faulkner primitive, an army corporal described as a re-resurrected Christ. The Corporal's moral gesture, like Nancy Mannigoe's, leads to immediate destruction, to the slaughter of two regiments of troops. The Corporal's romantic idealism and the Marshal's cynical faith in human evil represent opposing points of view that cannot be resolved except through ever-widening circles of rhetorical verbiage. In earlier novels the moral intuition of primitive figures and the self-destructive rationality of archetypal puritans tend to be related, if at all, only by dramatic juxtaposition and symbolic contrast. The failure of *Requiem for a Nun* and *A Fable* shows the inadequacy of Faulkner's stylized characterization when it is given the inappropriate function of direct moral statement.

19

NARRATIVE STRUCTURE in a Faulkner novel tends to be closely involved with the author's stylized psychology. In both *Light in August* and *The Sound and the Fury* the thematic contrast between rational puritans and primitive characters is reflected both in plot situations and in chapter organization. In *Light in August* Lena Grove's calm refusal to recognize moral dilemmas provides a dramatic and psychological framework whereby the nature and significance of Joe's torturous self-hatred can be readily perceived by the reader. The presence of opening and closing chapters devoted to Lena's arrival in Jefferson before Joe's death, and to her subsequent departure, suggests a symbolic relationship between the two characters, even though they never meet. In *The Sound and the Fury* the narration of the first section is associated with the idiot Benjy and the last section with Dilsey, the Compson servant. Benjy and Dilsey are both social outsiders, and their points of view establish a perspective by which the Compson social failure can be viewed. In many novels where primitive figures do not play an important part, there still exists a structural opposition between socially oriented figures and characters who stand apart from the social framework, often as victims of puritanism. Both Caddy in *The Sound and the Fury* and Charles Bon in *Absalom, Absalom!* are sympathetic characters who are rejected by their families and forced into a limbo of social isolation. In "Wild Palms" the puritan romanticism of Harry Wilbourne is opposed to the genuine capacity for love of Charlotte Rittenmeyer, the victim of Harry's moral anxiety. Although Charles Bon and Charlotte Rittenmeyer are sophisticated figures, the one a New Orleans aristocrat and the other an intelligent artist, both play a relatively passive role and allow themselves to be sacrificially killed by archetypal puritans.

These extreme personality contrasts and oppositions make it difficult for Faulkner to use traditional techniques of character revelation. His primitive figures are generally characterized by terms that do not involve ordinary social personality. Both Lena Grove and Eula Varner are usually described negatively, by their lack of activity and rational comprehension. Eula Varner's chief trait, at least in *The Hamlet*, is her unawareness of the sexual desire she arouses in the male population of Frenchman's Bend. A similar point can be made concerning nonprimitive victims of social puritanism. They usually remain in the background, and tend to be characterized in terms of the puritan obsessions of which they are the objects. Thus Charles Bon remains an enigma to most of the narrators of *Absalom, Absalom!* and Charlotte Rittenmeyer is seen largely through the distorted perceptions of her unhappy lover.

In contrast to Faulkner's primitives, his socially oriented heroes are generally described in terms of their rational obsessions or by their fanatical exertions of will, to the virtual exclusion of more commonplace qualities. Quentin Compson is characterized by a suicidal moral drive, Joe Christmas by his desperate sense of guilt, Thomas Sutpen by his ruthless ambition, and so on. Less important figures tend to be even more sharply drawn. The presentation of Jason Compson emphasizes his jealousy and avarice, and Percy Grimm in *Light in August* is described almost exclusively in terms of his overpowering racial hatred.

As a consequence of such stylized characterizations, Faulkner is forced to rely heavily upon features of style and narrative organization that illuminate not so much the characters themselves as their significance. The development of a novel or story often emphasizes the gradual resolution of an initial conflict between opposed characters or between a character and his social environment. Joe Christmas and Thomas Sutpen first appear to Jefferson citizens as friendless and hostile strangers, but by the end of each novel they are associated symbolically with the Yoknapatawpha social world. At the beginning of *Sanctuary* Temple Drake is raped unnaturally by Popeye, a dehumanized Memphis gangster; but later in the novel she is revealed as sharing to some degree his morally stunted attitudes. Temple's responsibility for her own disaster is implied by her false testimony during the trial scene near the end of the novel. In order to salvage a last vestige of respectability she protects Popeye and allows the innocent Lee Goodwin to be lynched.

Major figures in Faulkner's work are usually introduced under enigmatic circumstances that establish an atmosphere both of mystery and of symbolic meaning. *Sanctuary* opens with a meeting between Popeye, a gangster bootlegger, and Horace Benbow, an ineffectual lawyer trying to escape his shrewish wife. That both stylized figures represent distortions of nature is suggested by their standing on opposite sides of a spring in a country environment to which each seems to be alien. Each carries an object that indicates a false refuge, or sanctuary, from the natural world. Popeye's gun is a sex-surrogate, a symbol of his impotence, and Horace's book indicates his desperate rationality. The reader's attention is diverted from each character's status as a realistic individual to his symbolic role and to the significance of the confrontation. The thematic tension thus generated is later heightened and given a new direction by the introduction of another stranger, Temple Drake, into the same frightening environment.

IN HIS use of the above and related narrative techniques, and in his handling of social theme, Faulkner may be viewed as responding simultaneously to twentieth-century American naturalism, with its awareness of social issues, and to European technical sophistication, the tradition of Gustave Flaubert, Virginia Woolf, and James Joyce. Faulkner began writing in the middle 1920's, when the European experimental novel, in particular James Joyce's *Ulysses*, was in great vogue among American writers. Such contemporary writers as Thomas Wolfe and John Dos Passos were also concerned, although in different ways, with social behavior as seen through the medium of individual subjective responses. Yet Dos Passos was not content with the Joycean style of *Manhattan Transfer* (1925); and under the influence of a revived naturalism, following the stock-market crash and subsequent depression, he shifted his attention from the individual mind to the physical depth and breadth of American life. Wolfe also found European techniques too restrictive, and developed more expansive rhetorical techniques. Only Faulkner among the earlier Joyceans was able to reconcile effectively psychological interests and experimental techniques with the social spirit of the times.

The European tradition influencing Faulkner's work is associated with the elimination of the narrative voice as a distinct personality and with the substitution of symbolism as an author's primary means of establishing his moral authority. The effort to explore both tendencies to their logical end characterizes the interior-monologue technique, as developed by Dorothy Richardson, James Joyce, and Virginia Woolf. Such a technique, especially in Joyce's hands, directs the reader's attention to the pre-, or barely, rational formulations of the active human mind, and in this way eliminates, at least in principle, the unwanted commentary of the omniscient author. The narrative eye may shift from mind to mind, but it avoids making comments of its own or seeming to provide information for the sole purpose of aiding the reader. Necessary information is provided indirectly by the content of the characters' thoughts, by physical details reported by the characters, and in some cases by stylistic suggestion. The author's aim is both to create an atmosphere of psychological realism, and to force the reader to become more thoroughly involved with the characters and their actions.

In Faulkner's hands the interior-monologue technique helps to establish a sense of psychological realism and thus counteract the extreme stylization of character and situation. Faulkner's work represents a kind of answer to what Lionel Trilling has called the paradox of the liberal imagination, the tendency of morally conscious writers to allow their conception of what society should be like to warp their view of how it actually is. Faulkner is no better an observer of American society in its entirety than Theodore Dreiser or Sherwood Anderson, but in seeming to focus upon psychological rather than sociological reality he permits his moral and social preconceptions to go relatively unchallenged. If Faulkner succeeds in achieving the effect of profound social analysis, as he sometimes does, it is hardly, as Mr. Trilling has said, through his recognition of "the full force and complexity" of his subject matter,[3] but through his successful treatment of individual characters as archetypal social figures and by his mastery of sophisticated narrative techniques.

The difference between Faulkner's work and that of writers within the main tradition of American naturalism can be described in terms of his use of symbolic detail. Naturalistic writers tend to treat physical situations or events as symbolic of human concerns, as in the case of the Darwinian struggle between the lobster and the squid that opens Theodore Dreiser's *The Financier*. Faulkner occasionally uses descriptions of physical detail in this way, but he is more likely to create symbolism that reflects a character's interpretation of experience and does not necessarily describe the world in

[3] Lionel Trilling, *The Liberal Imagination* (New York, The Viking Press, 1951), p. 299.

23

which he lives. An example is the use of Christ-like characters in such works as *Go Down, Moses* and *Light in August*. The assumption by Ike McCaslin and Joe Christmas of such a role can be at least partly explained in terms of their moral obsessions. As self-conscious Southern puritans they seek deliberately to translate abstract moral doctrines into concrete actions. The Corporal of *A Fable* is a similar figure, even though he is implicitly described as an actual incarnation of Christ. In all three cases the symbolism is applied more to the characterization as a whole than to any single aspect. The Christian imagery provides a layer of meaning that is clearly available to the reader but, except in *A Fable*, is not necessarily forced upon his attention.

Faulkner's use of Christian symbolism was certainly inspired by the device, evident in the poetry of T. S. Eliot and the fiction of James Joyce, of imposing symbolic references to Greek or Christian mythology upon a modern scene. In *The Sound and the Fury* the Christian elements are imposed in precisely this manner. However, most of these references are deeply imbedded in the text and even if recognized do not necessarily seem important. It is likely that Faulkner originally intended to place more emphasis upon Benjy's similarity to Christ and upon the comparison between each monologue narration and a day within Holy Week.[4] But Faulkner may have either lost interest in his original scheme or chosen to emphasize other symbolic techniques.

Another example of Faulkner's relation to modern European writers is the manner in which he uses flashback narrations, especially those involving childhood experiences. Passages of this type in *The Sound and the Fury* and *As I Lay Dying* tell the reader almost nothing about the cause of a character's personality. Rather they provide a series of microcosmic scenes in which the attitudes or obsessions of important characters are shown to be already present. The psychological troubles of the Compson and Bundren children are closely related to environmental conditions, but the relationships remain symbolic. Faulkner never tries to show how such conditions actually shape the early lives of the children. He illustrates personal-

---

[4] See Carvel Collins, "The Interior Monologues of 'The Sound and the Fury,'" *English Institute Essays 1952*, edited by Alan S. Downer (New York, Columbia University Press, 1954).

ity differences and conflicting points of view as if they had always existed and were only magnified by particular circumstances. In the orphanage scenes of *Light in August* there is a clear description of traumatic experiences that could be said to explain Joe Christmas's later revulsion from sex, food, and money. But in my opinion such scenes have the primary functions of making Joe's stylized role more acceptable and of heightening the reader's awareness of his archetypal puritanism. Joe Christmas is not a realistic character, and although Faulkner strives to make his obsessions believable, he does not try to give him a realistic past.

But where he has used techniques associated with modern naturalism, Faulkner has adapted them to patterns of psychological investigation and to the creation of characters representative of social forces. Like many of his American contemporaries, Faulkner writes of the struggle between the individual and a corrupt social world. He appears to accept a conservative view that if the source of human corruption can be located at all it must be found in human nature and not in man's political and economic institutions. The result is a constant interest in social problems only as they involve the moral life of the individual. Like the novels of Henry James, Faulkner's work fuses characteristic American moral seriousness with uncharacteristic sophistication of craft. Like Melville and Hawthorne, Faulkner creates extremely stylized characters and concerns himself with morbid and self-destructive aspects of American puritanism. Thomas Sutpen pursues his wilful obsession as ruthlessly and privately as does Melville's Captain Ahab. *Absalom, Absalom!* is also comparable to Hawthorne's *The House of the Seven Gables* in its use of conventional Gothic elements: the sense of the past, the ancestral mansion, and the family curse.

Both Faulkner and his New England predecessors seek to analyze and interpret the Calvinistic view of experience. The relation between Hawthorne's *The Scarlet Letter* and Faulkner's *The Sound and the Fury* goes far deeper than a mutual interest in the social consequences of sexual promiscuity. However, the two authors differ radically in their treatment of puritan obsessions. Hawthorne seems unable to decide whether his characters are inhabited by the devil or merely hounded by personal neuroses. Although Faulkner is just as oriented toward moral and religious problems as Hawthorne, there is never any supernatural element in his work, apart from obvious fantasies, and the problem of motivation is always resolved in terms of private concerns or compulsions to action. Faulkner's handling of primitive nature somewhat resembles Hawthorne's treatment of Pearl in *The Scarlet Letter*. Yet nature in Faulkner's work is in no way associated with human sin; it functions in absolute contrast to puritan morality and not as a mirror in which the latter's excesses are viewed.

In his best novels, Faulkner presents the possibility of a moral earnestness free of corrupting rationality. Although a Southerner and no philosopher, Faulkner may be compared in this respect to New England's Jonathan Edwards, who delivered sermons of fire and brimstone but sought to define man's relation to God in the language of aesthetic harmony. Faulkner is also a Puritan seeking to reform puritanism by placing love and intuitive understanding above codified moral law.

Chapter Three

※

THE USE OF SOCIAL MYTH

UNDERLYING FAULKNER'S NOVELS can be discerned a vision of the collapse of society and the dehumanization of mankind. The situation in *Pylon* suggests the extent of this vision. A New Orleans reporter tries to assist a small group of penniless flyers and is himself infected with their despair and sense of coming doom. The reporter, whose given name is never revealed, is described as a "cadaverous" figure standing apart from the "flesh and time" (171) of the actual world. He is contrasted to Roger Shumann, the pilot of the group, who suggests an atmosphere of hard-and-fast action, divorced from thought. "Single-purposed, fatally and grimly," Shumann functions "without any trace of introversion or any ability to objectivate or ratiocinate" (171). Like his airplanes he seems to move "only in the vapor of gasoline and the filmslick of oil" (172).

27

The reporter and Shumann stand for the alienated extremes of mind and body. "Walking, they seemed to communicate by some means or agency the purpose, the disaster, toward which without yet being conscious of it apparently, they moved" (172).

By this sharp contrast Faulkner expresses a fear of man's virtual disappearance as a free moral agent from an increasingly mechanized world. In 1936, the year in which *Pylon* was published, Faulkner reviewed, in *American Mercury*, the memoirs of a test pilot. In this review he ironically predicts a "folklore of speed" to be written about the precision pilots of the future. According to this myth, the human pilots have been driven from their planes, and speed alone remains: mankind is vanishing "against a vast and timeless void filling with the sound of incredible engines, within which furious meteors moving in no medium hurtled nowhere, neither pausing nor flagging, forever destroying themselves and one another." Like Roger Shumann and his companions, the silent engines are racing "without comprehensible purpose toward no discernible destination." The few individuals who retain their human awareness are deprived of flesh and time; they are forced to melt into oblivion or to unite with the representatives of blind and meaningless destruction.

This grim choice explains the contrast between the ghostly reporter and the mechanized flyer. The reporter has preserved his moral feeling but cannot translate it into action. In the effort to help Shumann win the jack-pot air race, he provides the flyer with a dangerous plane. When Shumann crashes to his death, the reporter, who has not belonged to the lost world represented by the barnstormers, now joins them in their despair. "It was himself now who was the nebulous and quiet ragtag and bobend of touching and breath and experience without visible scars" (281).

Pylon is a weak novel because flat and allegorical characters, representing Faulkner's apocalyptic theme, are thrust into an environment incongruous because of its realism. The reporter is constantly associated with images of timelessness and death, but this ghostly aura has little to do with his heavy drinking and with the French Quarter world to which he belongs. There is a similar contradiction between the treatment of the individual barnstormers as lonely and pathetic human beings and their function as harbingers of mankind's doom. Shumann's death and the reporter's despair are described as if they were inevitable. Yet the reader can accept this inevitability only if he accepts the truth of Faulkner's social theme.

In other novels Faulkner avoids these contradictions of tone, not by raising his characters from symbolic flatness but by involving them in more openly contrived situations. In *Sanctuary* the principal figures are also two-dimensional, and the dramatic contrasts are equally extreme. However, the reader does not have to accept the action as realistic, as he does in *Pylon,* in order to recognize the validity of the theme. The exploration of moral despair in *Pylon* centers upon the death of Shumann and the dispersal of his group. Comparable events in *Sanctuary,* including Temple Drake's violation by Popeye and her experiences in a Memphis brothel, are not presented as the cause of Temple's degradation or even as a direct symbol of cultural decay. Rather, Popeye's violence functions as a catalytic agent which forces Temple to reveal a deeper and more socially significant moral failure.

Whereas the symbolism of *Pylon* is concentrated upon the surface action, in *Sanctuary* it moves parallel to the principal events and becomes evident only when Temple begins to like the brothel to which Popeye takes her. The reader learns late in the novel that her sick imagination was partially responsible for the initial rape. Shrinking from Popeye's touch, she imagines herself telling him: "Come on. Touch me. Touch me! You're a coward if you dont. Coward! Coward!" (262). She is a "poor little gutless fool" (70), in strong contrast to Ruby, an ex-prostitute, who tries vainly to protect her.

Temple's failure is comparable to that of Horace Benbow, a Jefferson lawyer, who tries to save Lee Goodwin when the latter is tried for a murder committed by Popeye. Like the reporter in *Pylon,* Benbow succeeds only in hastening the death of the man he tries to save. Yet his lack of manhood is far more effectively presented than the reporter's abstract despair. Benbow's futility is expressed by his relations with Belle, his unfaithful wife, who makes him carry home every Friday a leaking box of shrimp. "Here lies Horace Benbow," he tells Ruby, "in a fading series of small stinking spots on a Mississippi sidewalk" (19). Like Temple he is romantically innocent of evil and he holds desperately to a naive concept of justice, that breaks down before actual experience. Unrealistic to the end, he even romanticizes his despair. "Perhaps it is upon the instant that we realize, admit, that there is a logical pattern to evil," he thinks, "that we die" (265–266). He recalls an expression seen in the eyes of a dead child: "the cooling indignation, the shocked despair fading, leaving two empty globes in which the motionless world lurked profoundly in miniature" (266). Although he tries to be a moral agent, he is still the Horace Benbow of *Sartoris*, an ex-YMCA official and apprentice glass blower with an air of "fine and delicate futility" (161). In *Sanctuary* he plays both roles, and his moral impotency is made a fundamental part of the corrupted world that he tries to save.

Instead of depending upon the inevitability of the dramatic climax, as in *Pylon*, the moral theme of *Sanctuary* is expressed in the reactions of Temple Drake and Horace Benbow to the contrived situations forced upon them. The unbelievable action, far from being a weakness, is the principal means by which this vital interplay between character and situation is emphasized. It is true that Popeye functions, like Roger Shumann, as a symbol of the mechanized humanity described in Faulkner's *American Mercury* review. But in *Sanctuary* the mechanization that Popeye represents is so thoroughly inhuman that Faulkner makes little effort to give him realistic qualities, characterizing him largely through the reactions of others.

Popeye is no real agent of corruption; he is a symbol for the environment that Temple comes to accept as her own. He introduces the action and then recedes in importance, leaving Temple, Horace, and the aristocratic world they represent as the real agents of decay. In the trial scene, when Temple sends the innocent Lee Goodwin to his death, the rouge on her cheeks is compared to paper discs and her lipstick to "something both symbolical and cryptic cut carefully from purple paper and pasted there" (341). This recalls Faulkner's description of Popeye's "vicious depthless quality of stamped tin" (2) and suggests that she has replaced him as the novel's major representative of depraved humanity.

The theme of moral corruption in *Sanctuary* is embedded more in stylized characterization than in naturalistic action. The failures of Temple Drake and Horace Benbow are revealed by their reactions to a number of obviously contrived events. At the same time, this gradual revelation is a commentary upon the dying society which both characters represent, a society which never appears directly in the dramatic situation.

THE DEVELOPMENT of the technique displayed in *Sanctuary* can be traced through Faulkner's early work. In *Soldiers' Pay*, his first novel, a flyer returns to his Georgia home wounded and near death. On the train Donald Mahon is befriended by two strangers, Joe Gilligan and Margaret Powers. These self-appointed guardians, a soldier and a soldier's widow, escort the scarred and helpless hero to his home and stay to protect him from an indifferent or misunderstanding society.

Donald symbolizes all the wartime flyers, the men who "died" in the air above Europe and returned to earth as living ghosts. In a short story, "All the Dead Pilots," Faulkner explains how heroism in war can mean a spiritual death. "And that's all. That's it. The courage, the recklessness, call it what you will, is the flash, the instant of sublimation; then flick! the old darkness again. That's why. It's too strong for steady diet. And if it were a steady diet, it would not be a flash, a glare." [1] Donald's will to live has been extinguished by this flash of valor, and his death in Georgia is only a pale echo of what happened earlier. With his last breath, he passes into that day long past "that had already been spent by those who lived and wept and died, and so remembering it, this day was his alone: the one trophy he had reft from Time and Space. *Per ardua ad astra*" (293).

Although the living death of a returned war hero dominates *Soldiers' Pay*, its plot hinges upon the effort of Donald's two friends to bring about his marriage to Cecily, his "shallow characterless" fiancée of former years, who is now repelled by the scar on his face. They succeed in preventing the girl from breaking the engagement, but at the last moment she elopes with a younger boy who is already her lover. Although Margaret marries Donald instead, this fiasco hastens his inevitable death, leaving the two guardians confronted with their own failure and unable to find happiness together.

The novel unfolds as a series of oppositions and alienations—be-

[1] "All the Dead Pilots," in *Collected Stories of William Faulkner* (New York, Random House, 1950), p. 531.

tween actions and situations as well as between characters. Donald and his friends represent an atmosphere of violence and destruction which is thrust into a peaceful Trollope-like world, complete with a philosophizing rector (Donald's father) and his garden. There is no continuous action, but rather a series of disconnected events, such as Cecily's elopement and Donald's death, each with a separate waste-land significance.

Soldiers' Pay is unified by the theme of sexual longing, which is forcibly injected into the story at several points. The important women in the novel—Margaret, Cecily, and the rector's maidservant —have their frustrated lovers. The seduction efforts of Januarius Jones, a fat creature with yellow "obscene" eyes, are directed against all three. In this way Faulkner maintains his focus upon loneliness and the lack of binding human relationships, a theme that is burlesqued by Margaret's refusal to marry Joe: "I couldn't marry a man named Gilligan" (305). At the novel's end Joe and the rector hear gospel songs sung by a small Negro congregation. The author contrasts the patience and suffering embodied in the group singing to the frustrated desires of individual lives: "They stood together in the dust, the rector in his shapeless black, and Gilligan in his new hard serge, listening, seeing the shabby church become beautiful with mellow longing, passionate and sad. Then the singing died, fading away along the mooned land inevitable with to-morrow and sweat, with sex and death and damnation; and they turned townward under the moon, feeling dust in their shoes" (319).

Faulkner's second novel, *Mosquitoes*, is also divided into a number of fragmentary plots joined by a common theme of human loneliness. The characters on board Mrs. Maurier's pleasure yacht, just out of New Orleans, are separated into three static groups. In the first a number of artists and intellectuals, led by the novelist Dawson Fairchild (modeled on Sherwood Anderson), try to achieve reality through the spoken and thereby "dead" word. In the second the hostess's young niece tries to escape the yacht, symbol of loneliness, by eloping with the equally young steward. Their adventure is frustrated by her impulsiveness, by the boy's ineffectuality, and finally by a cloud of mosquitoes. The third group consists of passengers gathered about the hostess's card table. These include Mr. Talliaferro, a more affected but less sinister Januarius Jones.

Only Mark Gordon, a sculptor, dares to express an intensely personal despair. He is scornful of the intellectuals: "Talk, talk, talk: the utter and heartbreaking stupidity of words. It seemed endless" (186). From them Gordon turns to "the wet and simple prints" of the niece's bare feet on the deck; "he seemed to feel about him like an odor that young hard graveness of hers." Gordon can appreciate the girl's youth and vitality, but he is just as isolated from her as from the intellectuals: "ay ay strangle your heart," he concludes, "o israfel winged with loneliness feathered bitter with pride" (187).

The title of *Mosquitoes* indicates Faulkner's effort to unify his panorama of human frustration by a dominant symbol. In a prefatory paragraph mosquitoes are described as "pervading and monstrous but without majesty: a biblical plague seen through the wrong end of a binocular: the majesty of Fate become contemptuous through ubiquity and sheer repetition" (8). The failure of the mosquitoes to attain the dignity of Fate is paralleled by their weakness as a unifying symbol. Faulkner's lost souls are real enough, but the dramatic situations in which they are placed do little to make their plights interesting or significant. In the absence of strong plot action excessive emphasis is placed upon dialogue and description. Unfortunately, the dialogue is highly artificial, and flamboyant rhetoric mars the descriptive passages.

Like its predecessor, *Mosquitoes* expresses a direct condemnation of a world in which individual action is sterile and without consequence. It is a novel justly criticized by liberal critics for its negative point of view and the absence of any profound understanding of social forces. Faulkner's attitude may be described as an inverted romanticism, with a concentration upon the lack of harmony between the individual and his natural world. The early Faulkner hero perceives this separation self-consciously and accepts it as a personal fate. Thus Donald Mahon must draw a laborious breath in an alien world while his true existence lies in a different place and time. Mark Gordon is more annoying than Mahon largely because he is more articulate in defining his despair. Oddly enough, the best parts of *Mosquitoes* are the stories—the "empty words"— told by Dawson Fairchild. *Soldiers' Pay* is less intense, better constructed, and consequently more readable. Yet both works collapse

into a series of isolated vignettes or dramatic portraits, each permeated by the author's romantic gloom.

In *Sartoris,* the first Yoknapatawpha novel, Faulkner repeats the
situation of a returned aviator. But in the opposition between a lost
hero and an alien society, the burden of responsibility now rests
with the hero and his family tradition. The aura of fatality surrounding Bayard Sartoris is expressed almost solely by his self-consuming
pride. Instead of hastening Bayard's doom, the people around him
do everything possible to save him. But the young flyer is destroyed
by an inward despair, related symbolically to family tradition; and
no friendly effort by an understanding and sympathetic world can
prevent his death.

In this novel there are two characters named John Sartoris: a Civil
War patriarch and his great-grandson, Bayard's twin brother. Although both figures are dead, their personalities control the thoughts
of the living. The first John, "freed as he was of time and flesh," is
described as more palpable than his aging son, old Bayard, who is
bound by memory to the lost world of his father "and so drawn thin
by the slow attenuation of days" (1). Into this ghostly milieu comes
young Bayard, who quickly reveals a similar preoccupation with his
dead brother: "I tried to keep him from going up there on that goddam little popgun" (46). The only reality which the flyer recognizes
is located in the past, in "a life peopled by young men like fallen
angels, and of a meteoric violence like that of fallen angels, beyond
heaven or hell and partaking of both: doomed immortality and immortal doom" (126). With present existence rendered meaningless
by the death of his twin and the end of the war, Bayard can find
no refuge beyond a taste for fast driving and a yearning for death.

For a while Bayard is lured from his fate by work on the family
plantation and by a love affair with Narcissa Benbow, Horace's sister. He is kept submerged in a monotony of days, "snared by a
rhythm of activities repeated and repeated until his muscles grew
so familiar with them as to get his body through the days without
assistance from him at all" (204). But when sowing time is over
and this "hiatus that might have been called contentment" (203) is
ended, Bayard has no full-time recourse. He takes up reckless driving as a hobby, has an accident, and is nursed back to health by
Narcissa. She becomes his wife and bears him a son; but like the

power of the land, her love causes only a "temporary abeyance of his despair" (289). When old Bayard dies in young Bayard's car, the latter is consumed by guilt and cannot face his family. He flees town and later on, as a reckless test pilot, he crashes to his death.

The structure of *Sartoris* is more lucid than that of *Soldiers' Pay* because in the earlier novel the hero's illness and society's lack of sympathy and understanding tend to conceal the basic theme of personal maladjustment and despair. Bayard's physical vitality and his possession of all the comforts that organized society can offer emphasize by sharp contrast the intensity of his mental pain. But the importance of *Sartoris* in Faulkner's development as a novelist lies mainly in the connection established between young Bayard and his male ancestors, who are also destroyed by excessive pride and "thirst for vainglory." The relation between Bayard's reckless despair and the ruthless pride of old John Sartoris establishes violence and a thirst for fatality as traits which recur in each generation.

Aunt Jenny, priestess of this essentially male tradition, tells the story of a Sartoris who died during the Civil War in a pointless one-man raid upon a Yankee camp. Miss Jenny transforms this story involving the legendary Sartoris and the historical Jeb Stuart into a "finely tragical focal point to which the history of the race had been raised from out the old miasmic swamps of spiritual sloth by two angels valiantly fallen and strayed, altering the course of human events and purging the souls of men" (9). The images "fallen angels" and "meteoric violence" are applied to this Confederate Sartoris as well as to Bayard and his flying companions. At the end of the novel Narcissa christens her child "Benbow" instead of the traditional "John," not wanting him to become "just another rocket to glare for a moment in the sky, then die away" (358). "Do you think," Miss Jenny asks, "that because his name is Benbow, he'll be any less a Sartoris and a scoundrel and a fool?" (380).

This fusion of past and present is not an effort to explain the cause of Bayard's despair by invoking his Southern environment. Rather, it exemplifies Faulkner's method of exploring social attitudes in terms of individual compulsions to blind and self-destructive action. The behavior of Bayard's male ancestors is just as reckless and antisocial as his own; the flyer's actions are dovetailed into a family myth which in turn comments implicitly upon the Southern aristocracy. Bayard is an archetypal Southern aristocrat, even though his Sartoris fury is given a personal quality by his twin's death and by his own war experiences.

The ambivalent handling of social decline in *Sartoris* is in strong contrast to the treatment of the Sartoris family in a group of romantic and anecdotal Civil War stories published in book form as *The Unvanquished*. In these stories the center of focus is the courage and versatility of Rosa Millard, as viewed by her grandson, Bayard Sartoris. As a young boy, Bayard watches Granny Millard recover a trunk of Sartoris silver from the marauding Yankees. In the process the old woman stumbles upon a bizarre device for cheating the enemy out of a large number of mules, which she subsequently loans to suffering townspeople. This heroic and thoroughly absurd character becomes dangerously involved in the intricacies of mule stealing and is finally murdered by a poor-white ruffian. One of the stories deals with Bayard's part in the successful tracking down of the murderer. Another story concerns the forced marriage of Colonel John Sartoris to Drusilla, his tomboy cousin who has fought in his company.

The total collection of stories has little thematic unity, other than the general treatment of Southern courage and foolhardiness during the War. In *Sartoris* the theme of reckless pride is given the symbolic function of explaining the failure of the Southern aristocracy, but in *The Unvanquished*, as the title suggests, the characters' absurd behavior merely adds dramatic interest to the eulogy of a fallen society. The one story in which serious themes are broached, "An Odor of Verbena," is the only one not originally published. In this story an older Bayard Sartoris hurries home from his study of law to find his father dead and himself expected to avenge the murder, just as he avenged the murder of his grandmother. But Bayard recognizes the need to put an end to war and bloodshed, and refuses to take arms. Drusilla, his father's widow, leaves Jefferson when she discovers that Bayard will not carry out his family obligation. But she recognizes his courage in facing his father's enemy unarmed and by his gesture of bravery driving the latter out of town. She leaves a sprig of verbena, a symbol for courage, on his pillow, "filling the room, the dusk, the evening with that odor which she said you could smell alone above the smell of horses" (293).

In *The Unvanquished* the war is only a background against which Sartoris moral vitality is exercised. There are hints of a psychological destruction wrought by too much courage and honor, but there is no evidence that Bayard Sartoris, in spite of his excessive ratiocination, will not become as self-confident a Sartoris as his father. In *Sartoris* the theme of Sartoris spiritual death is uppermost; the war is not so much its cause as its symbol. The responsibility for Bayard's doom lies somewhere within the Sartoris way of life. Although the family heroes represent the elite of Southern society, they obey a selfish and destructive personal code. Living in a self-created world where honor and morality are rigidly defined, they blind themselves to reality and drive without hesitation to violent and meaningless deaths. Despite their social glamour, they lack consciousness of their true social role. Like Bayard when his grandfather dies, they are driven to destroy or pervert their noble aims and to evade responsibility for their actions.

THE MORAL PARADOX vitiating ante-bellum society is explored more thoroughly in *The Sound and the Fury* and *Absalom, Absalom!* In the latter novel Thomas Sutpen rises from West Virginia poverty to a rich and respected position in the Jefferson aristocracy. His actions suggest in allegorical terms the settlement of the Deep South and the efforts of its *nouveau riche* pioneers to establish a permanent society. Sutpen's loss of fortune and lack of descendants are symbols of the South's inability to achieve its aim. The planter is destroyed by what amounts to a contradiction between his democratic idealism and his status as a plantation aristocrat, committed to the doctrine of white supremacy. At the height of power and prestige Sutpen is confronted by Charles Bon, his part-Negro son by a discarded wife. In refusing to treat Bon with human consideration he brings ruin to himself and to others. Sutpen's self-destruction reflects the South's failure to reconcile its moral pretensions with social realities.

There is a clear relation in *Absalom, Absalom!* between the decline of Thomas Sutpen's fortunes and the collapse of Southern culture during and shortly after the Civil War. Yet the war appears in the novel less as an independent force than as a symptom of moral failure. Sutpen's desire to create a family tradition is frustrated by

37

the action of Henry Sutpen, the planter's acknowledged son, in murdering Charles Bon. Instead of accentuating this conflict, the war delays its climax for four years—while the half brothers fight side by side. Faulkner emphasizes Sutpen's responsibility for his own social failure in order to establish his central character as an archetypal aristocrat and to provide a psychological explanation for the South's tragic defeat. This maneuver is made possible by the presence of several witness-figures who identify with members of Sutpen's family and read their own destinies in the legendary events.

The full significance of the Sutpen allegory, with its terrible mixture of idealism and corruption, takes the form of a neurosis in the mind of Quentin Compson, the final witness. Himself a puritan Southerner, Quentin cannot fully accept his interpretation of Sutpen's failure. His answer to the question as to why he hates the South expresses a sense of frustration and defeat. "I dont hate it," he replies, thinking, *"I dont. I dont! I dont hate it! I dont hate it!"* (378). Faulkner seems to believe, like Quentin, that the Southern way of life was wrong and that a more humanized code of behavior should take its place. But Faulkner cannot discount the glamour of the Southern tradition, which is responsible for this strain of destructive pride. Without seeking to resolve the paradox, he expresses it dramatically in terms that transcend, for a moment, the need for judgment and resolution.

In *The Sound and the Fury*, perhaps his most important novel, Faulkner creates an aristocratic family only slightly less marked by reckless and violent behavior. The Compson lineage includes both a governor and a brigadier general, but after the war the family fortune and abilities decline rapidly. In Jason Lycurgus Compson, son of the general, the first open signs of decay appear. Oppressed by a tradition that he lacks the force of character to uphold, he takes to drinking and to classical studies. His self-pitying wife is a terrifying example of the functionless Southern Lady, and their four children represent varying degrees of social degeneration. Benjy is an idiot; the girl, Candace (Caddy), is promiscuous; Quentin drives himself to suicide by an obsession with his sister's dishonor. The last male Compson to survive, apart from Benjy, is the younger Jason, demonic and childless, who sells the house and repudiates the heritage it embodies. "It's a damn good thing we never had any kings and presidents; we'd all be down there at Jackson chasing butterflies" (247).

The main focus of *The Sound and the Fury* is upon Quentin's relation to Caddy. His self-appointed role of priest-brother parodies the moral idealism of previous Compson generations. Yet Quentin's sense of personal honor is fused with an excessive puritanism, which he tries to impose upon his sister, and his moral rage is in part responsible for her unhappy fate. Quentin's personal tragedy may be equated with the failure of moral effort described in *Pylon* and *Soldiers' Pay*. But *The Sound and the Fury* is saved from too rigorous a thematic structure by the subtle handling of dialogue and patterns of symbolism. Although Quentin's corruption is an important aspect of Compson degeneration, the boy is first presented dramatically as a witness of the family's decline. This contrast between Quentin and an immoral world is then complicated by the gradual revelation of the boy's own failure. Quentin's suicide is presented as less a reaction to Caddy's dishonor than a futile attempt to preserve his moral pride in the face of an unknown future that might rob him even of despair.

Instead of establishing an allegorical action which conveys the moral argument, Faulkner creates a series of implicit contrasts between the tormented Compsons and various unsophisticated characters that stand outside the social framework. Benjy's love for Caddy herself is set against Quentin's self-conscious rage at her behavior. The Compson servants are constant reminders of permanent values. An alliance between Benjy and Dilsey, the most important servant, is indicated by the scene, near the end of the novel, in which she takes the idiot to her Negro church. They both hear a visiting preacher, a "meagre figure, hunched over upon itself like that of one long immured in striving with the implacable earth" (310). In rising to a vision of "de power en de glory" (313), the minister illustrates the redeeming principle that is contrasted to the "sound and fury" of the Compson world. The preacher is a Christ-like figure, "a serene, tortured crucifix" (310), who transports his audience beyond the cares of the body to a spiritual reality void of spatial or temporal distinction. "With his body he seemed to feed the voice that, succubuslike, had fleshed its teeth in him. And the congregation seemed to watch with its own eyes while the voice consumed him, until he was nothing and they were nothing and there was not even a voice but instead their hearts were speaking to one another in chanting measures beyond the need for words" (310).

This acceptance of transcendent value is in strong contrast to the Compson concern for personal ownership, whether of sexual virtue or material wealth. Instead of accepting the flow of time, the Compsons are caught within it and struggle desperately to extricate themselves. Faulkner indicates this attitude toward experience by a series of time images. Quentin looks upon his suicide, an action foreshadowed by the breaking of his watch, as an effort to reduce time to an immobile instant in which past and present are one. Both his and Jason's monologues are crowded with time references expressing their effort to impose personal order upon recalcitrant experience. Benjy and Dilsey, on the contrary, stand apart from time: the one not aware of its passage, the other always seeing things in a simple but effective pattern of understanding. By contrasting these attitudes toward a central image or concept, Faulkner achieves a symbolic tapestry which itself comprises the moral theme. His characters are usually defined by such oppositions or by the language describing their personal obsessions. Only in the full context of the novel are characterizations and themes fully unveiled.

In *Sartoris* Faulkner combines Southern violence and pride with the death wish of a modern war hero. Both are made intelligible as wilful behavior rooted in private obsessions. In *The Sound and the Fury* and *Absalom, Absalom!* he deals more concretely with aristocratic failure and isolates its source more explicitly in the self-destructive moral drive, or puritan rage, of individual characters. Before *Sartoris*, his treatment of society is that of a disenchanted romantic. In *Sartoris* he locates a primordial source of evil in the hero's personality and not in the society which he confronts. Instead of trying to explain Bayard's taste for fatality in terms of his relation to a specific social environment, Faulkner relates him to a mythological family tradition. This mythology places the youth's despair and violence in a pseudohistorical context and so isolates its essential mystery. The solution of this mystery is to be found in the Sartoris response to society, not in society itself.

Chapter Four

MAN AGAINST NATURE

$\mathscr{I}$N *The Sound and the Fury*, the primitive figures of Dilsey and Benjy are contrasted to the more sophisticated Compsons. In *Light in August* a similar contrast is established between the demonic Joe Christmas and the rural "earth-goddess" Lena Grove. Joe's desperate effort to expiate or atone for his imagined Negro blood binds him to a series of frustrating and, as Faulkner reveals them, identical or interchangeable experiences. His destiny is likened several times to a single street, "savage and lonely" (225), which stretches indefinitely into the future. To Joe's constant struggle is opposed Lena's placid composure. Lena is a "shapeless and immobile" (10) figure whose life seems not a violent street but a "peaceful corridor" (4). Faulkner likens her to Keats's image of beauty in ideal fusion with truth: "like something moving forever and without progress across an urn" (6).

Joe Christmas's oppressive puritanism is revealed by the imagery associated with his actions. As with Quentin Compson, the major events of Joe's life are determined by his distorted moral concerns. The fate which drives him down his endless street is self-created and inescapable. This is implied by images that indicate constant movement or infinite repetition. Such imagery suggests a force impelling Joe into the future yet stamping each new action with the repeated imprint of the past. Language appropriate to Joe's obsession is used even when the narrator is only describing the character's environment. A steel fence is compared to a parade of starved soldiers. Street lamps march along, "spaced, intermittent with bitten and unstirring branches" (100). Lena Grove's experiences, on the other hand, seem to flow effortlessly, passing through a "long monotonous succession of peaceful and undeviating changes" (6). The world about her lacks rational demarcation. Abstract time, when it exists, seems to roll backward "like already measured thread being rewound onto a spool" (7).

Richard Chase has cited the large number of images indicating a simple geometrical form, and with this in mind has called the novel a "poetry of physics."[1] Associated with Joe or Lena, these images are usually based either upon the straight line divided into parts or upon the figure of a circle. Joe's street-of-days image is distinguished from the curved and self-contained surface of Lena's urn. However, the difference between these two motifs is not clearly maintained. Round or tubular objects, in particular, are often associated with Joe Christmas and combined with references to endless repetition. Mr. Chase suggests that whereas the curve image stands for Lena's strength, endurance, and hope, it represents for Joe a cage or prison which he must break out of—or else attack from the outside, as he gashes the whiskey tins he has buried in the woods. However, this description is misleading. Joe's entire life is a prison, and his desperate actions are affirmations of his destiny as well as efforts to escape it. Combinations of the two motifs, especially in the first half of the novel, are likely to represent Joe's hatred of anything which will not fit his puritan categories.

[1] Richard Chase, "The Stone and the Crucifixion: Faulkner's 'Light in August'," *Kenyon Review*, 10 (Autumn, 1948), reprinted in *William Faulkner: Two Decades of Criticism*, edited by Frederick J. Hoffman and Olga W. Vickery (East Lansing: Michigan State University Press, 1951), pp. 205–206.

Later in the novel, when Joe comes to terms with his destiny, the distinction between the two patterns of imagery—and the attitude toward experience which they suggest—is purposely blurred. While wandering in the country after his murder of Joanna Burden, Christmas feels himself in harmony with nature, "becoming one with loneliness and quiet that has never known fury or despair" (289). For the first time he is able to view his life in perspective, its pattern forming a closed circle. "I have never got outside that circle," he thinks, "I have never broken out of the ring of what I have already done and cannot ever undo" (296). This falling away of guilt is a source of strength and security; it gives Joe a feeling of "peace and unhaste and quiet" (295). He surrenders to social authority and even accepts a brutal lynching with a sense of calm certainty, his eyes "open and empty of everything save consciousness" (407).

By surrounding Lena Grove with an aura of temporal mysticism Faulkner prepares the reader for the Christ-like passivity with which Joe accepts his death. The tormented puritan passes beyond the need for violence and achieves a calm awareness that resembles Lena's primitive faith.

In spite of their early opposition, the two characters have some things in common. Both seem to project about them a strange, immobile world in which physical movement is held in a timeless stasis. In the first chapter Lena sees a slowly moving wagon which appears to be suspended in a "middle distance" (7). This expression is repeated a few pages later as Lena is riding in a similar vehicle. "The wagon creaks on. Fields and woods seem to hang in some inescapable middle distance, at once static and fluid, quick, like mirages. Yet the wagon passes them" (24). A similar lack of motion pervades the experience of Joe Christmas, but in his case the motionless exterior is usually contrasted to an inner world of raging emotion. Both characters see the world in simple terms, but for Joe it is the simplicity of an abstract order imposed arbitrarily upon experience.

The same combination of exterior calm and interior rage is associated with other puritan characters in this novel. When Joe is whipped by his stepfather for not learning his catechism, the latter's anger assumes an impersonal mask and his voice is "cold, implacable, like written or printed words" (130). Joe's expression is also outwardly calm; "it would have been hard to say which face was the more rapt, more calm, more convinced" (131). This duality is often extended to passages of omniscient description whenever such characters are involved. When McEachern, the puritan stepfather, rides toward the country schoolhouse where he believes Joe is committing the sin of dancing, the "slow and ponderous gallop" of his horse creates an effect of abstract unmoving motion: "He turned into the road . . . the two of them, man and beast, leaning a little stiffly forward as though in some juggernautish simulation of terrific speed though the actual speed itself was absent, as if in that cold and implacable and undeviating conviction of both omnipotence and clairvoyance of which they both partook known destination and speed were not necessary" (176–177). A few pages later Joe Christmas rides the same horse with the same "implacable urgency" and falls into the same two-dimensional composition. The result, as the author describes it, is "a strange, dreamy effect, like a moving picture in slow motion" (183). The suspended or transfixed emotional violence which Faulkner assigns to his puritans is carried over into the description of the world in which they live. Even a passing train is ascribed a paradoxical "effect of terrific nomotion" (386).

If the mask of calm certainty worn by Joe Christmas and other male characters implies a striving for emotional control, then Lena Grove, whose inner tranquility matches her outward appearance, is in part the fulfillment or the pastoral emblem of that puritan ideal. She symbolizes what Joe hopes to achieve by struggling against the dark and sensual forces that oppress him. The earth often appears to him as "tragic and inescapable," with a "damp rich" or "savage and fecund" odor. Nature represents to Joe the force of sensual desire, including the attractions of women and food, which he tries to escape or sublimate by an effort of will. The teeming Negro blood he imagines within his veins is a further symbol for this force. Whereas the world seems bestial and uncontrollable when he is oppressed by life's fecundity, it appears peaceful and harmless when his abstract designs have temporarily prevailed.

The victory of reason over nature is often represented by a strong, hard wind described as blowing "cool" or "hard and clean" (137). Christmas feels this wind blowing upon him in moments of violent purgation, especially during and after fights. He also feels it when his romantic effort to elope with Bobbie is frustrated and he first discovers his terrible loneliness. "What he was now seeing was the street lonely, savage, and cool. That was it: cool" (228). This cold wind blows for other puritans in comparable situations. It blows for Byron Bunch when he discovers that Lena Grove's former lover has fled and that he, Byron, is responsible for Lena's future. The wind he feels is cold and hard, "at once violent and peaceful" (373). It blows away "like chaff or trash or dead leaves all the desire and the despair and the hopelessness and the tragic and vain imagining too" (373).

The puritan ideal of inward calm is the product of an abstract morality, yet it represents a freedom from moral complexities. The cold, hard wind is both a purgation and an apotheosis of moral rage. Thus Gail Hightower speculates upon "the cool soft blowing of faith and hope" (321) of the Protestant church service, which he associates with the subsequent lynching of Joe Christmas.

Faulkner denies his puritan characters the right to control their own destinies consciously. His heroes are responsible for their own fates, but they are driven by forces of individual will which assume the form of fixed ideas or violent compulsions to action. These obsessions function as blind psychological drives which are not subject to self-conscious control.

Although Joe Christmas is responsible for his own destiny, he cannot alter or fully understand the logic of its unfolding. Such a hero can perhaps foresee what he will do in the future, but he cannot change that future. Joe predicts his murder of Joanna Burden only by imagining it as an action forced upon him and already committed: "He was saying to himself *I had to do it* already in the past tense; *I had to do it. She said so herself*" (245). The relation between his implacable destiny and his personal will is so ambiguous that even Joe cannot understand it. At one point he feels "like an eagle: hard, sufficient, potent, remorseless, strong" (151). But the narrator adds that "like the eagle, his own flesh as well as all space was still a cage" (151). "With calm paradox" he sees himself "the volitionless servant of the fatality in which he believed that he did not believe" (244–245).

Faulkner often describes his characters as acquiescing mentally to decisions that their emotions or their "bodies" have already made. In *Intruder in the Dust* Chick Mallison thinks he is going to turn in at the Edmonds' gate instead of following Lucas Beauchamp to the latter's cottage. "He still believed he was going to turn in at the gate and even after he knew that he wasn't or anyway hadn't, already beyond it now" (7). Again in *Light in August* the dietician at the orphanage is described as following herself "to see where she was going" (113). Joe Christmas is impelled by hunger to raid the kitchen of a strange house: "It was as though, as soon as he found that his feet intended to go there, that he let go, seemed to float, surrendered, thinking *All right All right* floating, riding across the dusk, up to the house and onto the back porch and to the door by which he would enter, that was never locked" (207). Even Mink Snopes, in *The Mansion*, uses the past tense in thinking of his projected murder of Jack Houston. Faulkner implies that a psychological force, primitive in nature, is superior to the individual's conscious will. The irony of this view is that the uncontrollable force is itself a creation, or rather a projection, of individual will. Thus Joe Christmas and other characters appear victims of a destiny which reflects their abstract reasoning but is not subject to rational control.

Faulkner describes man's rational faculties as inferior in two different ways. On the one hand, action which is motivated by conscious reason proves self-destructive or at best ineffectual. On the other hand, destructive rationality is often related to basic intuitive drives, indicating that puritan energy is more a perversion or misdirection of primitive vitality than an independent source of power. A passage introducing one of the flashback chapters of *Light in August* approaches a codification of this view. The implication is that the scenes of Joe's childhood which follow are unconsciously imbedded in his adult mind: "Memory believes before knowing remembers. Believes longer than recollects, longer than knowing even wonders. Knows remembers believes a corridor in a big long gabled cold echoing building . . ." (104).

In unscrambling the logic of this curious passage one learns that "memory" or "belief" precedes or is somehow prior to conscious recollection or knowledge. The passage is clearly Freudian, but the language is entirely Faulkner's own. Later on in the novel, when Joe is knocked out and lies in a coma on the floor, he experiences a type of awareness that precedes self-consciousness or the moment when the "severed wireends of volition and sentience" (192) are reknit, enabling him to move. In Joe's comatose state he is able to "look without actually seeing, hear without actually knowing; the two wireends not yet knit as he lay peacefully, licking his lips now and then as a child does" (193). When the functions of will and feeling return, he feels a pain in his head; he gets up, "and with his bloody head and his empty stomach hot, savage, and courageous with whiskey, he entered the street which was to run for fifteen years" (195). Faulkner describes a peaceful and childlike state in which consciousness exists but has not become self-directed and, consequently, a vehicle for moral self-torment. In its suggestion of a condition beyond the cares and problems of self, the passage recalls the tranquility of Lena Grove, who in part symbolizes this freedom.

Other passages in *Light in August* illustrate Faulkner's effective handling of this stylized psychological scheme. Byron Bunch accepts Lena Grove's pregnancy without actually believing in it. "I must have knowed," he comments afterward, "to have done what I have done: the running and the lying and the worrying at folks" (350). Yet Byron did not actually "believe" until he saw the child. It was as if he and Lena "were just a lot of words that never even stood for anything, were not even us, while all the time what was us was going on and going on without even missing the lack of words" (352). Faulkner describes Byron's thinking as something which moves "slow and smooth" (351)—slower, in fact, than human emotion—and has to get past a series of obstructions in order to influence action. Byron's dependence upon slow-moving reason explains his weak personality; his struggle between reason and emotion leaves him no match for Lena, who takes him as a substitute for her defaulted lover.

BY IMPOSING this unusual psychology upon such primitive figures as Lena Grove, Faulkner is able to make their complex symbolic roles believable. However, the characterization which lies behind the psychology brings up other problems. The moral function that Dilsey and Lena Grove are given cannot really be described by such eulogistic terms as "truth," "honor," or "understanding," which imply at least some degree of conscious awareness. Faulkner's primitives are usually distinguished by their total lack of rational sophistication, and when they act morally they cannot really be conscious of doing so.

In his later work, Faulkner uses such terms as "endurance," "suffering," and simply "love," all of which suggest emotional attitudes rather than moral awareness as such. But in the novels thus far considered, he establishes moral distinctions by the use of a highly abstract and to some extent artificial language. Time and space imagery dominate the structure of *The Sound and the Fury* and *Light in August* and help to explain the contrasts between rational and intuitive perceptions of reality. The implication is that rational experience posits a world arbitrarily divided according to rigid distinctions of time and space. The failure of such primitives as Benjy and Lena to perceive time differences isolates them from this self-destructive milieu which is more or less identified with human society. Such figures are therefore removed in a double sense from conventional reality. They have considerably fewer realistic traits than the socially oriented characters to whom they are opposed, who are themselves fictional distortions of the ordinary world. It is the very nature of Faulkner's primitives to resist exact description; and the qualities attributed to them tend to be negative or highly abstract.

Thus Eula Varner in *The Hamlet* is described largely by what she is *not*, by the system of rational order that her mere presence undermines and destroys. The thirteen-year-old girl is more than a match for the long history of sophisticated human endeavor, as represented by the village school and its ambitious young master. The young man's classroom has neither head nor foot: "It would have but one point, like a swarm of bees, and she would be that point, that center, swarmed over and importuned yet serene and intact and apparently even oblivious, tranquilly abrogating the whole long sum of human thinking and suffering which is called knowledge, education, wisdom, at once supremely unchaste and inviolable: the queen, the matrix" (116).

The Hamlet is a fragmentary novel which introduces Faulkner's most pessimistic social theme, the replacement of the aristocratic families as economic rulers of Jefferson by the new and irresponsible

Snopes clan. In terms of Yoknapatawpha mythology the Snopes victory is best symbolized by Flem Snopes's achievement in becoming president of the Sartoris bank in Jefferson, an event discussed and interpreted in *The Town* and *The Mansion*. But *The Hamlet,* a much superior novel, concerns the poor farmers of Frenchman's Bend, outside Jefferson. A number of separate incidents or stories, many of them published separately, are united by the serio-comic saga of the Snopes family as it becomes more and more prominent in the community and more and more disturbing to the other inhabitants.

In addition there is a strong contrast between Flem Snopes and the forces of nature to which he holds superficial title. Both the apparent success and the underlying failure of Flem's quest for social power are illustrated by his marriage to Eula, who is closely associated with the land: "the fine land rich and fecund and foul and eternal and impervious to him who claimed title to it" (119). Whereas she is an incarnate life force, Flem is a gnomelike figure, "without glands or desire" (119), and his title over Eula, who is pregnant with someone else's child, is made to seem absurd. Like Popeye in *Sanctuary,* Flem is almost totally lacking in human dimension. His eyes, the color of "stagnant water" (22), are set in a face "as blank as a pan of uncooked dough." He wears a gray cap, gray trousers, and a white shirt; his "machine-made" black bow tie is "a tiny viciously depthless cryptically balanced splash like an enigmatic punctuation symbol against the expanse of white shirt" (58). The other members of the family mirror some of Flem's traits, but they are given characteristics that seem more human and are therefore easier to dramatize. Lump, the clerk, is avaricious without having Flem's shrewdness; I.O., the schoolmaster, is an ambitious scatterbrain; Eck, the blacksmith, is good-natured but incompetent; and so forth. They are alike only in their capacity for prolific growth and their orientation toward self and clan as opposed to country and community.

Faulkner's characterization of both Flem Snopes and Eula Varner emphasizes their isolation, as stylized and incomprehensible figures, from conventional society. Although they are polar opposites and dominate the structure of *The Hamlet,* their personalities are too negatively shaped to be in strong dramatic conflict. The incidents

49

in which Flem or Eula appear derive their impact from the frustrated reactions of Yoknapatawpha males, who are either gulled by the silent Flem or sexually frustrated by the placid Eula. Within such separate episodes Faulkner's social pessimism is kept in the background and a spirit of comedy allowed to prevail.

The humor is made possible by the characterization of Eula and other pastoral figures as having a kind of mastery over the male world of self-conscious reason. Eula cannot use this power directly, but she invokes it by her mere presence, "as if, the drowsing maidenhead symbol's self, she possessed life but not sentience" (115). In the scene between Eula and Labove, the schoolmaster, her placidity so infuriates him that he tries to frighten her and, when this fails, to rape her. He is confounded not only by her greater physical strength but also by her failure to think that anything very important has happened. The realization that he can mean nothing at all to the moronic girl deprives Labove of his self-confidence and his ambition.

In another episode the force of primitive nature represented by Eula is associated with a romantic affair between an idiot and a neighbor's cow. Ike Snopes rescues his beloved from a burning barn and leads her away on a woodland honeymoon. The two are in idyllic harmony with the world of nature. For them "there is no distance in either space or geography, no prolongation of time for distance to exist in, no muscular fatigue to establish its accomplishment" (181). Time and nature are united: "from now until evening they will advance only as the day itself advances, no faster. They have the same destination: sunset" (186).

In opposition to these natural lovers stand the forces of organized society. Houston, the cow's owner, resembles the schoolmaster in his puritan frustration, his "helpless rage at abstract circumstance which feeds on its own impotence, has no object to retaliate upon" (191). A similar figure is the farmer who, consumed with "constant and unflagging" (194) rage at the theft of a small quantity of feed, laboriously tracks down the thieves, returns the cow to Houston, and collects his dollar reward.

One of the best stories in *The Hamlet* (first published separately as "Spotted Horses") describes a temporary alliance between the opposing principles represented by Eula and Flem. Flem takes advantage of his honeymoon in Texas to bring back a number of wild ponies, which he sells to his fascinated fellow townsmen. The poor farmers of Frenchman's Bend give up their savings to buy creatures too primitive and wild to handle, "animals which some of them had owned for seven and eight hours now but had not yet laid hands upon" (297). The theme of the story and the source of its comedy is the absurdity of man's effort to assert mastery over natural forces. The desperate farmers are afraid of the bunched herd but march in a body upon it. "Then an indescribable sound, a movement desperate and despairing, arose among [the ponies]; for an instant of static horror men and animals faced one another, then the men whirled and ran before a gaudy vomit of long wild faces and splotched chests which overtook and scattered them and flung them sprawling aside" (344–345).

Most of the remaining stories in *The Hamlet* are based upon similar oppositions between frustrated male puritans and primitive nature. Because Flem Snopes has little to do with this basic opposition, he tends to disappear from the action whenever this theme is emphasized. As a result, the theme of man's dehumanization which he symbolizes does not spoil the humor of each episode. He initiates the main action of "Spotted Horses," for example, but retires to the background once it has begun. His behind-the-scene role frees the reader to enjoy the struggle between man and beast without being directly concerned with Flem's knavery.

The reader is instinctively on the side of the wild ponies in their refusal to be harnessed, even though he feels sympathy and concern for their deluded masters. A serious moral contrast is perhaps associated with the opposition between the men and the ponies, but if so, it remains deliberately unstated. The victory of the animals is not acclaimed, nor is the consequent human misery deplored. Faulkner leaves the reader sufficiently detached from the action to enjoy the created scene and its blend of tragedy and humor, without inquiring after the social meaning.

THE PSYCHOLOGICAL OPPOSITIONS which dominate *Light In August* and *The Hamlet* are also present in the two novellas that comprise *The Wild Palms*. Both Harry Wilbourne and the convict are given the mental rigidity typical of Faulkner's puritans and are thrust into a series of contrived situations that expose this rigidity. Neither character can understand the human passions and natural events which are confronted, and neither can adjust old values and habits of mind to new situations. Harry Wilbourne is presented as abandoning medical school and a respectable future for a life of sexual freedom with Charlotte Rittenmeyer, a married woman with several children. But he corrupts the potential honesty and integrity of their relationship by forcing it within the puritan framework of sin and damnation. Wilbourne's moral guilt is symbolized by his mishandling of an abortion, which is followed by Charlotte's death. He is sent to prison to be alone with his self-torturing but nevertheless selfish memories. In "Old Man" a convict is sent out to do flood rescue work and finds himself lost upon the Mississippi River with a refugee woman about to have a baby. The convict delivers the baby and supports both it and the mother, but his dominant aim is always to carry out his initial instructions and return to a prison life regarded as a moral sanctuary.

One may view "Wild Palms" and "Old Man" either as two closely related but distinct works or as a single novel involving an interplay between a tragic and a comic plot action. In either case the interlacing of the two works can be called a brilliant and successful *tour de force* in which puritan minds are placed in conflict with natural forces that they seek to suppress or control. On the one hand Harry's self-destruction is brought about by his inability to reconcile his moral scruples with his sexual imagination. First he surrenders to imagination and then seeks to destroy or pervert its expression. On the other hand, the convict succeeds in defeating nature, as Joseph J. Moldenhauer [2] has pointed out, by keeping his struggle purely external, by keeping his morality and mentality all of a piece. His lack of imagination, and consequently of human personality, is symbolized by his namelessness. He preserves human dignity and self-respect at the expense of individuality.

Harry Wilbourne first appears to the reader in juxtaposition with a puritan doctor representing the destiny that Harry only by chance escapes. In ferreting out the nature of Charlotte's illness, the unnamed doctor reveals the fascination and disgust for illicit sexu-

[2] Joseph J. Moldenhauer, "Unity of Theme and Structure in 'The Wild Palms'," in *Three Decades*, pp. 305–322.

ality that characterize Harry's own reactions throughout the story. Instead of sacrificing everything for love, as Harry believes he is doing, he is trying to pervert his affair with Charlotte into what he calls "the passionate idea of two damned and doomed and isolated forever against the world and God and the irrevocable . . ." He despises Charlotte, whose ideal of freedom leaves no room for self-reproach, for her ability as a woman to "take the illicit love and make it respectable" (82). Charlotte is genuinely in love and considers her flight from husband and children as a desperate sacrifice of a limited value for a greater one. But her lover is only acting out his private moral drama. Harry becomes dissatisfied with his life with Charlotte whenever it approaches what he calls bourgeois respectability. He resents anything which would lessen, in his mind, his puritan struggle with forces that he believes have already doomed himself and Charlotte to moral and physical defeat.

Like the plot of "Old Man," the action of "Wild Palms" depends upon an accidental disturbance of the *status quo* followed by a character's effort to impose old categories upon the new situation. An incident that parallels the flood conditions of "Old Man" is Harry Wilbourne's accidental discovery of a wallet containing enough money to permit his departure with Charlotte. Instead of trying to resist the forces of circumstance, as does the convict, the intern accepts greedily the temptation which the money affords. But when chance provides Harry a steady income as the author of pornography—an ironical expression of his distorted puritanism—he makes a "wilful" decision to leave Chicago, where he and Charlotte are comfortably settled, for an unsavory medical job in Utah. In a long harangue he tells a friend that idleness and "fleshly pleasures" breed human virtues, whereas thrift, industry, and financial independence spawn all the vices—"fanaticism, smugness, meddling, fear, and worst of all, respectability" (133). Faulkner's intentions are clearly satirical. The context in which Harry's bohemian idealism is placed reveals it as a mere caricature of a true artist's love—manifested by Charlotte—for what is concrete and honest in human experience.

Harry derives his philosophy of idleness from Charlotte's supposed example. But her life cuts across his categories, showing thrift and industry as well as leisure. When they are living an "idle" life at an isolated lake, Charlotte swims and paints while Harry sleeps and worries about their dwindling supply of food. He is shocked by her habit of walking about naked; but later, in Chicago, he professes fear that with the advent of respectability they will be dressing and undressing privately and turning off the light before making love. The sophomoric Harry merely reverses his rigid puritanism without realizing that Charlotte's actions elude moral descriptions. His flight to Utah is not so much an effort to escape bourgeois respectability as a desire to rid himself of the pleasures of life that threaten to blur his clear image of their illicit love.

At the heart of Harry's demand for moral honesty is a fundamental disbelief in the very love upon which he and Charlotte stake everything. He explains to their friend that love cannot last, that "there is no place for it in the world today, not even in Utah" (136). His puritan sense of guilt conjures up an antagonist who destroys love by using the weapons of money and respectability, against which there is no defense. "So I am afraid. Because They are smart, shrewd, They will have to be; if They were to let us beat Them, it would be like unchecked murder and robbery" (140). He believes that it would really be immoral, "like unchecked murder and robbery" (140), for Charlotte and him to remain unpunished for their love. Because of this obsession, he cannot be reached by the friend's common-sense question: "But why go to Utah in February to beat it? And if you cant beat it, why in hell go to Utah?" (141). Harry wants martyrdom to love; he wants the cold and discomfort of Utah as an appropriate setting for his private drama of sin and damnation. In carrying out his plan, he destroys love and brings pain and death to Charlotte.

In "Old Man" the convict's denial of the freedom thrust upon him lacks the tragic atmosphere that pervades Harry Wilbourne's actions, but the same mental weaknesses are revealed. Like Harry, the convict cannot adapt himself to new circumstances. His deeds of apparent courage are performed only because fate forces him into situations from which he lacks the imagination to retreat. At the beginning of the story he is sent out by prison authorities to pick up a woman and a man caught in a flood and to return with both. After he and the pregnant woman are swept down the river, he tries to find help for her before her time comes. But when someone offers to take the woman off his hands, he refuses. He was sent out with specific instructions to return *with* the woman and the boat, and to give her up would violate the terms of a sacred contract. He chooses to stick to the ridiculous terms of the original instructions rather than allow the responsibilities of freedom to disturb his mental peace.

The woman's unborn child represents the same kind of alien force, from the convict's point of view, as the flooded river under him. It is "a separate demanding threatening inert yet living mass of which both he and she were equally victims" (154). He assists in the birth only because he has no alternative. "The convict felt exactly as he had in the fleeing skiff when the woman suggested that they had better hurry. He felt the same outrageous affronting of a condition purely moral, the same raging impotence to find any answer to it" (229).

Throughout the work the convict keeps his eyes down, both literally and metaphorically, ignoring the reality about him. His relation to the flood is expressed symbolically in a passage describing the three strata into which the flood waters are divided. First there is the "bland and unhurried surface"; then "the rush and fury of the flood itself"; and finally the original stream, seemingly oblivious of the flood's presence, "following undisturbed and unaware its appointed course and serving its Lilliputian end" (62–63). The convict's calmness barely covers a torrent of rage and frustration, comparable to the swift and violent currents of the flood. But deeper than his sense of outrage lies a refusal—like that of the undeviating original stream—to accept the changed world about him. Even when the full force of the flood strikes him, he continues his "Lilliputian" effort to row the skiff back to the landing. He persists even though the direction of the current has been reversed and the paddle itself has been hurled from his hand. "The convict . . . still waiting his chance to scream and still going through the motions of paddling though he no longer even had the paddle now, looked down upon a world turned to furious motion and in incredible retrograde" (157).

Occasionally the convict is forced into actions against his will, or even into a fleeting awareness of his immediate situation, but he nevertheless pursues his original and now ridiculous aim. Weeks later the flood subsides, and the convict works his way painstakingly back up the river, taking the woman with him. Wearing his carefully preserved uniform and emerging as if from nowhere, he surrenders to a deputy:

> "You a officer?" he said.
> "You damn right I am," the deputy said. "Just let me get this damn gun—"
> "All right," the other said. "Yonder's your boat, and here's the woman. But I never did find that bastard on the cottonhouse." (278)

The convict returns to a world that has written him off as dead, yet he acts as if he had just been sent out that morning. In this way he repudiates the intervening passage of time. The convict has defeated the world by refusing to take anything from it, even memories. The prison authorities give him ten extra years for "escaping"; but this gift of time, which the convict interprets as a refuge *from* time, is just what he wants.

The convict's effort to fulfill his absurd contract can be viewed as a comic parody of the blind rationality that characterizes such figures as Thomas Sutpen in *Absalom, Absalom!* and Quentin Compson in *The Sound and the Fury*. Faulkner's puritans usually destroy themselves through their attempts to fit new experiences into predetermined categories. The disaster which Harry Wilbourne brings upon Charlotte and himself exemplifies this kind of self-induced fate. The convict is ruled by a similar obsession; but he does not impose his rational will, if he can help it, upon the lives of others. He remains impervious to the implications of his new life and thus protects himself from a destructive conflict with the natural forces symbolized by the flood.

Faulkner's comic technique is illustrated by the description of the convict's participation in an alligator hunt. To everyone's astonishment and admiration he leaps into the water and kills his first animal with a knife in hand-to-hand combat. He performs this seemingly heroic action not through deliberate courage, but merely because he has no idea how alligators should be killed and is too proud to ask. Learning afterwards that he should have used a gun instead of a knife, he is naturally upset at the waste of time and energy. But he decides that "since I done already started out without one, I don't reckon I'll change" (261). For the next few days he performs the same desperate ritual before a small but faithful audience of Cajuns, "like the *matador* [before] his *aficionados*" (263). His actions appear heroic to his fellow hunters, but to the convict they represent "durn foolishness" and hard work. Only the reader, who sees the convict's role as both hero and fool, understands the comedy of the scene.

THE HUMOR of "Old Man" stems from the disparity between the convict's deep involvement in life and his desperate wish to remain uninvolved. A similar technique is found in *As I Lay Dying*. The surface action of the novel has all the accoutrements of a serious folk epic. Addie Bundren dies, and her husband and children carry out her dying wish to be buried with her own family in Jefferson, a few miles away. Yet nature plays a grim joke upon the Bundrens in the form of a powerful flood which washes out two bridges and forces the family to undergo great hardships before reaching their goal. But the most unpleasant consequence of this delay, the decay of the mother's body, causes the trip to seem grotesque and absurd. Moreover, the family's courage and apparent devotion to Addie's last wish are mocked and betrayed by the fact that each member of the family has a private and selfish reason for reaching or not reaching Jefferson. The extreme gap between public and private goals deprives the group effort of heroism, and such personal misfortunes as Darl's madness or Dewey Dell's pregnancy are robbed of dramatic pathos.

The novel is characterized by equally extreme contradictions of style. Rustic characters are made to express profound emotions in language sometimes colloquial and sometimes elaborately rhetorical. Wherever passages of high seriousness occur, they are rudely interlaced with others of light burlesque. The reader never quite knows what to take seriously and what to laugh at. Because of these artificial contradictions of tone, the total structure appears as fundamentally comic rather than tragic, as mock-epic rather than epic.

The comic structure is made possible by constant incongruity between the major characters and the situation in which they are involved. Usually the important characters in a Faulkner novel struggle against an environment to which, as the action develops, they are seen to be symbolically related. In this way the actions of styllized figures become vehicles for the revelation of serious themes. But in *As I Lay Dying*, even though the materials for thematic synthesis are present, Faulkner deliberately refrains from exploiting them. He goes to the opposite extreme and carefully eliminates from the epic venture every vestige of moral or social significance. The trip to Jefferson functions in a way comparable to the presence of Yoknapatawpha County in other works. But Faulkner deliberately avoids making the symbolic connections between the individual and his milieu. He could project serious social themes into his stylized plot situation, yet he carefully refrains.

Despite the comic atmosphere, *As I Lay Dying* illustrates Faulkner's creation of stylized puritan figures. Anse Bundren suggests the potential inertia of a mind committed to arbitrary principles and unwilling to relax them, regardless of the circumstances. Dewey Dell is driven by a passion and Jewel by a fury comparable to the emotions of Joe Christmas and Thomas Sutpen. Like Quentin Compson, Darl Bundren is obsessed with the passage of time and the enigma of selfhood. To both characters, and to Faulkner's puritan figures in general, the evolutions of nature are savage and intolerable; man is only a clotting soon dissolved in the stream of time.

A unique feature of *As I Lay Dying* in this connection is the absence of primitive figures fully comparable to Dilsey in *The Sound and the Fury* or Eula Varner in *The Hamlet*. Dewey Dell is too forceful a personality to function in this way. Vardaman is only a child, but his vivid imagination does not seem to represent natural intuition. He is perhaps the archrationalist of the family, even though his reasoning processes are surrealistic. The result is the absence in the novel of any dramatic conflict between opposed attitudes toward experience. The personalities of the Bundrens are very different, but the differences are not themselves related to serious moral themes.

As a family group, the Bundrens win a victory, although a meaningless one, of the individual human will over nature. Their victory is possible because they keep their eyes on limited, concrete aims (as does the convict of "Old Man") and do not waste their strength by fighting abstract moral battles. More characteristic Faulkner heroes pursue to the death some kind of abstract ideal: Thomas Sutpen wants to begin a family dynasty, Quentin Compson wants his sister to be either pure or morally damned, Joe Christmas desires self-punishment, and Harry Wilbourne craves martyrdom for love. But the Bundrens are not usually concerned with moral sin or the unfolding of an absolute destiny. Apart from the dead mother only Darl explores absolute questions seriously, and only he suffers permanent destruction. The rest of the Bundrens merely flirt with the problem of selfhood and the puritan conception of an irrevocable destiny. When the action of the novel is resolved all the remaining characters seem to retire from such philosophical frontiers.

The comic figures of *As I Lay Dying* and "Old Man" may be called puritan heretics who combine Protestant habits of mind with isolated personal goals. To this degree they cast light upon Faulkner's methods of characterization. They reflect a kind of self-satire, as if Faulkner were aware of his rigid mythological and psychological devices and were trying to parody both.

In *Light in August* and *The Hamlet*, Faulkner demonstrates his ability to use extreme contrasts between psychological archetypes as a basis for narrative structure. In *Light in August*, where Faulkner is concerned with the presentation of serious social themes, the characters in greatest opposition, Joe Christmas and Lena Grove, do not appear in the same scenes. The greater stylization of Lena Grove, as well as the lighter tone associated with her nonpuritan behavior, is useful as a foil to the presentation of the guilt-ridden Joe Christmas. The less serious themes and even greater stylization of *The Hamlet* enable Faulkner to place his primitive figure, Eula Varner, into direct conflict with other characters, and to make her a center of narrative focus. In this pleasant and loosely organized work there is no central puritan figure comparable to Joe Christmas, or Thomas Sutpen, or even Quentin Compson. Minor puritan characters, like Jody Varner or the schoolmaster, are in destructive opposition to the forces of primitive nature; but the personal tragedies which result are not of major concern. Moreover, the consequences of rational man's struggle with nature are made to seem less important thematically than the unifying concern for Snopesism and its rise to power. At the same time Flem Snopes's ability to gull the inhabitants of Frenchman's Bend is traceable to the use he makes of natural forces, as illustrated by his profitable marriage to Eula and by his successful sale of the wild Texas ponies. Faulkner insists that Flem cannot "possess" the symbols for nature that he holds title to; but he is sufficiently shrewd to use nature to his own advantage.

Important characters representing primitive nature are lacking in *The Wild Palms,* and there is no such character in *As I Lay Dying,* with the possible exception of the pregnant Dewey Dell. But in both these works natural realities are suggested by the environmental forces with which the individual characters are in conflict. Harry Wilbourne is destroyed by his effort to give natural facts a personal moral interpretation, but the members of the Bundren family make no effort to impose their will upon nature, except in the sense of achieving limited physical goals; and as a family group they are not destroyed. In *As I Lay Dying* and "Old Man" Faulkner creates comic effects out of the material of personal tragedy.

All these works illustrate Faulkner's creation of a stylized characterization involving an extreme opposition between rational or puritan man and the natural world in which he must live. Faulkner's ability to make this stylization serve the aims of either tragedy or comedy reveals his ability to control the emotional reactions of his reader, and indicates the extraordinary versatility of his art.

Chapter Five

❧

EXPERIMENTS IN NARRATION

$\mathscr{I}$N HIS FIRST THREE NOVELS Faulkner pays relatively little attention to problems involving the point of view of narration. He employs a traditional third-person and semiomniscient point of view, with only an occasional intrusion into the inner lives of his characters. However, his next two novels, *The Sound and the Fury* and *As I Lay Dying*, rely heavily upon the Joycean interior monologue, radically modified, as a basic technique. These two important works place Faulkner (along with Henry James, James Joyce, Virginia Woolf, and others) in the tradition of the modern psychological novel. Yet Faulkner never breaks completely from conventional modes of narration. Many of his monologues are interior in appearance only and do not contain stream-of-consciousness writing. They are often third-person accounts cast arbitrarily in the form of first-person discourse. Instead of eliminating his detached narrator, Faulkner gives him a stronger voice and often identifies him with a character whose language may or may not be used. This enables Faulkner to cross barriers of time and space, make arbitrary stylistic changes, and grant extraordinary linguistic ability to idiots, children, and other primitive characters. These distortions and contradictions of tone are kept under strict control and help to create an atmosphere of psychological analysis.

Before Faulkner's monologues can be examined in detail some definitions and comparisons must be established. I shall use "interior" or "internal" monologue to signify a particular narrative method, and "stream-of-consciousness" to mean either a type of novel or the impressionistic effect created by individual passages. In a stream-of-consciousness novel, the author seeks to explore the full range of individual thought processes and may or may not employ the monologue technique. Dorothy Richardson's *Pilgrimage*, James Joyce's *Ulysses*, and Virginia Woolf's *The Waves* are all stream-of-consciousness novels, although in each case many and varied techniques are used. A typical device is that of alternating between the actual thoughts of a character and indirect paraphrases of what is said or thought. The narrative voice sometimes quotes and sometimes merely reports or summarizes what is passing through a character's mind.

The Sound and the Fury and *As I Lay Dying* employ stream-of-consciousness writing, but it is doubtful whether they can be classified in the genre created by James Joyce and Dorothy Richardson. For one thing, Faulkner's use of first-person narration automatically rules out methods involving indirect discourse. The result is a lack of the flexibility required for a full-scale exploration of mental reality. Faulkner compensates for this limitation by emphasizing dramatic action where Joyce or Virginia Woolf would stress subjective experience. His monologuists are also narrators of the physical events taking place around them. In many cases Faulkner creates characters who are themselves detached witnesses of the main action and whose monologues are interior in form only. Even in genuine stream-of-consciousness passages there are many shifts to ordinary discourse and to conventional flashback description.

There is nothing in Faulkner's work suggesting even remotely the uncontrolled thought processes of the Molly Bloom episode of *Ulysses*. Nor does Faulkner often try to indicate indirectly the nature of a character's unconscious mind. It should be remembered that interior monologues usually consist of words presumed to be passing through individual minds. It cannot, therefore, be directly associated with the unconscious mind. Mental activity below the level of consciousness must be indicated by words, if at all; but the words cannot be described as actually framed by or in the mind. All words framed by the mind can be ascribed to conscious mental processes, whether the individual is aware of making them or not. For an individual to hear his own words during animated discourse of any kind is the exception rather than the rule. The rush of words ascribed to Molly Bloom may suggest a deeper layer of consciousness than that ascribed to an inspired lecturer, but there is no essential difference of type apart from considerations of origin. Both involve formulated words never really heard by the speaker.

When the line is crossed between conscious and unconscious areas of the mind, the literary break must be sharp. The writer must turn from what he knows through experience to what he can only infer through an understanding of psychology and linguistics. The verbal content of his work cannot pretend to be naturalistic, and the monologue form, as such, must be abandoned. In breaking down the distinction between conscious and unconscious areas of the mind Joyce is forced virtually to abandon both narrative realism and the interior monologue form. He invokes mythological or hallucinatory roles, collapses temporal and spatial barriers, and in general employs distorted language patterns. In *Ulysses* he uses the minds and personalities of his central characters as a kind of stage upon which his narrative and poetical skills are freely exercised. The frequent result is a shift from the exploration of individual minds to the creation of archetypal figures or types of mental behavior. In *Finnegan's Wake*, where these techniques are brought to an extreme development, Joyce may be said to transcend even the stream-of-consciousness genre. Seeking to create a universal consciousness or monolithic dream awareness, he forces a deliberate fusion of dramatic experience and psychological theory.

In *The Sound and the Fury* and *As I Lay Dying*, Faulkner follows closely the experiences and points of view of his narrating characters. The distinctions in technique are not between the near and far reaches of the mind, as in *Ulysses*, but between degrees or intensities of controlled rational thought. Consequently the stream-of-consciousness passages are usually associated with the more self-conscious and intellectual members of each family. Faulkner often crosses temporal and spatial barriers, but he seldom tries to eliminate them. The confusions of time and space in his work are deliberately unrealistic and are usually associated in some way with the personality of the narrating characters, as in the Benjy section of *The Sound and the Fury* and in the Darl Bundren monologues of *As I Lay Dying*. Although his work is deeply influenced by Freudian ideas, Faulkner is mainly concerned with the dramatic realities and he does not need the hypothesis of the unconscious mind. The past comes fully alive to Faulkner's rational characters; it almost never works in secret. One might call Faulkner's use of the monologue technique a deliberate misunderstanding of Freudian theory and Joycean practice.

In the opening monologue of *The Sound and the Fury* Faulkner gives the impression that an idiot's unconscious mind is somehow responsible for the narration. But the function of the monologue is to provide dramatic exposition while creating the misleading atmosphere of psychological chaos. A major portion of the monologue is devoted to actions which the idiot cannot understand and to conversations which do not involve him. Instead of trying to explore an idiot's mind—an absurd task—Faulkner adopts a narrative point of view which follows Benjy's actions but reports in a detached and impersonal manner what the idiot sees and experiences. The events which are narrated occur in several contrasted layers of time. Each layer or chronological grouping is divided into fragments, which are rearranged to give the impression of a primitive chain of association. These disorganized episodes are later recognized by the reader as introducing key scenes or symbol patterns which recur in more intelligible contexts.

Two sets of related episodes dominate Benjy's monologue. In the present world of "April Seventh, 1928," a man-sized idiot celebrates his birthday by following Luster, Dilsey's grandson, as the Negro boy searches for a missing quarter. The corresponding day in the past is that of the grandmother's death and funeral, when the Compson children spend the afternoon playing by a small stream in the pasture and are later sent to the servant cabins in the back. Both actions provide points of transition in which Benjy switches from one scene to the other, or to other scenes, such as Caddy's wedding or to the rainy day in which Benjy is given a new name. These transitions are made possible by similar locations, similar actions, or phrases common to more than one level of time. Faulkner is often able to define the idiot's thoughts by the nature of these shifts. When Benjy hears a golfer shout "caddie," the narration immediately changes to a time when his sister Caddy and not a Negro boy is holding him by the hand. Benjy's ability to "smell" death in the family is also indicated by his time shifts from one scene of death to another. Through this obsession with death, Faulkner is able to load Benjy's narration with references to important scenes that are described in greater detail in other sections of the novel.

By these devices, Faulkner avoids any direct statement by Benjy of his one clearly defined emotion, his love for Caddy. The idiot never describes this emotion except through ambiguous and impersonal phrases, such as "She smelled like trees" (91). His attitude is revealed almost solely by the focus of the narration upon her behavior, as viewed by the idiot, or upon scenes in which she comforts him.

Occasionally Benjy makes a gesture or begins to cry, but these actions are usually described as if they were an impersonal feature of the physical scene. The narration stops just short of his consciousness and indicates unknown thought processes by a restrained factual narration. There is no interior world at all in Benjy's monologue; everything is externalized. This explains the bewildering time shifts: it cannot reasonably be argued that an idiot is capable of reliving the past, but neither can it be said that he "lives" the present as ordinary individuals do. Faulkner assumes that if an idiot could remember the past at all, he could not distinguish it from the present. The confusions of past and present are in their way realistic, as long as the reader accepts an idiot as narrator.

Quentin Compson's monologue, which follows Benjy's, is much closer to the *Ulysses* model. Faulkner continues his use of a detached voice which reports everything it sees or hears, including Quentin's thoughts, in the first person. This voice is also capable of crossing temporal barriers and describing events in the past as if they were taking place in the present. The principal difference between the two flashback techniques is that Quentin appears to *remember* events in their entirety and only occasionally does he seem to *relive* them as Benjy does. The past underlies Quentin's Harvard world and seems to intrude upon his consciousness at every possible opportunity. These intrusions are facilitated by a series of parallels between Harvard acquaintances and members of Quentin's family. The presence of Gerald Bland causes the boy to remember scenes involving both Dalton Ames, who first seduced Caddy, and Herbert Head, who married her. Quentin's lengthy speculations concerning Gerald's moral character clearly reflect his obsessed interest in the two background figures. In a similar way, his analysis of Mrs. Bland reveals indirectly his feelings toward his own mother. Through a strange flirtation with a small Italian girl, whom he calls "sister," Quentin both expresses and recalls his past life with Caddy.

Toward the end of his monologue, Quentin is listening to Gerald Bland's boasting. Without warning, the narration shifts from the Harvard picnic scene to past events which involve Quentin, Caddy, and Dalton Ames. Only typographical changes (the punctuation marks are removed) indicate that the traumatic events are remembered and not actually taking place. Faulkner achieves a stream-of-consciousness effect simply by shifting from present to past reality and making it seem that the earlier scene is passing through Quentin's memory. When Quentin is knocked out by Dalton Ames, the narration shifts back to the picnic scene. It is then revealed indirectly that while remembering the past and perhaps confusing it with the present, Quentin tried to hit Gerald Bland and was knocked out by him.

In telling Quentin's story, Faulkner uses essentially three points of view or modes of narration. The first and most common mode is Quentin's description in the past tense of his actions upon the day of his suicide. The second mode is a direct recording of Quentin's thought processes during this final day. The narration often shifts back and forth from one point of view to the other, from Quentin describing a past action to Quentin's thoughts describing a present action as he experiences the action. This oscillation is prevented from disturbing the reader by the constant focus of Quentin's Harvard thoughts upon events occurring in his Mississippi past. Very cleverly, Faulkner has the past-tense narration deal with the narrative present and the present-tense recording of the narrative present concentrate upon Quentin's recollection of events prior to his life at Harvard. This makes an easy transition possible since both modes of narration make use of past-tense verbs. For example, Quentin Compson describes in the past tense his act of boarding a Harvard streetcar. Then he begins to quote or paraphrase his own recollections, which are also expressed in the past tense. "The only vacant seat was beside a nigger. He wore a derby and shined shoes and he was holding a dead cigar stub. I used to think that a Southerner had to be always conscious of niggers. I thought that Northerners would expect him to. When I first came East I kept thinking . . ." (105). And so on for about three pages of summarized thoughts and recollections concerning Quentin's experience with Negroes, told with the immediacy of Quentin's presence on the streetcar. These recollections are terminated only when his seatmate leaves the car. The past-tense voice of the narrator Quentin is blended with a paraphrase of the thoughts of the streetcar Quentin, who, speculating in the present about the past, also uses the past tense. The distinction is dissolved between a narrative of Quentin's actions as he thinks and a summary of the thoughts themselves. Quentin moves from an exterior point into his own mind; he becomes simultaneously himself and his own detached historian.

A third mode of narration occurs when the reader is projected directly into Quentin's Mississippi past. The narrator is now a Quentin who experiences the past events directly but does little more than report impersonally what he sees or hears, again in the past tense. The result, as in Benjy's monologue, is basically a conventional third-person account which generates an atmosphere of intense stream of consciousness. Since the reported events consist almost entirely of dialogue, there are few past-tense verbs and the narration has the effect of remembered words passing through the character's mind. The impersonality of the narration and the emphasis upon dialogue suggest that Quentin, in his distraught state, is temporarily reliving past events, or at least *hearing* past words.

Occasionally Faulkner has great difficulty in controlling these various types of discourse and in establishing smooth transitions from one to another. He begins Quentin's monologue as if the point of view would remain in the past tense. "When the shadow of the sash

appeared on the curtains it was between seven and eight oclock and
then I was in time again, hearing the watch." A discussion of the
history and meaning of Quentin's watch is then given from what
appears to be the same point of view ("when Father gave it to me
he said . . ."). This is followed by more action and by Quentin's
thoughts upon awakening—thoughts framed in indirect discourse
from a later point in time: "As soon as I knew I couldn't see it, I
began to wonder what time it was." And: "If it had been cloudy I
could have looked at the window, thinking what he said about idle
habits" (95–96). At this point the first major shift occurs. The narrator ceases to be a Quentin looking back upon his last day of life
and becomes the Quentin actually lying in bed and thinking about
his sister's marriage:

Thinking it would be nice for them down at New London if the weather
held up like this. Why shouldn't it? The month of brides, the voice that
breathed *She ran right out of the mirror, out of the banked scent. Roses.
Roses. Mr and Mrs Jason Richmond Compson announce the marriage of.*
Roses. Not virgins like dogwood, milkweed. I said I have committed incest, Father I said. Roses. Cunning and serene. If you attend Harvard
one year, but dont see the boat-race, there should be a refund. Let Jason
have it. Give Jason a year at Harvard. (96)

The progression is by natural chain of association, but the past-tense
point of view indicated by the word "thinking" is quickly abandoned, and the reader is confronted with the words actually passing through Quentin's mind. In later passages Faulkner makes no
effort to establish a grammatical transition, as he does here, but
moves easily from the narrator speaking in the past tense to the
present-tense "thinking" Quentin. Another feature of this passage is
the transition from the youth's active speculation to remembered
words that flow through his consciousness. "The month of brides"
is Quentin's bitter comment on the present June morning, but "the
voice that breathed" is from the title of a song associated with
Caddy's wedding. "Not virgin like dogwood, milkweed" (a comment on roses) is again a fresh thought; whereas "I have committed
incest, Father" is remembered dialogue. Other scraps of past conversations, later clarified, complete the passage.

This distinction between Quentin's active thinking and his passive memory prefigures the later and much sharper distinctions between narration of past and of present action. In the early part of the monologue, the interpolated dialogue is carefully integrated with Quentin's conscious speculations. But as the monologue continues, such remembered fragments become longer and more unified until they transcend the framework of the monologue form, as in the passage leading up to Quentin's fight with Dalton Ames. The long flashback accounts accumulate toward the end of the monologue, when the reader has recognized the force of Quentin's fascination with past events. Many but not all of the extreme shifts from present to remembered reality are indicated by italics, elimination of punctuation, or some other typographical aid. Faulkner is deliberately inconsistent in the use of such devices. If he were consistent the arbitrary nature of the transitions might become obvious, and the effect of psychological realism might not be as strong.

Faulkner is virtually unique in his use of first-person interior monologues. In creating stream-of-consciousness narration most novelists employ a third-person observer whose point of view is almost identical with that of the character in question. The narrator of the early part of *Ulysses* shifts easily from brief descriptions of physical action to internal thought processes. In fact, interior monologues would appear to require such a third-person narrator if the effect of realistic narration is to be maintained. No character can be represented as quoting his own stream of consciousness unless compensating narrative techniques are used.

The advantage Faulkner gains by first-person narration is the opportunity to contrast a strong dramatic action to the mental reactions through which the action is filtered, without a corresponding difference of tone. In *Ulysses* there are similar oppositions between physical events and the thoughts of Joyce's Dublin characters, but the events associated with the narrative present are relatively few and static. An emphasis is placed upon remembered events and upon abstract or universalized motivations, such as Stephen's search for a father or Bloom's quest for identity, which can be adequately dramatized without much reference to a physical world.

In both *The Sound and the Fury* and *As I Lay Dying*, the thoughts of the characters, though often abstract, are focused upon clearly defined physical situations. Both novels are crowded with scenes in which character is revealed solely through dramatic action objectively narrated. If Faulkner had settled for a third-person narrator pure and simple, the amount of genuine interior-monologue narration would necessarily have been negligible. He maintains an emphasis upon psychological reactions by the simple device of having character-narrators report actions and their own thoughts interchangeably. But this creates a basic problem. A third-person narrator that mirrors the point of view of a single character can still move freely from objective to subjective narration, as the Joycean narrator does. But if such a narrator is given a personality, he must always be inside his own mind looking out and thus unable to report his thoughts except by quoting them. Like any other narrator, he can be expected to have a realistic position in space and time.

This realistic point of view is precisely what Faulkner's narrators are *not* given. Faulkner's typical procedure is to write a semiomniscient account in which the third-person detached voice is arbitrarily replaced by the first person "I." The narrator retains his freedom, but the pretense is nevertheless established that the character is telling his own story. This device works splendidly in the Benjy section, where the idiot narrator is given no interior consciousness. The first-person point of view remains consistently detached, and is thus the virtual equivalent of a third-person point of view, in spite of the devices by which Benjy's love for Caddy and his lack of rational sophistication are revealed. The very absurdity of an idiot narrator distracts the reader from the problem of an impersonal narrator posing as an "I" voice.

Difficulties occur when the first-person narrator is an important actor in the scene being described. Although Quentin's monologue is more realistic than Benjy's in other respects, there are more potentially disturbing transitions from detached narration to psychological revelation. Similar transitions are found throughout Jason's monologue. For example, a paragraph begins: "I opened her letter first and took the check out. Just like a woman. Six days late. Yet they try to make men believe that they're capable of conducting a business" (208). If the first sentence is emended to read "He opened her letter . . ." the unrealistic shift from description to immediate statement by the same voice is eliminated.

Experiments in Narration

FAULKNER'S USE of the interior-monologue form in *As I Lay Dying* is neither as pretentious nor as startling as in *The Sound and the Fury*. Instead of four large sections, this novel is divided into fifty-nine monologues varying in size. The shorter narrations enable Faulkner to make an extensive use of present-tense narration by first-person speakers. This daring attempt to have a character tell his own story as it occurs is especially effective when the speaker is intently watching the scene he describes. Thus Dewey Dell is desperate with fear that Anse will turn the family wagon down the New Hope Cemetery road instead of taking the mother's body on to Jefferson. She watches the signpost where the road turns off:

Now it begins to say it. New Hope three miles. New Hope three miles. *That's what they mean by the womb of time: the agony and the despair of spreading bones, the hard girdle in which lie the outraged entrails of events.* Cash's head turns slowly as we approach, his pale, empty, sad, composed and questioning face following the red and empty curve; beside the back wheel Jewel sits the horse, gazing straight ahead. (422)

The perception of external events is continuous with Dewey Dell's interior thoughts. The point of view is not realistic, but the writing is keyed so high that the reader does not mind. Here, as in other passages of the novel, the language of a relatively primitive character is full of rhetorical flourishes. At the same time, the narration of the physical action is couched in simple and tightly controlled language. Faulkner combines his detached narration with a voice identical with that of the speaking character. The narrator perceives as Dewey Dell perceives, and thinks as she thinks; but the author uses his own language.

The use of impersonal flashback narrration in *The Sound and the Fury* corresponds in the later novel to the strange ability of the narrating characters to report what they see with a minimum of distortion. Even though Darl Bundren's thoughts are dominated by jealousy and despair, he is made the chief narrator of the trip to Jefferson. Darl is pictured as so much absorbed in the world outside him that his emotions do not interfere with the narration. The novel opens with a description by Darl of himself and Jewel going home from work: "Jewel and I come up from the field, following the path in single file. Although I am fifteen feet ahead of him, anyone

71

watching us from the cotton-house can see Jewel's frayed and broken straw hat a full head above my own" (339). Darl's narration continues to be objective, in this restrained manner, until he reaches the yard where Cash is making a coffin for the dying mother:

He holds the two planks on the trestle, fitted along the edges in a quarter of the finished box. He kneels and squints along the edge of them, then he lowers them and takes up the adze. A good carpenter. Addie Bundren could not want a better one, a better box to lie in. It will give her confidence and comfort. I go on to the house, followed by the

Chuck   Chuck   Chuck

of the adze. (340)

This passage is effective because of the vibrant restraint and the use of factual details and conventional sentiments out of harmony with the atmosphere of death. Even Darl's thoughts seem as impersonal and detached as the events he describes. Yet the obvious irony of the description suggests a repressed fury that Darl is trying to keep under control. As in *The Sound and the Fury*, the reader is given information that enables him to see beyond the physical scene to the character's complex feelings.

In other passages Darl's capacity for objective narration is made a direct function of his developing madness. His obsession enables him to transcend spatial barriers, just as a neurosis allows Quentin Compson to cross temporal ones. When his mother dies, Darl is with Jewel on a wagon many miles away. The wagon mires down, and as Jewel strains at the bogged wheel, Darl imagines himself telling his brother the news: "Jewel, I say, she is dead, Jewel. Addie Bundren is dead" (375). This simple announcement is broken into by a long portion of the death scene narrated by Darl in the present tense.

Darl's brief moment of heightened consciousness, as he watches Jewel try to lift the wheel, is a starting point from which the impersonal narration moves freely in time and space. On the one hand, Darl seems to sacrifice his personality whenever this abnormal awareness is exercised. On the other hand, his relatively few passages of genuine introspection, as at the end of this particular monologue, appear abstract and philosophical, as if his consciousness were completely divorced from concrete experience. The result is a virtual split between two narrators, one an objective witness of the world's scene and the other completely withdrawn from it. Darl's madness causes an absolute division between these two narrating selves or opposed points of view. In his final monologue, Darl refers to himself in the third person and describes his own actions as if his consciousness were entirely disembodied: "Darl is our brother, our brother Darl. Our brother Darl in a cage in Jackson where, his grimed hands lying light in the quiet interstices, looking out he foams" (527).

Faulkner makes dramatic use in *The Sound and the Fury* of the reader's difficulty in understanding the complicated and superficially disorganized monologues of Benjy and Quentin. In *As I Lay Dying*, where the plot situation is more clearly defined, an even greater use is made of confusions and contradictions of detail. Faulkner introduces a number of characters whose sole function is to narrate the action from points of view outside the Bundren family. However, these witnesses are often guilty of errors of fact, especially in matters involving human emotion. Pitfalls for the careless reader are also created by the multiplicity of narrators and by the lack of a clearly defined chronology of events. Doc Peabody tells how Addie forces him to leave the sickroom before calling out the window for her son Cash. In the next monologue, narrated omnisciently by Darl, the reader learns that Addie first asks for the absent favorite, Jewel, and only calls for her oldest son to make sure the coffin will be ready. Then she dies. In this way Faulkner presents the outline of a major event—the last words of the dying Addie Bundren—before revealing the meaningful context.

In many cases the reader is given conflicting versions of the same event. Cora Tull reports that, appearing before his mother for the last time, Darl is silent, even when Dewey Dell asks him what he wants. "He didn't answer," according to Cora. "He just stood and looked at his dying mother, his heart too full for words" (355). In the next monologue, narrated by Dewey Dell, the reader is given a different version:

He stands in the door, looking at her.
"What you want, Darl?" I say.
"She is going to die," he says. And old turkey-buzzard Tull coming to watch her die but I can fool them.
"When is she going to die?" I say.

"Before we get back," he says.
"Then why are you taking Jewel?" I say.
"I want him to help me load," he says. (356)

The reader must assume that this conversation takes place only in Dewey Dell's imagination, yet it is consistent with Darl's characterization. The presence of Cora's factual account reveals not that Dewey Dell is wrong, but that she does not distinguish what she actually hears from what she knows Darl to be thinking. The result is a breakdown of narrative realism for the sake of psychological intensity. Objective truth becomes involved with personal imagination, and Dewey Dell, because of her own inward torment, is capable of understanding Darl's.

AFTER *The Sound and the Fury* and *As I Lay Dying* Faulkner makes no important use of the interior-monologue technique. The psychological intensity of the Joycean method makes it difficult for any author employing it to have a strong plot action or to make strong moral judgments. Faulkner was able to do so successfully only by fusing the interior monologue with contradictory techniques.

In later works Faulkner presents his moral themes more explicitly and, as a rule, points them more directly to social problems. He needs far more panoramic action than can be sustained by interior monologues, however supplemented by *tour-de-force* techniques. He turns to narrative devices which lend themselves to psychological analysis but leave the author free to create without subterfuge a swiftly changing dramatic scene. These techniques often involve the creation of witnesses who may or may not be directly involved in the action. Like Quentin Compson and Darl Bundren, they describe a dynamic and often violent plot situation. But these witnesses tend to be detached from the events they narrate, and their reports to the reader are generally organized by conventional logic. Such characters may speak in the first person and recount events to a definite audience, often a close friend; or their point of view may deeply influence an otherwise omniscient narration. In both cases the action which they view or describe takes on the color of their thoughts and obsessions.

In *Sanctuary* and *Light in August*, as well as later novels, the narrative eye often follows these witness-characters and quotes either their words or their interpretations of the action. In both novels the chronology is discontinuous, and symbolic language carries the burden of establishing atmosphere and theme. In *Sanctuary* Faulkner is mainly concerned with individual futility and despair in the society represented by Horace Benbow and Temple Drake. The narration is thus permeated by the language of Benbow's defeatism. Thus Popeye is seen to jerk his hat "in a dull, vicious gleam in the twilight" (5). As Benbow approaches a house, it lifts "its stark square bulk" above "a black, jagged mass of trees" (6). And so on. This personal view prevails even when Horace or a comparable witness is not present. The moron Tommy watches Temple Drake lying on a bed, "her hands crossed on her breast and her legs straight and close and decorous, like an effigy on an ancient tomb" (84). At the end of a fight an atmosphere of anger and violence blows away, "gone like a furious gust of black wind, leaving a peaceful vacuum in which they moved quietly about" (85).

Light in August is permeated by religious imagery, which is related symbolically to the puritan obsessions of Joe Christmas and other important characters. Occasionally the narration quotes Joe's presumed language, but more often the attitudes of major characters are described in language appropriate only to an omniscient narrator.

When his stepmother brings the young Joey a tray of food, in violation of her husband's order, the boy is outraged. He dumps the tray in a corner of his room. "Then he returned to the bed, carrying the empty tray as though it were a monstrance and he the bearer, his surplice the cut-down undergarment which had been bought for a man to wear" (135). The imagery reflects the boy's inverted religious drive, even though terms are used which are not his own. As in *Sanctuary*, this type of personal imagery is employed in the relatively few scenes involving omniscient description. The language is that of a narrator who, in spite of his freedom to move and speculate at will, has become saturated with the dominant symbolism of the novel.

Another characteristic of Faulkner's later novels is the extensive use of the author's own rhetorical voice. There are hints of this development in *The Sound and the Fury* and *As I Lay Dying* when the author appears to be speaking through, instead of quoting, the thoughts of the monologuists. Yet the language forced upon such figures as Benjy Compson and Darl Bundren remains appropriate to their characterization. In works later than *As I Lay Dying* the author's moral and social attitudes seem to be more directly expressed. Correspondingly, the introspective characters lose their identities and appear to function more and more as the author's spokesmen. This loss of dramatic immediacy is often compensated for by the removal of such characters, both in space and time, from the action with which they are concerned. The author's numerous witness-participants are gradually supplanted by figures who are introduced for the express purpose of reporting events to the reader. The Compsons of *Absalom, Absalom!*, V. K. Ratliff of *The Hamlet* and *The Town*, and Gavin Stevens of *Intruder in the Dust, Requiem for a Nun*, and *The Town* are narrators in this sense.

Faulkner's witnesses are never entirely divorced from the action they narrate. Even when most removed physically, as in *Absalom, Absalom!*, they are deeply involved emotionally and symbolically. Quentin Compson and his Harvard roommate identify themselves with Henry Sutpen and Charles Bon, whose exact relationship they are trying to discover: "Four of them there, in that room in New Orleans in 1860, just as in a sense there were four of them here in this tomblike room in Massachusetts in 1910" (336). The identification in this case works both ways, transporting the two ante-bellum Southerners into the twentieth century and the narrators into the past. Quentin and Shreve McCannon are associated both with the reader, in their effort to understand what actually takes place, and with the author, in their conscious fabrication of much of the action. An important dialogue between Charles and Henry is presented as a kind of interior monologue intuited by the combined intelligences of Quentin and Shreve. The reader is never given a definitive statement of what happened; he must accept the final speculation of the witnesses as approximate truth. Author, reader, and witness coalesce into a single active consciousness which transcends all distinctions between past and present and between the action and the contrived manner of its presentation.

As in *The Sound and the Fury* and *As I Lay Dying*, the use of symbolic imagery in all these later works is closely involved with the narrative point of view. The imagery of the two interior-monologue novels is traceable to the subjective experiences of the monologuists. The clocks and shadows of *The Sound and the Fury* are time and death symbols, but only because Quentin Compson sees them in this way. The flooded river of *As I Lay Dying* is a time symbol because the Bundrens view it as a barrier which they are fated, and not privileged, to cross. In *Light in August* important symbols are geometric shapes or such psychological events as the presence of an imaginary cool wind, expressive of puritan moral ecstasy. The imagery underlying both types of symbols is involved with the subjective nature of perception—Joe Christmas's street of days and Lena Grove's corridor of time—rather than with the material objects of perception.

In *Absalom, Absalom!* many of the important uses of figurative language are associated with the interpretations of the narrating witnesses. Miss Rosa speaks of Sutpen as an "ogre" as well as a "demon." Through Mr. Compson's eyes the reader sees Ellen, Sutpen's second wife, as a symbolic chrysalis or incipient butterfly. Even Sutpen is at times a commentator upon his own destiny: he recognizes the symbolic connection between the front door where he is insulted as a youth and the gate beyond which Henry will not let Charles Bon pass. In fact his recognition of the connection influences the events of the novel.

The dramatic force of Faulkner's best novels depends to a great extent upon the fusion of the symbolic imagery with the attitudes of self-conscious puritan heroes. In his less successful novels the symbolism is still linked with psychological reactions; yet it tends to be associated with the attitudes of witnesses who do not take part in the central dramatic action. An exception is *Absalom, Absalom!*, where this potential weakness is redeemed by the intensity with which the witnesses read their own regional fate into the action they narrate. In most of Faulkner's novels after *Absalom, Absalom!* the figurative language employed by witness-narrators becomes even more identical with the author's own point of view or, more specifically, with a direct statement of his moral themes. The result is often a display of rhetorical virtuosity at odds with the characterization.

In *Go Down, Moses* a witness imposes a grandiose theological imagery upon stories dealing with hunting parties and plantation

77

scandals. Ike McCaslin is seldom the center of dramatic focus except as a narrator or witness, yet his gradually developing moral consciousness assumes a dominant role. This awareness is typified in Ike's description of an old bear as a symbolic forest deity, and the hunt for the bear as a ritual of loving worship. In earlier novels the major events exhibit a dramatic force distinct from the symbolism which renders them socially and morally meaningful. But the events of "The Bear" cannot be separated in this way from their symbolic function. Though Ike McCaslin is a fascinating character, he is given little personality apart from his insistence upon treating life as a religious allegory.

The action of *Intruder in the Dust* is a further example of Faulkner's increasing tendency to subordinate characterization and plot to the direct illustration of moral ideas. In *Go Down, Moses* Ike McCaslin speaks of the Negro race as free of the moral corruption of the white race, and therefore eligible, at some future time, for social supremacy. The narrative action of *Intruder* follows this ideological pattern closely. A white mob threatens to lynch a Negro for a social crime actually committed by the mob's own leader. Thanks to the redeeming gesture of an old woman and a young boy the mob is forced to recognize the Negro's innocence and its own symbolic guilt. The Negro, whose grandfather was a white aristocrat, maintains throughout the action a dignity far superior to that of any white person.

This is far removed from the type of social allegory in such novels as *Sanctuary* and *Absalom, Absalom!* The action of *Intruder in the Dust* is a direct projection of the author's conception of the present and future of the South, and not an indirect interpretation of the present in terms of the past. What is dramatized is not social history so much as sociological theory, however attractively it might be presented. The symbolism is made evident not only to the reader but to virtually all of the characters who take part in the action.

A similar effort to convert a private symbol into a public image is responsible for the unreasonable behavior of characters in *Requiem for a Nun*. An idealistic conception of the function of the Negro race as a potential savior of white society is illustrated by a servant's murder of a white child in order to save its parents' marriage. Such characters seem to reflect Faulkner's effort to solve complicated

social problems by means of language alone. In earlier novels, introspective characters deal with such problems in a manner that reflects
their own obsessions. In later works the introspection is Faulkner's
own, but much of the bizarre stylization remains and continues to
dominate both language and action.

IN *The Sound and the Fury* and *As I Lay Dying,* the reader sees
the dramatic situation only through the minds of several narrating
characters. Even though physical events are reported with apparent
objectivity, as in the various flashback scenes, they are still made to
seem mental creations. Faulkner's use of the interior-monologue
form emphasizes the vital role which human consciousness plays in
the stabilization, and to this extent in the actual formulation, of
everyday experience. In addition, Faulkner creates characters whose
obsessions or mental limitations determine the very nature of the
world in which they live. The reader is able to compare these private
worlds and evaluate each character accordingly, as in *The Sound
and the Fury;* but unless the reader creates it, there is never an objective reality standing apart from the various private visions.

The obsessions of Quentin Compson and Jason Compson are
integral parts of the experiences which they narrate. Both live in
worlds which simultaneously reflect and bolster their inward rage.
Their brother Benjy is a primitive character without rational awareness, but his unsophisticated love for Caddy is revealed by means of
the narrative details that his impersonal "monologue" contains. In
the case of Darl Bundren, the relation between the flooded river and
the passage of time is an empirical fact of the world that he describes. Faulkner generally pays less narrative attention to what
characters think than to the actions and situations they think about.
Yet the sympathetic reader is encouraged to interpret the physical
details as tantamount to psychological revelation. In many cases the
impression of stream of consciousness is supported by the reader's
willingness to attach psychological importance, as in Benjy's
monologue, to whatever seems deliberately obscure.

Most of the vagaries and complexities of Faulkner's style stem
from this basic strategy of forcing the reader to supply much of the
psychological revelation. The surface complexities which make any
first reading of *The Sound and the Fury* very slow and perhaps

laborious are not efforts on Faulkner's part to capture the surge of intuitive consciousness. They represent technical devices which slow the reader down and control his awareness of what is going on. The reader must grope to a simultaneous understanding of the action and its moral and psychological meaning.

An extreme example of gratuitous distortion is the passage toward the end of Quentin's monologue in which the boy explains to his father his intention of committing suicide. In this passage the speeches are run together, all punctuation is eliminated, and there is no typographical indication of a change of speaker. Anyone who takes the trouble to supply the punctuation and to arrange the words in orthodox dialogue form is rewarded by a highly sophisticated (and carefully reasoned) argument by which Quentin defends his coming suicide as a victory over time. The obscuration may seem perverse, but the result is a successful shift of emphasis from the details of Quentin's argument to the general significance of its presence. By giving the dialogue as an implied rush of memory Faulkner minimizes its effect as logical argument and yet conveys the youth's tendency to reduce everything to logical terms. The apparent obscurity of the passage contributes to an atmosphere of stream-of-consciousness narration, yet the details of Quentin's argument are available to the reader who wishes to analyze the youth's self-defeating sophistry.

The success of such passages depends upon a kind of double vision forced upon the reader. On one hand, Benjy's and Quentin's monologues should be read as if they were genuine streams of consciousness. On the other hand, the reader must envision the dramatic scenes which are carefully invoked and objectively described. The reader must uncover the essential *tour de force* and yet appreciate its imaginative strength and dramatic purpose. Neither *The Sound and the Fury* nor *As I Lay Dying* can be effectively understood until the reader has explored deeper than the stream-of-consciousness surface. Once this is done, the reader has the privilege of viewing the extraordinary world of the novel with an imaginative awareness comparable to the author's. The personalities of Quentin Compson and Darl Bundren seem all the more vivid, because any weakening of the illusion of realism is compensated for by the reader's sense of Faulkner's intense creative vision.

Experiments in Narration

Faulkner's pragmatic use of stream-of-consciousness narration indicates his knowledge that the interior-monologue form is a literary device no closer to "reality" than any other mode of prose narration. Breaking without hesitation the rules established by Joyce, Dorothy Richardson, and Virginia Woolf, he succeeds in freeing a whole body of interrelated narrative techniques from an artificial naturalism, itself based on arbitrary assumptions about the relation of language to human truth.

The use of witness-narrators in Faulkner's later novels performs much the same function as that performed by the experimental techniques of *The Sound and the Fury* and *As I Lay Dying*. Both methods have the effect of uniting dramatic action to psychological awareness and endowing even brute violence with the sharp but unreal quality of a mental projection. This emphasis upon perception itself rather than upon the world which is perceived reflects Faulkner's interest in obsessive and self-destructive Southern Protestant thinking.

The manner in which the puritan mind projects its distorted moral and social vision upon the world is Faulkner's major thematic concern. In characterizing both rational fanatics and unsophisticated primitives, he thus emphasizes the structure rather than the content of experience. Such an emphasis is expressed in two principal ways. One is the use of imagery patterns as a means of psychological revelation. In most instances, the language by which Faulkner explores mental reality is based upon geometrical and philosophical abstractions or other de-materialized concepts. The other is the use of monologuists and other witness-characters who filter narrative events through points of view which seem contrived or intensely personal. The plot action of each novel is no less important than the mental reactions, as in the typical stream-of-consciousness work, but it is made an integral part of the psychological analysis.

This is not to say that the social environment of Faulkner's novels has no realistic function. The Yoknapatawpha County novels, with their elaborate social mythology, are refutations of such a claim. However, the events of such novels receive their sociological importance through their symbolic function. The action is related first to the obsessions of the major characters and only then to the social themes which these characters typify. It becomes quickly evident that Thomas Sutpen is an archetypal Southerner and that Joe Christmas is driven by Protestant fanaticism. This atmosphere of social meaning, supported by the consistency and force of the characterization, prevents the reader from balking at the arbitrary situations in which characters often appear. By psychological "realism" of this sort Faulkner convinces the reader that Yoknapatawpha County is a genuine though distorted mirror of the South.

The treatment of the physical scene as a means of enhancing the symbolism helps to explain the artificial contrasts in Faulkner's work between the individual and his social world. Once having isolated his major figures in this way, Faulkner withdraws his controlling hand and, in the manner of a typical twentieth-century author, affects a passive, uncreative role. What is unique about this assumed passivity is the intensity with which Faulkner's characters take over the function of imaginative creation. Not only do they sometimes fabricate the action, as in *Absalom, Absalom!*; they are philosophically concerned with the nature of past reality and the problem of rendering experience in a verbal medium.

Faulkner's self-conscious characters, whether narrators or not, often despair at the difficulty, or impossibility, of saying anything with words alone. The tortured quality often present in the author's rhetoric is related to the effort of such figures as Quentin Compson, Darl Bundren, and even Miss Rosa Coldfield to find meaning for themselves—through a definition of past and present experiences— in a shifting temporal world. This is one reason why narrating characters never seem entirely detached from the action they describe: the events assume their ultimate form only through efforts to understand them.

Many critics have pointed out the crowded or choked quality of Faulkner's long sentences, especially those in *Absalom, Absalom!* These intricate rhetorical units, like the finely polished circumlocutions of Henry James, are efforts to capture the multiple thrusts of the mind during distinct phases of consciousness. As Warren Beck points out, "Faulkner is trying to render the transcendent life of the mind, the crowded composite of associative and analytical consciousness which expands the vibrant moment into the reaches of all time, simultaneously observing, remembering, interpreting, and modifying the object of its awareness." To this end, each sentence, constituting a separate unit, "is made to hold diverse yet related elements in a sort of saturated solution, which is perhaps the nearest that language as the instrument of fiction can come to the instantaneous complexities of consciousness itself." [1]

The saturated sentences in Faulkner's work are almost always associated with a character who makes a conscious effort to express his thoughts upon a particular subject. Even when Faulkner's rhetoric is not associated with a specific speaker, as in the historical sections of *Requiem for a Nun,* the narrative pose is still that of an onlooker who tries to express to the reader an elusive private vision. Faulkner concentrates upon definite events or situations as they are filtered through the intense and involved reflections of a witness. He is more concerned with the social and moral implications of the mind's grasp of experiences than with its general function.

Throughout his work Faulkner deliberately subordinates dramatic exposition to an exploration of how the mind confronts experience and seeks to reduce it to understandable terms. He uses this technique even in the clarifying appendix, written for *The Sound and the Fury* years after the publication of the novel. Instead of explaining ambiguities, Faulkner gives the reader new facts, often contradicting old ones, that concern the reservoir of Compson history from which the novel appears to be drawn. The conflicting testimony suggests the author's unconscious assumption of the point of view of a witness who has thought deeply concerning the actual events but has forgotten their precise details. The preface is one more monologue to be added to Benjy's, Quentin's, and Jason's—no one of them representing necessarily the final truth.

AT THE HEART of Faulkner's technique lies the interest of a literary scientist in the reaction of individual minds to the controlled plot situation into which, as in a laboratory experiment, they are cast. Each novel corresponds to a separate experiment, and the Yoknapatawpha world—an aggregate of stylized novels in which individual puritan obsessions are dramatically explored—implies the outlines of a general hypothesis concerning human behavior that the scientist-novelist wishes to test. In employing his instruments of

[1] Warren Beck, "William Faulkner's Style," *American Prefaces,* 6 (Spring, 1941), reprinted in *Three Decades,* p. 153.

analysis, the scientist, like the mathematician, can only explore the limitations of his instruments and thus establish in logical and detailed form the conception of reality that their very use entails. In a similar way, Faulkner seeks to render more coherent and reasonable a series of dramatic situations which are intended not as realistic images of society but as devices for exploring and analyzing the minds of his characters.

After establishing the controlled conditions of his narrative world, Faulkner adopts the pose of a detached reporter whose duty it is to describe the reactions which occur. Like the scientist, he declines to interfere with the course of the experiment once it has begun. However, he creates characters that reflect his personal interest in the proceedings, and in some cases his preconceptions. He allows such characters to speak for themselves directly or to express their feelings and reactions through a neutral mediating voice.

The focus is simultaneously the physical action and the psychological milieu. Faulkner's use of arbitrary violence, of distorted characterization, and of sharp breaks between characters and their environment are means of bringing psychological or inward reality to the dramatic surface. Qualities of mind emerge out of the conflicts and distortions, just as qualities of a chemical element are revealed through its behavior under controlled circumstances. The interior monologues and witness voices make these revelations possible and emphasize their thematic significance.

The reader may be compared to a laboratory assistant asked to observe the results of each experiment and, in many cases, to correlate them with other results. The reader must share in the author's creative act; he must know what the subject of the literary experiment is and what narrative techniques are employed. His attention is usually directed to a series of conflicting narrative voices. He must commit himself emotionally to each and yet place each in the larger framework provided by the novel's symbolic structure. What the author and his reader-assistants derive from a successful literary experiment is not a clear picture of reality, or truth, but an insight into the psychological forces, the thrusts of consciousness, that make human reality and truth possible.

PART TWO

The Major Novels

Chapter Six

※

RAGE AGAINST TIME:
THE SOUND AND THE FURY

WHETHER OR NOT *The Sound and the Fury* is Faulkner's masterpiece, as many critics claim, the novel has a central position in the author's work and best illustrates his use of techniques of psychological revelation to explore social themes. To my mind Faulkner's narrative genius reaches its highest point in the skilful handling of characterization and dialogue in this novel. The success of *The Sound and the Fury* rests finally upon the vivid quality of conversations and fragments of dialogue, especially those remembered by narrating characters or presented in some way as passing through their minds. The reader is not so much confronted with a character's inner life as permitted intense glimpses of dramatic events remembered by the narrating figures.

This emphasis upon past events recreated in a character's imagination is closely associated with themes involving the passage of time and with patterns of imagery involving clocks, bells, and other time symbols. Only the middle two sections of the novel focus directly upon temporal concerns, in particular the fatalism of Mr. Compson and the obsessive rage against time of Quentin Compson and his brother Jason. But the novel's structure involves an implicit equation between a character's possession of moral value and his freedom in some sense from a destructive puritan struggle against time. Such freedom is negatively associated with the emotional simplicity of Benjamin, Quentin's idiot brother, and positively equated with the religious wisdom of Dilsey, the Compson servant. The opening and closing sections of the novel deal primarily with these two characters and provide a narrative perspective or dramatic framework by which complex issues of the novel are compressed to a basic contrast between love and understanding on the one hand and rational self-destruction on the other. Faulkner deliberately obscures this extreme contrast; he forces the reader to work it out for himself by following the leads suggested by the symbolism.

The opening monologue of *The Sound and the Fury* is only superficially the representation of an idiot's stream of consciousness. Because it renders dramatic events objectively, Benjy's account is less confused than the monologues of Quentin and Jason, in which details are occasionally distorted by the narrator's emotions or perversions of will. One must also distinguish between the moral role ascribed to Benjy and the account which Faulkner gives of his personality and motives. Benjy's lack of a moral point of view, in contrast to the puritan obsessions of his brothers, is a means by which their false or destructive "morality" is exposed. Yet it is a mistake to think of the Compson idiot as a moral agent or a symbol for a moral point of view. Carvel Collins has argued persuasively that an extraliterary origin of Faulkner's handling of Benjy may be found in the Freudian concept of the id, an area of the mind in which no moral distinctions of any kind have a place.[1]

Benjy's love for Caddy, like Ike Snopes's love for a cow in *The Hamlet*, could be described as blindly sexual. But whether Benjy's

[1] Carvel Collins, "The Pairing of 'The Sound and the Fury' and 'As I Lay Dying'," *The Princeton University Library Chronicle*, 18 (Spring, 1957), 114–123.

attitude is given a Christian or a Freudian interpretation, it cannot really be described as selfish. Unlike his brothers, Benjy is incapable of rationally conceived self-interest. Faulkner emphasizes this negative quality of Benjy's role—his lack of a conscious self—and gives it an implicit moral function. This role is illustrated by the frequent dramatic and symbolic relations between Benjy and Dilsey, even though the idiot does not have the latter's capacity for sympathy and understanding.

Because Benjy is helpless and cannot put his feelings into words, he must depend upon the love and understanding of others without giving any return. His presence is a catalytic agent by which the virtues and vices of other characters are quickly and effectively revealed. The boy Jason expresses his greed and innate cruelty by cutting up Benjy's dolls. Mrs. Compson is always trying either to discipline Benjy or to get him out of the way when his actions threaten to embarrass her. Quentin is more sympathetic toward his idiot brother, yet he sees him as an inhuman symbol of family disintegration.

Only Caddy appears to have a genuine love for Benjy. She understands his desires and feelings better than anyone else and is always trying to comfort him or protect him from the rest of the family. In one childhood scene, Benjy and Caddy are sitting by the fire when Mrs. Compson calls her idiot son over to mother him. Although Caddy asks her to wait, Mrs. Compson insists that the reluctant and now crying boy be taken to her. Caddy advises her mother to hold Benjy on her lap, but again Mrs. Compson is selfish and obstinate: "a five year old child. No, no. Not in my lap. Let him stand up." Caddy tries to give Benjy a cushion that will soothe him, but her mother orders it taken away: "He must learn to mind." When Benjy refuses to stop howling, his mother collapses into a crying fit and has to be led upstairs so that, as Caddy puts it, she "can be sick." The patient girl then leads Benjy back to the hearth, where he once more watches the "bright, smooth shapes" and hears "the fire and the roof". (82–83).

Benjy's monologue includes a number of scenes in which Caddy's sexual experiences are mirrored in Benjy's reactions. When the young girl uses perfume, her brother's wailing leads her to wash her face and give the bottle to Dilsey. When she has been seduced by

Dalton Ames, Benjy senses a loss or violation and pushes her to the bathroom. When she is in the swing kissing a lover, she allows Benjy to pull her away:

Caddy and I ran. We ran up the kitchen steps, onto the porch, and Caddy knelt down in the dark and held me. I could hear her and feel her chest. "I wont." she cried. "I wont anymore, ever. Benjy. Benjy." Then she was crying, and I cried, and we held each other. "Hush." she said. "Hush. I wont anymore." So I hushed and Caddy got up and we went into the kitchen and turned the light on and Caddy took the kitchen soap and washed her mouth at the sink, hard. Caddy smelled like trees. (67)

Though Benjy's emotional response is primitive, it is uncorrupted by rational puritanism. He reacts not to his moral interpretation of Caddy's experiences, as Quentin does, but to his awareness of Caddy's own sense of shame. He feels instinctively that sex and puritan guilt are the forces that will drive Caddy from him.

Once the reader is well into the second monologue he discovers that Benjy's love for Caddy is a commentary upon Quentin's rational obsession with his sister's moral life. Instead of seeing Caddy as a human being Quentin makes her an abstract symbol for the moral chaos around and within himself. Whereas Benjy reacts in pain to Caddy's misadventures, Quentin takes refuge in moral fantasies. The idiot's attitude is implicit in his impersonal narration: he appears to remember only what he sees and hears and what happens to him, never what he does or thinks. Quentin's descriptions of the past, on the other hand, reflect his desire to change or in some way exorcise the memories that torment him. The flashback scenes in the second monologue are impersonally told, but their subject matter and location in the narrative point directly to the youth's obsession. Benjy's recollections actually return him to the past, whereas Quentin's only make the present more unbearable.

Benjy's characterization suggests a comment in *A Fable*: "the witless know only loss and absence: never bereavement" (296). The idiot is never conscious of losing Caddy forever because, unlike Quentin, he has never claimed abstract possession. As Faulkner writes in the appendix, Benjy loves three things: firelight, the pasture which is sold to make a golf course, and his sister Candace.

He "lost none of them because he could not remember his sister but only the loss of her, and firelight was the same bright shape as going to sleep, and the pasture was even better sold than before" (19). A slipper which invokes Caddy's presence can always be used to quiet Benjy's crying. But memory of his sister only reinforces Quentin's neurosis and drives him to suicide.

In early childhood Caddy is little more than a symbol for innocence and natural affection. She develops her sense of guilt under the impact of her brother's puritanism. The extent of Quentin's responsibility is established by three related scenes, all involving water imagery. The first scene takes place by the small creek in the Compson pasture and is reported by Benjy. Caddy is playing with the other children in the creek and, having gotten her dress wet, decides to take it off to dry. Although Quentin is only a child, he makes a moral objection. When Caddy pays no attention to him, he splashes water on her. Jason is not concerned with morality but tells on them both out of meanness.

This scene is paralleled by a later one, described by Quentin, in which the youth tries to make his schoolgirl sister ashamed of her flirtation with boys. He taunts her: "What did you let him for kiss kiss." Caddy replies, "I didn't let him I made him." Quentin slaps her and rubs her head in the grass to which Caddy retorts: "I didnt kiss a dirty girl like Natalie anyway" (152–153). The monologue narration, representing Quentin's memory, then shifts to a scene in which Quentin and Natalie, a neighbor girl, are "dancing sitting down" in the barn when Caddy appears accusingly in the door. Quentin hurls abuse at the frightened Natalie and then turns on Caddy, taunting her with his own sexual obsessions. "She had her back turned I went around in front of her. You know what I was doing? She turned her back I went around in front of her the rain creeping into the mud flatting her bodice through her dress it smelled horrible. I was hugging her that's what I was doing. She turned her back I went around in front of her. I was hugging her I tell you" (155–156). Refusing to accept the fact of his sister's innocence, Quentin tries to make her see the world through his puritan eyes. When Caddy answers, "I dont give a damn what you were doing," he splashes her with the mud in which he has rolled. "You dont you dont I'll make you I'll make you give a damn. She hit my hands away I smeared mud on

91

her with the other hand I couldn't feel the wet smacking of her hand I wiped mud from my legs smeared it on her wet hard turning body hearing her fingers going into my face but I couldn't feel it even when the rain began to taste sweet on my lips" (156).

A third water scene takes place the day of Caddy's seduction, when Quentin finds her lying in the creek. His anger is directed not at her loss of innocence but at her failure to recognize her action as sinful: "Caddy you hate him dont you dont you" (169). When the girl refuses to speak words of hatred, Quentin holds a knife at her throat. This gesture, like the attempted seduction which follows, is more an expression of Quentin's despair than a genuine effort to escape it. Caddy becomes a helpless victim both of her capacity for love and of her brother's efforts to pervert that love into abstract morality. Her promiscuity reflects the self-hatred which Quentin has helped to force upon her. "There was something terrible in me," she tells Quentin, "sometimes at night I could see it grinning at me I could see it through them grinning at me through their faces it's gone now and I'm sick" (131). Although the natural expression of love has become a poison to Caddy, she drinks it to excess and after her summer vacation becomes pregnant—feeling "dead" inside. Her hasty marriage is foredoomed to failure, and, as her mother phrases it, she quickly turns into a "fallen woman" (237).

To Quentin the idea of sexual union means death, and is associated with water and shadow imagery. It is significant that Gerald Bland, in Quentin's mind a surrogate for Caddy's lovers, is viewed as he rows upon the Charles River: "the wet oars winking him along in bright winks and female palms" (130). It is by the creek where Quentin hurled mud at his sister that he tries to fight with Dalton Ames, who according to Caddy has "crossed all the oceans all around the world" (169). In thinking of Ames with his sister, Quentin conjures up "whispers secret surges smell the beating of hot blood under wild unsecret flesh watching against red eyelids the swine untethered in pairs rushing coupled into the sea" (195). After following Caddy to her meeting with Ames, he watches "her shadow high against his shadow one shadow" (173). Later on Quentin refers to "shadows of things like dead things in stagnant water" (176). Such imagery expresses the boy's sick puritanism and indicates the strength of his corrupting influence upon Caddy. She finally admits to her brother: "I died last year I told you I had but I didnt know then what I meant . . . but now I know I'm dead I tell you" (142–143). This explains the phrase by which Quentin refers to Caddy's promiscuous summer vacation: "found not death at the salt licks" (121). The implication is that since Caddy died morally at the Indiana resort town, French Lick, she should have died a physical death as well. The phrase "death at the salt licks" also suggests the bones of dead animals associated with salt licks, perhaps implying that Caddy's animal sexuality deserved a similar end. The passage explains Quentin's comparison of the empty trunks assembled for the trip to "coffins" (114). Quentin associates all these images and references with Caddy's ill-fated wedding. There is consequently a brutal irony in his Harvard roommate's bantering question, "Is it a wedding or a wake?" (101) when he sees Quentin dressed up in preparation for death. Quentin cannot understand his sister's behavior and hides from reality in his own morbid rage. The events of his life take on the color of his obsession and reflect back only a blurred outline, or shadow, of his selfish agony.

ALTHOUGH QUENTIN is largely responsible for Caddy's disgrace, he finds its reality intolerable. His concern for family and personal honor compels him, since the past cannot be recalled, either to change his memory or to destroy himself. At first he tries to alter the nature of Caddy's dishonor by sheer force of will. This is why Quentin tries to convince his father that he and Caddy have committed incest. As Mr. Compson puts it, he wishes "to sublimate a piece of natural human folly into a horror and then exorcise it with truth" (195). If he could cast himself and his sister into hell, Faulkner writes in the appendix, "he could guard her forever and keep her forevermore intact amid the eternal fires" (9).

Quentin may be compared to Henry Sutpen, in *Absalom, Absalom!*, who is willing to permit incest—though not miscegenation—between his sister Judith and her half-brother, Charles Bon. "At last he could be something even though that something was the irrevocable repudiation of the old heredity and training and the acceptance of eternal damnation" (347). In his effort to impose some kind of meaning upon the past, Quentin tries to defeat time by denying what he knows to be the truth. His incestuous design is egocentric in origin and is a perverse response to a self-created problem.

When his attempt to change the past fails, Quentin decides to commit suicide. His despair is linked to that of his father, who stands at the junction of the Compsons' past glory and future degradation. "No battle is ever won," Mr. Compson tells his son. "They are not even fought. The field only reveals to man his own folly and despair, and victory is an illusion of philosophers and fools" (95). In the opening paragraph of Quentin's monologue Mr. Compson gives his oldest son a watch that belonged to General Compson, the boy's grandfather. Instead of representing family pride and prosperity, the watch has become "the mausoleum of all hope and desire" (95).

Both father and son look upon the passage of time as the source of inescapable human frustration. Life is only a battle against time, the very terms of which ensure man's defeat. "One day you'd think misfortune would get tired, but then time is your misfortune Father said. A gull on an invisible wire attached through space dragged. You carry the symbol of your frustration into eternity" (123). The close relation between Quentin's concern for Caddy's virtue and his attitude toward time is indicated by the source of this gull imagery. He has seen a gull "poised" high above the figure of Gerald Bland, his symbolic enemy, rowing upon the Charles: "the one terrifically motionless, the other in a steady and measured pull and recover that partook of inertia itself, the world punily beneath their shadows on the sun" (139–140). One is reminded of similar contrasts between man's puny effort and time's inexorable force in *As I Lay Dying*.

The imagery of struggle against time dominates Quentin's monologue and, to a lesser extent, the novel as a whole. When he wakes up on the morning of his intended suicide, Quentin turns his watch face down and lies in bed trying to ignore the unbroken "parade of time" (95) which its ticking suggests. As soon as he cannot see the watch, he begins to wonder what time it is. "Father said that constant speculation regarding the position of mechanical hands on an arbitrary dial which is a symptom of mind-function. Excrement Father said like sweating. And I saying All right. Wonder. Go on and wonder" (96).

Quentin is trying to establish a kind of permanent identity in the face of a shifting and ambiguous reality. This attitude underlies his suicide, which is not an act of deliberate self-destruction, but an attempt to free his consciousness from the inevitability of change and decay. Quentin wants to live forever in the moment when consciousness still exists but when time, which alone can bring death, has been forever stopped. In this abstract moment, a defeated or dead time will release the full potentiality of the human self, and in this sense be paradoxically alive. "Because Father said clocks slay time. He said time is dead as long as it is being clicked off by little wheels; only when the clock stops does time come to life" (104). Quentin hopes that in death life's candle will burn its brightest, that his memories of the past will fuse with present reality. "You are not thinking of finitude," his father tells him, "you are contemplating an apotheosis in which a temporary state of mind will become symmetrical above the flesh and aware both of itself and of the flesh it will not quite discard you will not even be dead" (195–196).

Although this argument for suicide is specious, it is consistent both with Quentin's character and with the style of his monologue. The manner in which past experiences impinge or intrude upon his present world illustrates his absorption in the past and his desire to break the temporal barrier which separates him from it. Moreover, the sense of unreality surrounding the youth's Harvard actions explains and justifies his matter-of-fact and impersonal narration of them. Here, for example, is the account of how he breaks his grandfather's watch: "I went to the dresser and took up the watch, with the face still down. I tapped the crystal on the corner of the dresser and caught the fragments of glass in my hand and put them into the ashtray and twisted the hands off and put them in the tray. The watch ticked on" (99). This act of mutilation symbolizes to Quentin his intention of committing suicide, but no direct hint of this is given in the narration.

Quentin is aware of his plans for suicide, but he recoils from any conscious association between the events of his last day and the forthcoming event. He allows his actions to be controlled by this blind intention, as if he were the victim of a fate set into motion long ago and now taken for granted. Though he seems impelled toward a future action, he absorbs himself in retrospection. Ritual and inertia dominate his thoughts about the present, even when he leaves his Harvard room for the last time. "Before I snapped the light out I looked around to see if there was anything else, then I saw that I had forgotten my hat. I'd have to go by the postoffice and I'd be sure to meet some of them, and they'd think I was a Harvard Square student making like he was a senior. I had forgotten to brush it too, but Shreve had a brush, so I didn't have to open the bag any more" (197). Because Quentin does not speculate about his suicide, he is all the more impelled toward it. He is doomed because in the rigidity of his mind he cannot harbor the possibility of the suicide's not taking place.

The success of Quentin's monologue rests largely upon the harmony Faulkner achieves between the boy's obsession and the manner in which he narrates events. The reader is projected into a physical universe where suicide does mean a victory of consciousness over the passage of time. As Jean Paul Sartre has pointed out,[2] the very fact of a first-person narration told in the past tense implies the existence of a consciousness looking back upon the events described. Yet the narration seems to take the reader up to the moment of death. The implication is that the point of view from which Quentin narrates is the moment in which his death has, as he anticipated, destroyed time without depriving him of consciousness. With the elimination of time, every object of perception, whether in the past or in the present, has equal reality. Quentin can narrate from a point of view that shifts back and forth yet holds events in a constant perspective.

This shifting point of view, which reflects Quentin's despair, is far from identical with the author's attitude. Through the perspective established by the other monologues, the reader learns that the boy's private world is distorted. Quentin cannot evade responsibility by turning his back upon the living present. This judgment is strengthened by implied contrasts between Quentin's temporal despair and the attitudes of other characters. The boy's effort first to defeat time and then to destroy it is in direct contrast to Benjy's acceptance of temporal experience. The idiot's ability to accept the present enables him to possess the past and future as well. The very form of his

[2] Jean Paul Sartre, "A Propos de 'Le Bruit et la Fureur': La Temporalité chez Faulkner," *La Nouvelle Revue Française,* 52 (June 1939) translated and reprinted in *Three Decades,* p. 230.

monologue indicates that he can move backward and forward in time without imposing his personality on the events thus recovered.

Closely related to the time symbols is the use of shadow imagery. When Quentin wakes up on the morning of his suicide he recognizes the approximate time by watching the shadow of his window sash on the curtains. The presence of this and other shadows joins time and death in Quentin's mind. In a number of passages the boy is aware simultaneously of his own shadow and of clock chimes. "The chimes began again, the half-hour. I stood in the belly of my shadow" (119). And again: "The chimes ceased. I went back to the postoffice, treading my shadow into pavement" (119). Quentin tries to eliminate his shadow by treading upon its "belly" or by trampling its "bones" into the concrete walk. Quentin's shadow is proof of the temporal existence which he wishes to eliminate by suicide. Once, while leaning over a rail by Boston harbor, he sees his shadow leaning flat upon the water and resolves to "trick it" or "blot it into the water, holding it until it was drowned" (109). He comments: "Niggers say a drowned man's shadow was watching for him in the water all the time" (109).

Quentin's description of this "trick" played upon his shadow is a direct reference to his coming suicide and a speculation upon its success. In another passage he applies this shadow concept to the decline of his family and to his own despair. He recalls a picture from a childhood book depicting "a dark place into which a single weak ray of light came slanting upon two faces lifted out of the shadow" (191). The faces symbolize his parents. "I'd have to turn back to it until the dungeon was Mother herself she and Father upward into weak light holding hands and us lost somewhere below even them without even a ray of light" (191). The parents are barely out of shadow, and their children are lost in utter darkness. It is this shadow-of temporal fatality falling upon his family and himself that Quentin seeks to overcome by suicide.

In another scene Quentin lies in bed smelling the rain and the honeysuckle, all mixed up and symbolizing "night and unrest" (188). He imagines himself lying neither asleep nor awake and looking down a long corridor of gray halflight "where all stable things had become shadowy paradoxical all I had done shadows all I had felt suffered taking visible form antic and perverse mocking without relevance inherent themselves with the denial of the significance they should have affirmed" (188). Once more, shadows suggest temporal instability, opposed to the permanence of self that Quentin hopes to achieve.

A related pattern of imagery is that of mirrors and other reflecting surfaces. By this mirror imagery, Faulkner tightens the connection between the bodies of water which Quentin associates with Caddy on the one hand and, on the other, her lovers and the imagery of time and fatality surrounding Quentin's Harvard experiences. There are two important mirrors in the action of the novel, a real one in the family living room and the symbolic mirror-surface of the Charles River. When Quentin recalls Caddy's flight from her wedding to comfort Benjy, he speaks of her running out of the mirror. "She ran right out of the mirror, out of the banked scent. Roses. Roses. . . . In the mirror she was running before I knew what it was. . . . she ran out of the mirror like a cloud, . . . running out of the mirror the smells roses roses the voice that breathed o'er Eden" (96–100). Quentin is standing by the home altar and watching a reflection of Caddy running down the aisle. In this symbolic passage Quentin sees Caddy only in "shadow," or only in the distorting perspective of his obsessive puritanism.

The mirror in which Quentin sees Caddy is presumably the same mirror in which Benjy watches reflected fire from the grate. Lawrance Thompson makes the point [3] that this piece of furniture, which Benjy loves, is sold when the Compson fortunes decline. Benjy is left with a sense of pain and a dark place on the wall where, according to Jason, he rubs his hands, slobbering and moaning. Throughout the novel the primitive Benjy treats reflections in mirrors as if they were real. To him the fire is actually "on the walls" or "in the mirror." Quentin, by contrast, translates everything into shadows. The mirror by which he views life is broken or distorted. Looking at the Charles River by twilight he sees the deadly surface of the water in which he will drown himself as supine and tranquil, "like pieces of broken mirror" (188). The image reminds him of Benjy's peaceful but unbroken mirror: "Refuge unfailing in which conflict tempered silenced reconciled" (188–189).

[3] Lawrance Thompson, "Mirror Analogues in 'The Sound and the Fury'," in *English Institute Essays, 1952*, p. 84.

Rage against Time

ALTHOUGH Quentin Compson can be said to inherit his fatalism from his father, the two characters differ in their consequent behavior. Mr. Compson tries to take refuge in despair. He ridicules Quentin's obsession with Caddy's lost honor, arguing that virginity is a male concept. "Women are never virgins. Purity is a negative state and therefore contrary to nature. It's nature is hurting you not Caddy" (135). Yet Mr. Compson is no less upset than Quentin over his daughter's promiscuity: at the time of her disastrous summer he begins to drink himself to death. Mr. Compson employs cynicism and irony in order to escape what his puritan mind, like Quentin's, cannot tolerate. He reveals his contempt for a weak-willed and philandering brother-in-law: "I admire Maury. He is invaluable to my own sense of racial superiority. I wouldn't swap Maury for a matched team" (62). When his wife, crying, defends her brother's behavior on the grounds of ill health, Mr. Compson adds despair to his irony:

"Of course." Father said. "Bad health is the primary reason for all life. Created by disease, within putrefaction, into decay. Versh."
"Sir." Versh said behind my chair.
"Take the decanter and fill it" (63).

In this passage, as in many others, Mr. Compson ends by turning his mockery upon himself.

At the end of a serious discussion with Quentin, Mr. Compson refers satirically to the corrupted tradition of male gentility—a tradition partially responsible for his self-contempt: "Then you will remember that for you to go to harvard has been your mothers dream since you were born and no compson has ever disappointed a lady" (196–197). In *Absalom, Absalom!* the same Mr. Compson remarks of the garrulous Rosa Coldfield: "Years ago we in the South made our women into ladies. Then the War came and made the ladies into ghosts. So what else can we do, being gentlemen, but listen to them being ghosts?" (12). The collapse of the budding Southern aristocracy did more or less deprive its women of any satisfactory cultural function, leaving them a prey, as in the case of Quentin's mother, to a selfish and unjustified social pride. Mr. Compson realizes and yet seems to evade the truth that, for him,

99

past ideals have become ghostly forms, his precious gentility having no more substantial object of service and devotion.

Unlike his father, Quentin makes no effort to sublimate his despair through cynicism or dissipation. Both his attempted incest and his successful suicide are efforts to preserve his despair and to render it permanently meaningful. Mr. Compson learns of his son's plan for suicide, but refuses to believe that Quentin will carry out the threat. Applying his own philosophy, he accuses the boy of ignoring "that part of general truth the sequence of natural events and their causes which shadows every mans brow even benjys" (195). The gamble of death, he argues, is too great for any man to face "under the first fury of despair or remorse or bereavement." A man will choose suicide, he tells Quentin, "only when he has realised that even the despair or remorse or bereavement is not particularly important to the dark diceman . . . no, you will not do that until you come to believe that even she was not quite worth despair . . ." (196). Mr. Compson sets up the extreme nature of Quentin's obsession as a safeguard against any reckless action. He believes that a year at Harvard will cure not Quentin's despair but the moral romanticism which would focus that despair upon a single object.

Yet the Compsons, we learn from the appendix, were all gamblers, "provided the gambit was desperate and the odds long enough" (5). Quentin agrees that time will soften his moral fury, but it is precisely this threatened loss that he finds intolerable. He tries to halt time by committing suicide; not to escape his anguish but to preserve it. He is determined to act while he is still young and naive enough to care about honor and truth. The last words of his father which Quentin remembers are "its not despair until time its not even time until it was" (197). In other words, the passage of time which creates despair also tends to undermine the immediacy of the experience upon which the despair is focused. By suicide Quentin intends to stabilize the elusive *I was* of the recent past and so preserve his moral feeling intact. In a society suffering from inward collapse Quentin tries desperately to transform his awareness of decay into a self-redeeming quality. This very effort to achieve a permanent self, linked as it is to extreme self-absorption, proves fatal.

Quentin sees through his own argument toward the end of his monologue when he refers openly to his coming death. Recalling the whiskey that his roommate keeps in a trunk, Quentin compares it to a death which obviates both the present and the past: "I am. Drink. I was not" (193). The sale of Benjy's beloved pasture, he thinks, has made possible nothing more than a wasted year at Harvard. "A fine dead sound we will swap Benjy's pasture for a fine dead sound. It will last him a long time because he cannot hear it unless he can smell it" (193). This reference to Benjy's ability to "smell" misfortune and loss indicates another contrast between the two brothers. Benjy reacts only to the presence of death, while Quentin carries the idea of fatality within him. It can be argued that Quentin's defense of death as a means of preserving life is a product of self-deception, of his inability to accept his own despair. Despite his protestations to the contrary, Quentin does seek the irrevocable *I was not* of death. He cannot think openly of his own plans for suicide (except inadvertently) because his real desire to escape reality through oblivion would then be exposed. He cannot face his own motivations.

THE THIRD MONOLOGUE in *The Sound and the Fury* is that of Quentin's younger brother, Jason, whose absolute corruption is a grotesque reflection of Quentin's more complex failure. Jason appears in the first two sections only as a spoiled crybaby and tattletale, with a penchant for petty shopkeeping and secret maneuvering. His fate, like that of his brothers, is linked to Caddy's downfall. Jason is outraged by her actions, but the reason for his hatred is the perverse conviction that her behavior has cost him the banking job promised by Herbert Head, Caddy's fiancé. This sense of injury is Jason's justification for stealing the money which Caddy sends to Jefferson for the support of her daughter.

The organization of Jason's sections is based upon his two primary obsessions, his quest for the "golden fleece" of financial profit and his hatred of both Caddy and her daughter Quentin. Much of his monologue narration is devoted to business affairs, in particular his exploitation of the two women and his futile efforts to make money by cotton speculation. Other sections of his narration are devoted to a flashback account of Mr. Compson's funeral, where Jason's financial arrangements with Caddy are initially made, and to his disastrous efforts to catch his niece with her carnival lover, "a man that would wear a red tie" (260).

It is significant that "time" for Jason is the equivalent of money. His practical obsession with the passage of time is a virtual parody of Quentin's more philosophical concern. Perrin Lowrey has shown in detail how Jason can never catch up with the fast-moving events around him.[4] He dashes convulsively from place to place, always trying to get somewhere and always being late. His cotton speculation is a case in point. The market is so unpredictable that Jason has to keep on the alert for any sudden rise or fall. Time gets the better of him when an important message comes through while he is out spying on his niece. He arrives at the telegraph office an hour after the cotton market has closed. Jason's method of exploiting Caddy is to accept and cash her checks in his mother's name. Mrs. Compson mistakenly thinks that the checks she is burning represent Caddy's tainted income, and that the money regularly paid into her account comes from Jason's salary. However, Jason has run out of blank checks to prepare for his mother's ritual of destruction and must search frantically, with very little time, for check blanks that will do.

Jason's hatred of Caddy is related to his most characteristic phobia, the smell of gasoline. Mrs. Compson says that Jason has had this weakness since a child, but it might well have originated with the car which Caddy's fiancé gives her, and which reminds Jason of his lost job. Jason's own car is paid for with the money originally used to buy him a share in the general merchandise store where he works. The headaches from gasoline fumes cause Jason great trouble, in the final section of the novel, when he tries to recover the money stolen by his niece.

He has no camphor-soaked handkerchief to allay the gas smell, and the drugstores are all closed on Sunday. His headaches and the use of camphor relate him to his mother, who uses her illness as a focal point for self-pity and often as a means to escape or reject her responsibilities. Like his brother Quentin, Jason never drinks alcohol —a frequent sign in Faulkner's work of moral impotency. Even Benjy gets drunk on "sasparillah." The virginal Quentin neither smokes nor drinks, but during his last day he buys his first cigar and takes two puffs before giving it away. Like the cigarette rolled by

[4] Perrin Lowrey, "Concepts of Time in 'The Sound and the Fury'," in *English Institute Essays, 1952.*

Dalton Ames and the expensive cigars which Herbert Head imports from Havana, this cigar which Quentin cannot smoke seems intended as a sign of masculinity.

In spite of his ruthless treatment of others, Jason's mind is filled with moral clichés traceable to the family tradition of public integrity and personal honor. Like Quentin, who cleans his vest and brushes his teeth before committing suicide, Jason has a ludicrous concern for personal appearance. His selfishness and cruelty are known to everyone, yet he refers constantly to his mother's "good name" and the family's "position" in the community. Jason even convinces himself that he is the loyal guardian of his niece Quentin. Seeing her playing truant from school with a boy friend from the circus, he gives reckless chase: "Me, without any hat, in the middle of the afternoon, having to chase up and down back alleys because of my mother's good name. Like I say you cant do anything with a woman like that, if she's got it in her. If it's in her blood, you cant do anything with her. The only thing you can do is to get rid of her, let her go on and live with her own sort" (250). Outwitted by the pair, Jason shifts his self-dramatization to that of a betrayed uncle: "It's not playing a joke that any eight year old boy could have thought of, it's letting your own uncle be laughed at by a man that would wear a red tie" (260). Jason is a product of a decayed gentility and not, like Flem Snopes of *The Hamlet*, a symbolic outsider devoid of any feeling for morality and justice. His cruelty rests to a great extent upon self-deception and is heightened dramatically by his role as a genuine though perverted Compson.

In Jason's monologue, the "present" world of April 6, 1928, comes more clearly into dramatic focus. Quentin and his father are dead; Caddy is exiled, and only Jason, his mother, and Benjy are left of the original family. The past does not figure prominently except in the scene during Mr. Compson's funeral when Caddy agrees to send Jason money for Miss Quentin's upkeep. However, the relation between Jason and his niece recalls the more veiled one between the boy Quentin and Caddy. Even as Jason robs the young girl of her rightful money, he badgers and bullies her, driving her finally to desperate rebellion. She robs Jason of his precious and ill-gotten savings and runs off with the carnival man. Whereas the corrupting influence of the older Quentin over Caddy is subtle and is veneered with professions of love, that of Jason over his niece is brutal and open. The girl's reaction, in turn, is neither complex nor restrained. "I don't care," she tells him. "I'm bad and I'm going to hell, and I don't care. I'd rather be in hell than anywhere where you are" (207). Again, she tells Jason: "Whatever I do, it's your fault . . . If I'm bad it's because I had to be. You made me. I wish I was dead. I wish we were all dead" (277).

Jason's inhumanity is too severely drawn to be traceable to his environment alone, but his character is influenced by Mrs. Compson, his whimpering mother. She spoils Jason outrageously and sets him apart as a "Bascomb" (her own maiden name) from the rest of her children. In a remarkable passage she reveals her hatred for all her children except Jason. Speaking to Mr. Compson, she contrasts Jason to the promiscuous Caddy:

What have I done to have been given children like these Benjamin was punishment enough and now for her to have no more regard for me her own mother I've suffered for her dreamed and planned and sacrificed I went down into the valley yet never since she opened her eyes has she given me one unselfish thought . . . except Jason he has never given me one moment's sorrow since I first held him in my arms I knew then that he was to be my joy and my salvation . . . I was unfortunate I was only a Bascomb I was taught that there is no halfway ground that a woman is either a lady or not but I never dreamed when I held her in my arms that any daughter of mine could let herself dont you know I can look at her eyes and tell . . . that's it go on criticise Jason accuse me of setting him to watch her as if it were a crime while your own daughter can I know you dont love him that you wish to believe faults against him . . . you must let me go away I cannot stand it let me have Jason and you keep the others they're not my flesh and blood like he is strangers nothing of mine and I am afraid of them I can take Jason and go where we are not known I'll go down on my knees and pray for the absolution of my sins that he may escape this curse try to forget that the others ever were. (121–123)

Jason reports the incident of Mrs. Compson's wearing a black dress and veil and refusing to speak a word the day after she sees a boy kissing her fifteen-year-old daughter. After Caddy's real disgrace, she will not allow the girl's name to be spoken in the house and does not inform her when Mr. Compson dies. Mrs. Compson deprives her husband of a true wife and her children of a mother. It is no wonder that Quentin thinks "If I'd just had a mother so I could say Mother Mother" (190) and that he comments at one point, "Done in Mother's mind though. Finished. Finished. Then we were all poisoned" (121). The unsuccessful marriage of Mr. and Mrs. Compson is a nucleus of disintegration underlying the more tragic failures of their children.

The final section of *The Sound and the Fury* is primarily concerned with Dilsey's preparation of the Compson breakfast and her subsequent trip with Benjy to attend Easter services at a small Negro church. The semiomniscient narration seldom leaves Dilsey except to trace Jason's futile effort to recover the stolen money, and to listen to Benjy's howling as Luster drives him the wrong way around the town square.

Dilsey's mere presence, like Benjy's in the opening narration, is an implicit moral comment upon the behavior of other characters. Mrs. Compson torments Dilsey with selfish requests, calling her name again and again with "machine-like regularity" (286). In one effective scene Mrs. Compson waits until the aged servant has labored up the stairs to dress Benjy before telling Dilsey that Benjy is still sleeping:

Dilsey said nothing. She made no further move, but though she could not see her save as a blobby shape without depth, Mrs Compson knew that she had lowered her face a little and that she stood now like a cow in the rain, as she held the empty water bottle by its neck. (288)

Although Dilsey is a passive witness of Compson decay, she pays active attention to Benjy's emotional needs, and in this way substitutes as best she can for Benjy's missing sister. She provides Benjy with a cake on his birthday, and near the end of the novel she directs Luster to put a splint on the broken stem of Benjy's narcissus, a flower that is damaged again by Jason.

Dilsey's ability to endure misfortune is in strong contrast to the weaknesses of Benjy's two brothers, as outlined in earlier sections of the novel. Dilsey never asks abstract questions and never finds the passage of time a matter of destructive concern. At breakfast time, hearing the old kitchen clock sound five strokes, she announces

105

"eight o'clock" (290), automatically making the proper correction. Her action is an ironical comment upon the Boston scene in which Quentin is fascinated by unwound clocks in a jeweler's window, and is unable or unwilling to realize that clocks must be regulated and set before they can tell the correct time. More importantly, Dilsey is associated with the vision of timeless reality that dominates the Negro congregation during Reverend Shegog's sermon. It is immediately after this Easter service that Dilsey makes her enigmatic statement to her daughter Frony, "I've seed de first en de last" (313). Dilsey is adapting the Christian paradox to social concerns, to the symbolic fusion of the first and last Mississippi Compsons. During the sermon itself two tears are described as sliding down Dilsey's fallen cheeks, "in and out of the myriad coruscations of immolation and abnegation and time" (311). Dilsey becomes herself a time symbol, her sunken cheeks representing human events and her sliding teardrops the flow of time. Her role suggests the destructive impact of time and indicates the possibility of a religious vision by which the individual can free himself at least from despair. Dilsey is the prophetic time-keeper of the Compson family, even though her role is unrecognized by those she would like to save.

The contrast between Dilsey and the Compson world is illustrated by the narrative point of view brought to bear upon her actions. In watching Dilsey emerge out of "a moving wall of grey light" (281) into the Compson kitchen, the reader himself seems to escape the gray interior world of aristocratic delusion and decay. Yet the artificial rhetoric by which Dilsey and other characters are described is comparable to the filtering of past events through a narrator's consciousness. Faulkner invests Dilsey with an atmosphere of heroic dignity and at the same time mocks his own narrative technique. Dilsey's gaunt hand is compared to "the belly of a fish" (281) and her indomitable skeleton is seen to rise "like a ruin or a landmark above the somnolent and impervious guts." Her ancient and collapsed face gives the impression of the bones themselves being outside the flesh, "lifted into the driving day with an expression at once fatalistic and of a child's astonished disappointment" (282). As Dilsey "coordinates" the Compson breakfast, she sings something without particular tune or words, "repetitive, mournful and plaintive, austere" (286).

The same technique is applied to other characters, especially Benjy. The reader is startled to see the idiot for the first time, his skin "dead looking and hairless" and his thick mouth open and drooling, but his clear eyes "of the pale sweet blue of cornflowers" (290). Far from being an objective witness, the narrator of the final section is anxious to establish figures like Benjy and Dilsey as symbolic archetypes. Once having established the illusion of naturalistic description, by references to Dilsey's "nether garments" (281) or Benjy's drooling lips, the narrator goes on to heighten the symbolic status of his characters. Benjy's bullfrog or foghorn voice is now the kind of "slow hoarse sound that ships make, that seems to begin before the sound itself has started, seems to cease before the sound itself has stopped" (304). Benjy's need for food is "hunger itself inarticulate" (292) and the sound of his wailing "might have been all time and injustice and sorrow become vocal for an instant by a conjunction of planets" (303–304). Even Jason is not spared this rhetorical technique. He becomes the human individual blundering through the "cluttered obscurity" (325) of events he cannot control or even understand. In being forced to recognize the existence of a reality "opposed to all nature and contrary to the whole rhythm of events" (324) he senses his "invisible life ravelled about him like a wornout sock," and for a moment he forgets Jefferson "as any place which he had ever seen before, where his life must resume itself" (329).

The language of Dilsey's section suggests the point of view of a reader who has struggled long and arduously with *The Sound and the Fury*, and who now recognizes beneath the "cluttered obscurity" an extraordinary clarity of action and theme. The reader views events with a double vision: on the one hand he recognizes the sordid Compson reality for what it is, and on the other hand he raises the family tragedy to a universal status. The serio-comic effect of the language brilliantly mirrors the reader's hesitating acceptance of stylized characters, isolated from realistic social conventions, as symbols for moral order and social stability.

Chapter Seven

A MODERN MOCK-EPIC:
AS I LAY DYING

$\mathcal{F}$AULKNER'S NEXT PUBLISHED NOVEL, *As I Lay Dying*, is very similar to *The Sound and the Fury* in both characterization and the handling of symbolic detail. In the two works Faulkner employs interior monologues as a means of contrasting the behavior of a family with the obsessive thoughts of individual members. Anse Bundren and his oldest son Cash are unique creations, but the rest of the Bundrens correspond in relative age and personality to the Compsons. The psychopathic Darl and the child Vardaman are close parallels to Quentin Compson and his idiot brother Benjy. The two girls, Dewey Dell and Candace, are lone daughters with promiscuous habits, and both are closely watched by introverted brothers. Jewel Bundren and Jason Compson are spoiled by their mothers and alienate themselves from the others. The similarity between Mrs. Compson and Addie Bundren is less obvious, yet both are complaining figures whose selfish natures are partially responsible for the destructive obsessions of their children. Even Anse and Mr. Compson are comparable in their unhappy marriages and relative isolation from the world's affairs.

The connection between the patterns of symbolism in the two novels is even more apparent. Common themes of death and mental disintegration are emphasized and linked with characterization. The dominant concept in both is that of human rage directed against a personified concept of time. In *The Sound and the Fury* the social degeneration of the Compson family and the despair of those members who recognize it are summed up in Quentin's hatred of time and his desire to halt its abstract motion by an act of suicide. Quentin's attitude is matched in *As I Lay Dying* by Darl Bundren's obsession with time as a dehumanizing and self-alienating force. Since Darl is the chief narrator of the action, the reader looks upon the flooded river, and by implication the trip to Jefferson, through Darl's possessed, time-ridden eyes. The success of the laborious trip depends not so much upon personal courage as upon a group inertia of movement, as if time rather than space separated the family from its goal. The pregnant Dewey Dell is herself a "time" symbol, and the buzzards which follow the coffin are constant reminders of time's presence.

As I Lay Dying differs radically from *The Sound and the Fury* in the absence of references to the social and moral decay of a dying culture. In the latter work Quentin's priest-brother treatment of his sister Caddy is linked to his awareness of moral failure both in himself and in his immediate society. His narration helps to create the structural pattern that gives social meaning to the passive endurance of Dilsey and to the demonism of Jason. The personal defeats and frustrations in this novel are in every instance involved with implicit moral and social themes. In *As I Lay Dying* there is little if any social meaning to be derived from the action. The Bundrens live in virtual isolation, without a significant past and without a sense of any social role to be maintained in the world's face. Even Jason in the earlier novel is vaguely aware of the Compson past—if only because of his desire to repudiate it—and talks about maintaining his mother's "name" in the community. *As I Lay Dying* is also about family relations and group effort, but the social world enveloping the Bundrens is wholly private and lacks the implications of social myth found in other Faulkner novels.

This absence of mythological themes in *As I Lay Dying* is all the more striking in view of the atmosphere of family loyalty and epic heroism which dominates the action. The Bundrens carry the mother's body past all manner of unforeseen obstacles, including two washed-out bridges and a barn fire, in order to fulfill her wish to lie in Jefferson with her ancestors. In portraying the sacrifices and ordeals of an entire family carrying out the wishes of the dead mother, Faulkner creates the paraphernalia of a folk epic. But Faulkner undermines the heroic atmosphere by revealing hidden personal motives and by depriving the trip of any intrinsic value beyond the fulfillment of the immediate group aim. The supposed idealism which underlies the trip, the devotion to Addie Bundren's memory, is transformed into a joke played upon the reader—or upon the Bundrens. Dewey Dell's enthusiasm for the trip is a consequence of her being pregnant and hoping to find something in Jefferson to cure her trouble. Anse wants a set of false teeth, and Vardaman wants to see an electric train which Dewey Dell has described to him. Personal tragedies beset the Bundren children, but they are deprived of much of their seriousness by the manner in which Faulkner subordinates them to the over-all success of the trip. At the same time this success is undermined by its failure to affect the majority of the Bundrens in any lasting way. The novel contains elements both of group heroism and of personal misfortune, but no consistent heroic or tragic theme can survive such disparities between public and private motives. Faulkner reconciles the consequent breaks and contrasts of tone by investing the entire work with a kind of mock-epic structure employing both the serious and the burlesque, the meaningful and the absurd, to gain an essentially comic end.

As I Lay Dying is not a mock-epic work in the traditional sense of possessing a style too grandiose for the action. The element of comedy does not pervade such isolated passages as Addie Bundren's monologue or the scenes in which Darl Bundren struggles to escape madness. But the over-all contrast between public and private reality produces a comparable effect. Thus the failure of Anse Bundren to live up to his superficial role of family patriarch establishes the atmosphere of the entire novel. In spite of his pride, Anse is content to let others, whether family or neighbors, do his work and thinking for him. Yet he is the only Bundren who manages to fulfill all of his secret expectations upon reaching Jefferson. Like the convict in "Old Man," Anse is driven by a rigidity of mind that often makes him seem more imaginative than he really is. "I notice how it takes a lazy man," a neighbor remarks of him, "a man that hates moving, to get set on moving once he does get started off, the same as he was set on staying still, like it ain't the moving he hates so much as the starting and stopping" (417). When Anse is told that the last bridge to Jefferson is down, he takes the news with neither disappointment nor anguish, "like he would be kind of proud of whatever come up to make the moving or the setting still look hard" (417). His team is killed in the river crossing, but Anse turns down Armstid's offer to lend him a team for the trip. "I thank you," he replies, "She'll want to go in ourn" (474). He is bent on choosing the path of least resistance, even if it means sacrificing the money he has saved for a set of new teeth. Anse is not motivated by loyalty to his dead wife, as demonstrated by his quick marriage at the end of the novel. He is not driven by pure selfishness either. He is a predominantly comic figure because his inertia or hesitation to change an original plan is even stronger than his love of self.

Faulkner qualifies Anse for his comic role by depriving him of any human qualities which might support his public mask of grieving widower. The same technique of dehumanization enables Faulkner to heap misfortune after misfortune upon other characters without making them the objects of the reader's pity or empathy. Cash fractures his leg; Jewel surrenders his beloved horse; Darl is betrayed by his family and sent to an asylum; and Dewey Dell is first made pregnant by a lover and afterwards degraded by a soda jerk posing as a pharmacist. Cash, who is the most unfortunate victim of chance and human stupidity, is also a primary source of comedy. As an expert carpenter he builds Addie's coffin, and as a general technician he directs the dangerous crossing of the river. But his efficiency is purchased with the last vestige of human emotion. When asked how far he fell from the church steeple when he broke his leg, Cash replies with absurd precision: "twenty-eight foot, four and a half inches, about" (402). His first monologue, given while his mother lies dying, is merely a tabulation of his reasons for designing and constructing the coffin as he does. When the coffin has been overturned in the river and Cash's leg has broken again, he assumes the role of the frustrated rationalist, forced to live in an insane world. "It wasn't on a balance. I told them that if they wanted it to tote and ride on a balance, they would have to—" (458). One of the most pathetic and yet ridiculous scenes of the novel occurs when Cash submits to having his leg cast in ordinary concrete merely because his family has already purchased the cement. Once he accepts the situation, he cannot help giving his brothers instructions on how to do the mixing. Throughout the novel Cash is so caught up in questions of theory and technique that he pays no attention to the facts of his own situation.

The emotionally charged Jewel is the antithesis of Cash in personality, but his restless and ungovernable temper renders him equally inhuman. We learn the extent of his aimless fury in the opening scene when Darl describes the two of them returning from the fields. Darl circles around a cotton house in their path, but Jewel, "looking straight ahead," steps doggedly through the window, "his pale eyes like wood set into his wooden face" (339); and in four strides he is across the floor and out again, walking "with the rigid gravity of a cigar-store Indian dressed in patched overalls and endued with life from the hips down" (339). Jewel takes no part in the planning of the trip, but once it has begun, he supports it frantically. "I don't give a damn," he tells Cash. "Just so we do something. Setting here, not lifting a goddamn hand" (443). Twice he saves the coffin from destruction, once when the wagon is floundering in the river and once when the coffin lies in a burning barn. His surrender of his horse toward the purchase of a second team appears to be a genuine sacrifice on his part to ensure the completion of the trip. But Jewel is too reckless and impulsive to accept the trip as a real family obligation. Like the other Bundrens he seems to adapt to the requirements of each separate situation rather than to make any deliberate choice of action. By the time his mother has reached Jefferson his devotion to Addie's memory, though genuine, seems burned out or transferred into hatred for Darl.

Faulkner implies that the dynamic and forceful Addie Bundren has used the formless energy of her favorite son as an instrument by which to reach her longed-for grave. In his only monologue Jewel creates an egocentric fantasy in which he and Addie are together on a high hill, isolated from the world, "and me rolling the rocks down the hill at their faces, picking them up and throwing them down the hill, faces and teeth and all by God until she was quiet" (347–348). This corresponds to Addie's prophecy to Cora Tull that Jewel is her cross and will be her salvation. "He will save me from the water and from the fire. Even though I have laid down my life, he will save me" (460). Faulkner has Addie make a kind of theological pun which equates her "salvation" and her trip to Jefferson to be buried. At first Cora thinks it is God who Addie believes will "save" her, but then she realizes that Jewel is being referred to. "[Addie] just sat there, lost in her vanity and her pride, that had closed her heart to God and set that selfish mortal boy in His place" (461).

Addie Bundren's daughter, Dewey Dell, is the strongest conscious force behind the trip. Though she seems devoted to her mother, her desperate need to reach a Jefferson drugstore leaves her no "time" in which to mourn. "I heard that my mother is dead. I wish I had time to let her die. I wish I had time to wish I had. It is because in the wild and outraged earth too soon too soon too soon. It's not that I wouldn't and will not it's that it is too soon too soon too soon" (422). When she learns that the second bridge over the swollen river is out, she turns her blazing eyes upon Anse, in the fear that he will decide not to go on. "You promised her," she tells him. "She wouldn't go until you promised. She thought she could depend on you. If you don't do it, it will be a curse on you" (417). Dewey Dell speaks in idealistic terms, but her real motive, the belief that she can buy medicine to cause an abortion, is wholly personal. Her acceptance of a drugstore clerk's argument that a second fornication will negate the consequences of the first is not in itself comic but is rendered so by a deliberate excess of pathos, and by the girl's passivity. Dewey Dell suffers from men, like Caddy in *The Sound and the Fury*, but her emotional life is so thoroughly self-centered that unlike Caddy she is not really affected.

Darl and Vardaman suggest the psychological extremes of madness and childish imagination; at the same time they are serious witnesses of the narrative action and try in vain to understand and evaluate it. Darl associates his personal insecurity with his mother's death and the effort to bury her far away in Jefferson; he tries at all times to halt or delay the trip. Vardaman is also absorbed in the question of personal existence and its relation to his mother, and through an act of childish imagination he tries to deny her death by identifying her with a fish that he has seen alive and has caught. Darl is self-absorbed in the manner of Quentin Compson, but he has Benjy's capacity for reporting events objectively. He is the chief narrator of the action, and his monologues dominate the reader's attention. Vardaman suggests a Benjy stripped of his role of objective narrator, even though the boy is fiercely imaginative and twists the facts of experience into personal images of which the idiot is incapable.

The two brothers, Darl and Vardaman, represent contrasting minds directed upon the same basic action and placing it in opposed emotional contexts. Together they provide the reader with a means for viewing the action in some perspective, but with no formula for drawing moral or social implications. In this important respect the roles of Darl and Vardaman differ drastically from those of Quentin and Benjy. Darl's madness is derived from his concern for family relationships, but his narrative point of view, though personal, tends to be amoral. Vardaman is a comic figure reacting with childish absurdity and not a pastoral creation whose natural reactions bring into focus the moral failure of others.

Little use is made of the past in As I Lay Dying, and consequently there is no need for a contrived monologue, such as Benjy's, in which past and present events are juxtaposed. In the earlier novel, the opening and closing sections function as impersonal accounts which cast light upon the two inner monologues in which events are distorted and given a highly personal stamp. In the later novel this use of multiple points of view is maintained—there are fifty-nine separate monologues—yet the world which emerges is darkly subjective, with no relieving rays of light apart from the general burlesque atmosphere. Instead of clearing up confusion, the reports by outsiders such as Vernon Tull or his wife only give an incorrect picture of the main characters, and force the reader deeper into the single-track minds of Dewey Dell or Darl in search of truth.

Within this subjective world madness and fury tend to remain isolated in the minds of individuals and not projected into a social context. In *The Sound and the Fury* the behavior of Caddy is directly influenced by Quentin and that of her daughter by Jason. The moral failure of the Compson children is related to the selfishness of the mother and the ineffectuality of the father. In *As I Lay Dying* Addie Bundren is given a comparable responsibility, but among the characters she is unique in this respect. Although Darl is aware of Dewey Dell's sexual adventure, he is not overly concerned with its moral implications. Darl knows that his mother has sinned with the Reverend Whitfield, but his reaction is only increased jealousy toward Jewel, the preferred son. In a similar way Jewel's restless fury is not directed at other members of the family but focused upon outsiders such as Vernon Tull, the Jefferson stranger, and the half-wild horse that Jewel makes into a scapegoat figure. Dewey Dell's virtue is no more important to her father or to the rest of the family than it is to Darl. She has a close relationship with Vardaman, suggesting that of Caddy with Benjy, but its driving force seems to be selfish interest rather than selfless love. In general the Bundrens are closely involved with one another, but they seldom love or hate, and the misfortunes caused by their actions are almost always their own.

There are two principal arenas of action in *As I Lay Dying*, the exterior public world and the interior realm of personal emotion. The reader is made to grasp almost simultaneously the Bundren saga as it appears to others and as it appears to the individuals taking part. These two arenas of action are established by contrasting monologues. On the one hand the reader is given direct insight into the obsessions of such family members as Dewey Dell, Vardaman, Darl, Jewel, and Addie Bundren. On the other hand he can watch the Bundrens as they are seen by outsiders that they meet along the way. Darl's monologues, with their combination of personal and impersonal narration, mediate between these opposed views.

Through the subjective accounts the reader takes the trip to Jefferson as deadly serious—but of a seriousness divorced from any sense of obligation to Addie's dying wish. Through the witness accounts the reader looks upon the venture as either epic or absurd; in either case it is fused with the real or imagined family responsibility. The result is a series of multiple views of the same central action that systematically deprive the reader of any consistent attitude. The only possible relief of tension, and the expedient forced upon the reader, is that of withdrawal of sympathy from the tormented Bundrens and a full appreciation of the comic or mock-epic elements.

This withdrawal enables the reader to look upon the novel as a dramatic *tour de force* and to appreciate the balance which Faulkner achieves between the public and private aspects of the Bundren venture. The journey still may be considered heroic, but no heroic force, either personal or social, can be described as underlying it. Only the comic inertia of such figures as Anse and Cash, supported by the secret emotions and desires of the other Bundrens, enables the family to achieve its goal. What personal heroism survives is destroyed, once Jefferson has been reached, by the sudden appearance of Anse with a new wife, "a kind of duck-shaped woman all dressed up, with them kind of hard-looking pop eyes like she was daring ere a man to say nothing" (531). Her appearance enables the novel to fulfill the formal requirements of comedy by symbolizing a new family stability that proves stronger than the threatened chaos. But acceptance by the family is a further betrayal of Addie and the public motive behind their trip. No solution is given to the problem of Darl's madness, Dewey Dell's pregnancy, or Cash's broken leg. This lack of a fully comic or tragic resolution is part of the elaborate interplay between the serious and the burlesque that provides the novel with its mock-epic structure.

IN SPITE OF the comic structure of *As I Lay Dying*, the wholly serious aspects of the novel, which exist in relative independence, cannot be ignored. In his treatment of Addie Bundren and the troubles of her children Faulkner takes up the problem of individual isolation and man's desperate effort to achieve personal security in an insecure world. In her private life Addie declines to make the social gestures of love and acceptance of family responsibility, and her resulting alienation is mirrored in the maladjustments of her children. In her one monologue, presented after her funeral has been described, the reader is given the impression that even in death she dominates and corrodes the family emotional life.

A Modern Mock-Epic

As an unmarried schoolteacher Addie hates her young charges. She tells of waiting for the last child to leave, "with his little dirty snuffling nose" (461), and then going down the hill to the spring to "hate" them. Involved with her scorn is a strong sense of personal isolation. She compares herself and the children to spiders dangling by their mouths from a beam, "swinging and twisting and never touching." Only by sadistic whippings can she bridge this gap and make "my blood and their blood flow as one stream" (463). "I would look forward to the times when they faulted, so I could whip them. When the switch fell I could feel it upon my flesh; when it welted and ridged it was my blood that ran, and I would think with each blow of the switch: Now you are aware of me! Now I am something in your secret and selfish life, who have marked your blood with my own for ever and ever" (461–462).

It should be evident from the preceding quotation that Addie desires to impose her personality upon others rather than just to escape her isolation. Her belief that abstract words such as motherhood, fear, pride, and love are meaningless must be read as an indication that she rejects her family and the mere words that unite her to it. She rejects Anse's love but accepts the birth of Cash, their first son, because it is a relationship of pain and blood. "I knew that living was terrible and that this was the answer to it" (463). Through the pain of giving birth her "aloneness had been violated and then made whole again by the violation: time, Anse, love, what you will, outside the circle" (464). Instead of trying to escape her isolation through human relationships she wants to make it permanent by an act of temporary violation. When Darl is born, the pain is no longer a symbol for self-identity. She feels that Anse has tried to break down her isolation altogether, and she reacts by repudiating him and his family. She imagines Anse retiring behind a paper screen of words and ceasing to exist except as a meaningless name.

At this point Addie tells Anse to bury her in Jefferson with her own family and not with the Bundrens. Only by lying with her "blood" family can her isolation (her permanent death) be complete. Her only reason for living, as she puts it, "is getting ready to stay dead" (467). She has a significant image of Jewel nursing and then "the wild blood" boiling away to silence. "Then there was only the milk, warm and calm, and I lying calm in the slow silence,

117

getting ready to clean my house" (467). What Addie wants is not death so much as the absolute identity which it paradoxically affords. The very title of the novel, *As I Lay Dying*, suggests that Addie has a power of awareness that looks back from death to a period covered by the action of the story. Only when the coffin is buried does Addie withdraw her influence from the family she has rejected.

After Darl is born, Addie takes the Reverend Whitfield as a lover. "I would think of sin as I would think of the clothes we both wore in the world's face, of the circumspection necessary because he was he and I was I; the sin the more utter and terrible since he was the instrument ordained by God who created the sin, to sanctify that sin He had created . . . I would think of the sin as garments which we would remove in order to shape and coerce the terrible blood to the forlorn echo of the dead word high in the air" (466). What she wants is not love, a mere word, but religious sin as a garment to cover and protect a transcendent isolation. Her attitude recalls Quentin Compson's view of incest as an act which would isolate both him and Caddy from a disintegrating world. The quest for sin by both characters represents an attempt to find some kind of personal meaning in the midst of a damned and forsaken Old Testament world where Divine justice is rigorous and without mercy. However, this desire to be condemned rather than forgotten by God proves selfish and dehumanizing. Quentin's excessive puritanism corrupts his sister's innocence and helps to cause the degradation that his abstract rage feeds upon. In *As I Lay Dying* Addie Bundren's thirst for a relationship of "blood" strikes at the heart of family unity. Addie sacrifices her family to the demands of self, but her sacrifice is hardly spiritual. She rules her actions by an inhuman logic, as when she construes the birth of Dewey Dell as a means of "negativing" Jewel, her son by Whitfield. Vardaman, born later, is a replacement for the child she has robbed Anse of. Thus she divides her children between herself and Anse. Two of them, Jewel and Cash, belong to her, or to them both, and the three others "are his and not mine" (467). In refusing to share even her children with Anse she destroys her marriage and sows jealousy and hatred among her children.

Addie's favorite child is of course Jewel, the product and the symbol of her redeeming sin. Cora Tull recognizes this preference but falsely believes that Jewel has no love to return. Jewel both conceals and expresses his attachment to Addie—openly stated in his single monologue—by a perpetual warfare with his beloved horse. His treatment of the unnamed animal suggests the alternate coddling and whipping which Addie, according to Darl, has invested in him. At one point Jewel is described as forcing the horse's head back painfully with one hand and caressing its neck with the other. Even as he curses the horse, he pulls down extra hay for it. "Get the goddamn stuff out of sight while you got a chance, you pussel-gutted bastard. You sweet son of a bitch" (346).

Jewel's virtual identification of his mother and his horse is confirmed several times by Darl. As a transference of emotion it is paralleled by Vardaman's belief that his dead mother has become a live fish. The boy catches this fish, "nigh long as he is" (358), on the day of Addie's death, and chops it up in preparation for cooking. He dramatizes his mother's death in terms of the whole fish becoming pieces of not-fish. "Then hit want. Hit hadn't happened then. Hit was a-layin' right there on the ground. And now she's gittin ready to cook hit" (378). The exact nature of Vardaman's reasoning is not clear, but he seems to feel that if it can be proven that the fish really existed as a fish before being chopped up, then his mother will be alive. He walks the four miles to Tull's place not to tell them of Addie's death, as they believe, but to get Tull's confirmation that the fish was once whole. His third monologue reads in its confident entirety: "My mother is a fish" (398).

Transferring his mother into a fish, Vardaman is able to think of her body as something still alive. He remembers his own horror at being once locked up in a corn crib and becomes afraid that his mother will suffocate. First he opens the window above her bed, exposing her body to the wind and rain. Then, after the body is placed in its coffin, he takes Cash's auger and bores breathing holes, two of them going into her face. Here is a further example of horrible experiences put into such a ridiculous context that the reader is sheltered from their full impact.

Though Vardaman's behavior is far from psychologically inevitable, it is completely justified by its symbolic function. Jewel's horse and Vardaman's fish enable the two characters to keep their mental

119

equilibrium in the face of bereavement. Their success in doing this is contrasted to Darl's failure. Darl taunts Jewel with knowledge of Addie's sin: "Your mother was a horse, but who was your father, Jewel?" (494). Yet Darl cannot escape his jealousy as well as his belief, like Quentin Compson's, that he has no real mother. In a dialogue with Vardaman, reported by the latter, Darl equates his own lack of personal existence with this absence of a mother-substitute:

> "Jewel's mother is a horse," Darl said.
> "Then mine can be a fish, can't it, Darl?" I said.
> Jewel is my brother.
> "Then mine will have to be a horse, too," I said.
> "Why?" Darl said. "If pa is your pa, why does your ma have to be a horse just because Jewel's is?"
> "Why does it?" I said. "Why does it, Darl?"
> Darl is my brother.
> "Then what is your ma, Darl?" I said.
> "I haven't got ere one," Darl said. "Because if I had one, it is *was*. And if it is was, it can't be *is*. Can it?"
> "No," I said.
> "Then I am not," Darl said. "Am I?"
> "No," I said.
> I am. Darl is my brother.
> "But you *are*, Darl," I said.
> "I know it," Darl said. "That's why I am not *is*. *Are* is too many for one woman to foal" (409).

Believing that he lacks a true mother, Darl argues that he has no personal existence, no *is*ness. Even if he had a mother once, she has now become *was*. Vardaman reasons that since Darl is his brother, then Darl too must exist. "But you *are*, Darl," Vardaman states. The boy intends "*are*" as a second-person singular verb, implying a single existent. But Darl chooses to interpret this "*are*" as standing for a plural "you are" in which both himself and Jewel are included. Thus Darl cannot have a mother, because "*are*" (meaning plurality here) would be "too many for one woman to foal." In other words Addie can have only one real son. The use of the word "foal" associates Addie with Jewel's horse and implies that she, like any mare, can nurse only one offspring at a time.

When his mother is upon the point of dying, Darl persuades Anse to send him and Jewel on an overnight trip to transport a load of wood. Cora Tull reports afterward that Darl was against the trip and Jewel for it. But her emotional account is contradicted by the facts as reported by her husband. Darl knows that Addie will die that night, and by taking himself and Jewel away he avoids the death scene and makes sure that Jewel is not present when Addie calls for him. Once they are gone, he uses his knowledge of what is taking place to taunt his brother: "It's not your horse that's dead" (405).

But that night Darl's suspicion that he does not really exist causes him to think about his mother's death. "I don't know what I am. I don't know if I am or not." Hearing rain strike the loaded wagon outside, he interprets its *was*ness (for rain is only heard as it ceases to fall) as a symbol of his mother's death. "Yet the wagon *is*, because when the wagon is *was*, Addie Bundren will not be. And Jewel *is*, so Addie Bundren must be. And then I must be, or I could not empty myself for sleep in a strange room" (396). In this passage, which strongly resembles Vardaman's speculations about his fish, Darl's effort to believe that his mother is still alive is a last defense against mental chaos. For as long as he can keep her symbolically alive, as Jewel and Vardaman have done, then his own existence as a human being is beyond question.

Later on, as he travels with the rest of the family and the coffin, Darl refuses to admit the fact of Addie's death. It is this need to think of her as being alive that causes him to set fire to the barn in which her body has been placed. Darl associates the trip to Jefferson with Addie's permanent death, and hopes by halting the trip to prevent her burial. This is also why he leaps from the wagon when it is threatened by the flooded river instead of staying with it to protect the coffin as Jewel does. Darl seems to echo his mother's implicit belief that only in a Jefferson grave, away from the Bundrens, can her process of "dying" become complete. Darl is the only member of the family to realize that Addie's desire to be buried away from her children is a selfish act that repudiates symbolically her responsibilities as a wife and mother.

After Jewel has rescued the coffin from the burning barn, Vardaman finds Darl lying upon it and in tears. With unconscious irony the boy tries to console him. "You needn't to cry . . . Jewel got her

121

out. You needn't to cry, Darl" (503). In conjunction with his failure to drown Addie's body in the flood or cremate it in the fire, and by either means to halt the trip, comes Darl's madness or complete loss of self. This is illustrated in Darl's final monologue by an absolute division between his narrating consciousness and his physical self. The speaker describes the actions of a third person "Darl" instead of the previous "I."

Like Quentin Compson, Darl Bundren is obsessed with family relations and the problem of personal existence. Yet Faulkner makes no use of structural relationships in *As I Lay Dying* as a means of condemning this distorted perception of reality as false or morally inadequate. In *The Sound and the Fury* it is impossible for the reader to separate Quentin's personal concerns from the character's puritan rage at the corruption about him. Darl's attitude on the other hand is more consistently abstract and is expressed in nonsocial language. His attitudes toward Addie and Jewel are responsible for his madness, but he struggles to save himself, whereas Quentin does not. Quentin is destroyed by his false morality, whereas Darl is destroyed by the world itself as it reflects back his self-doubts.

Throughout *The Sound and the Fury* Faulkner carefully defines the motivation for Quentin's suicide as his need to annihilate time. This motivation may seem obscure at first reading, but the passages which refer to it are numerous, explicit, and thoroughly consistent. In *As I Lay Dying* the motivation for Darl's attempted cremation of his mother's body is apparent only if the reader knows what happens to Darl after his failure, and draws the necessary conclusions. The surface action of the novel is not so difficult to follow as that of *The Sound and the Fury*, but the characterization is less precise and the reason for action is often left obscure or vague. Moral responsibility exists in the novel, but it is less important than the imaginative control which is maintained over language and tone. In effect the "dying" mother carries all such responsibility with her into the grave. By handling her characterization in this way Faulkner is able to establish the personal tragedies as subordinate to the trip which the dead mother has willed and somehow staged. The arrival in Jefferson and the appearance of a new wife represent no victory against time or destiny, but stand for the completion of a temporal cycle and a return for the Bundrens to the timeless present from which the death of Addie has dislodged them all. It must be remembered that in lacking a family or cultural tradition the Bundrens also lack a past and a future. By creating for themselves a future goal the Bundrens project themselves into time and, in a sense, into history. When their goal is achieved, they find themselves released from time and back at their point of origin with neither hopes for the future nor regrets for the past. Only Darl loses himself irrevocably in time—and he is eliminated from the family.

LIKE ITS COMPANION NOVEL, *As I Lay Dying* is dominated by images suggesting the passage of time. The family journey is made temporally urgent by the increasing decay of the mother's body. Moreover the eventual arrival in Jefferson, like the advent of the future, is always taken for granted. The Bundrens are not victims of a preconceived fate, but as a family group they accept a responsibility which determines or actually creates their future. Since they are driven by inertia rather than courage or determination, it is simply a matter of time before they reach their goal. At one point Darl watches Jewel's horse in the distance and describes the movement of the wagon on which he is riding as being "so soporific, so dreamlike as to be uninferent of progress, as though time and not space were decreasing between us and it" (413). As a group the Bundrens move with the flow of time, but as individuals they struggle desperately against time and become its inevitable victims. The river, a principal time-symbol, is associated with Darl's sense of isolation. He imagines the river to be an "irrevocable quantity" which separates him from members of his family on the opposite shore. "It is as though time, no longer running straight before us in a diminishing line, now runs parallel between us like a looping string, the distance being the doubling accretion of the thread and not the interval between" (443). Time is not a road upon which the individual travels, moving from point to point; it is a force that irrevocably separates individuals. Darl's comparison means that time is itself in motion and not individuals within time. The movement of time is circular, like the looping of a string, but the distance between individuals is never shortened. This is why Darl views the river as an alive and malignant force, "as though just beneath the surface something huge and alive waked for a moment of lazy alertness out of and into light slumber again" (439).

Within this isolating milieu of time the human individual is a static "clotting which is you" that breaks the flowing surface for a brief moment and then disappears into the "myriad original motion." Human sight and hearing are blind and deaf, "fury in itself quiet with stagnation" (458). Human reality consists of a few empty gestures made in the futile struggle to achieve a permanent self. "How do our lives ravel out into the no-wind, no-sound, the weary gestures wearily recapitulant: echoes of old compulsions with no-hand on no-strings: in sunset we fall into furious attitudes, dead gestures of dolls" (491). This fatalism strongly resembles Quentin Compson's insistence that time is man's misfortune, "a gull on an invisible wire attached through space dragged" (123). Quentin finds escape through suicide, but Darl's obsession drives him to madness. To use Darl's own terms, he eventually surrenders his pretension to existence and melts away into time. "If you could just ravel out into time," he thinks. "That would be nice. It would be nice if you could just ravel out into time" (492). A similar passage occurs in *The Sound and the Fury* when Quentin recalls his wished-for incest with Caddy and his vision of the "clean flame" (135) that would isolate them from the world. "That's it if people could only change one another forever that way merge like a flame swirling up for an instant then blown cleanly out along the cool eternal dark" (194–195).

Both characters experience the anguish of struggle for personal stability in a world where time always leads the individual out of himself and isolates him from the rest of humanity. In Quentin's case this view is involved with his social despair and is expressed as an incestuous love for his sister Caddy. In Darl's case it is linked to his jealousy of his brother Jewel and is expressed, more abstractly, as a concern for the nature of time and human existence.

Darl's struggle against time is mirrored by Dewey Dell's resistance to the fact of being pregnant. "That's what they mean by the womb of time," she thinks, "the agony and the despair of spreading bones, the hard girdle in which lie the outraged entrails of events" (422). She imagines her body, her bones and flesh, "beginning to part and open upon the alone, and the process of coming unalone is terrible" (382). Unlike Lena Grove in *Light in August,* Dewey Dell refuses to accept the natural condition thrust upon her. She is not less moral because of her resistance—at least in terms of the novel at hand—but her action does bring to mind Addie Bundren's selfish denial of family responsibility. The girl's desire to put an end to the process of becoming "unalone" is comparable to her mother's effort to maintain her isolation by having it first "violated" and then made whole again by the violation.

In a striking passage Dewey Dell establishes a contrast similar to Darl's distinction between the human self, "the clotting which is you," and time's restless dynamism. She reverses the terms by equating her pregnancy with the assertion of time, or growth, within a static and dead external world:

The sky lies flat down the slope, upon the secret clumps. Beyond the hill sheet-lightning stains upward and fades. The dead air shapes the dead earth in the dead darkness, further away than seeing shapes the dead earth. It lies dead and warm upon me, touching me naked through my clothes. I said You don't know what worry is. I don't know what it is. I don't know whether I am worrying or not. Whether I can or not. I don't know whether I can cry or not. I don't know whether I have tried to or not. I feel like a wet seed wild in the hot blind earth. (384)

The success of this passage illustrates Faulkner's ability to have his primitive characters express personal emotion in language that often borders on the metaphysical. The same technique is used in the passage, previously referred to, where Darl's obsession with Addie, his jealousy of Jewel, and his doubts concerning his own existence are all fused. The reader does not have to follow the subtlety of Darl's argument to understand its dramatic impact, yet the argument is logically consistent. At times Faulkner seems to create an imaginative world in which personal anguish lies too deep for normal descriptive language to express, and must be conveyed by the concepts of philosophy.

There are numerous other passages throughout the novel in which characters are concerned with the problem of personal existence amid the flux of time. Associated with these passages are images involving blood, a cool or warm breeze, and the concept of secret and primitive forces of nature. When Vardaman flees to the barn after Addie's death, he thinks of Jewel's horse as "an illusion of a co-ordinated whole of splotched hide and strong bones within which, detached and secret and familiar, an *is* different from my *is*" (379). The language is hardly that of a small boy, but the obsession is appropriate to his characterization.

In one passage Dewey Dell compares her human trouble to that of a cow, moaning to be milked. "She nuzzles at me, snuffing, blowing her breath in a sweet, hot blast, through my dress, against my hot nakedness, moaning" (382). When Dewey Dell knows that Anse is driving the wagon past the road to the Bundren cemetery, affirming his intention to go on to Jefferson, she feels the wind blowing cool out of the pines, "a sad steady sound." She is reminded of lying in bed half-asleep and being unable to remember her own name, where she was, or even "time" itself. "I couldn't even think I nor even think I want to wake up nor remember what was opposite to awake" (423). Then she knows suddenly that "something was it was wind blowing over me it was like the wind came and blew me back from where it was I was not blowing the room and Vardaman asleep and all of them back under me again and going on like a piece of cool silk dragging across my naked legs" (423). Darl too lies in bed feeling the "cool silence" (344) of the wind as it shapes his naked body and brings him existence. In both cases the wind is associated with an erotic experience that symbolizes the awareness of having a self.

The image of blood and the concept of an alien and "secret" life are joined by Addie Bundren's single monologue, as in this comment about her schoolchildren: "I would have to look at them day after day, each with his and her secret and selfish thought, and blood strange to each other blood and strange to mine" (461). Both obsessions are shared by other characters, as in Vardaman's reference to Jewel's horse. In one passage Darl imagines himself and Cash looking at one another "with long probing looks, looks that plunge unimpeded through one another's eyes and into the ultimate secret place where for an instant Cash and Darl crouch flagrant and unabashed in all the old terror and the old foreboding, alert and secret and without shame" (439). In Darl's encroaching madness, just before he tries to cremate Addie, he imagines her alive in her coffin and talking "in little trickling bursts of secret and murmurous bubbling" (494). The blood image is emphasized by Vardaman's "bloody" appearance after butchering his fish.

In one of Dewey Dell's monologues the image of blood, Vardaman's fish symbolism, and her own hatred of Darl for knowing about her shame are all fused:

> Once I waked with a black void rushing under me. I could not see. I saw Vardaman rise and go to the window and strike the knife into the fish, the blood gushing, hissing like steam but I could not see. . . . That was when I died that time. . . . I rose and took the knife from the streaming fish still hissing and I killed Darl. (422–423)

The reference to having "died that time" recalls Caddy's similar phrase in *The Sound and the Fury;* and the idea of a "black void" rushing under Dewey Dell brings to mind Temple Drake's comparable experience in *Sanctuary.*

Of particular interest is the number of references in *As I Lay Dying* to eyes and their effect upon other characters. We know little of Jewel's physical appearance beyond his flat lean figure, looking as if it were "cut cleanly from tin" (498) or carved out of wood, and his "pale eyes like wood set into his wooden face" (339). Darl refers several times to Jewel's pale wooden eyes, which are also described as "like marbles" (409), "like pieces of a broken plate" (427), and as "pale as two bleached chips" (442). Once in the moonlight Darl sees them as "spots of white paper pasted on a high small football" (494). Attention is also paid to Darl's eyes, which are associated with his abnormal perception. Dewey Dell senses their power: "the land runs out of Darl's eyes; they swim to pin-points. They begin at my feet and rise along my body to my face, and then my dress is gone: I sit naked on the seat above the unhurrying mules, above the travail" (422). Vernon Tull thinks of Darl's eyes as getting into the "inside of you, someway. Like somehow you was looking at yourself and your doings outen his eyes" (426). Dewey Dell's and Vardaman's eyes are also extensively described. Dewey Dell's look like blazing pistols when she tries to convince Anse that he should go on to Jefferson. Vardaman's eyes are "round and black in the middle like when you throw a light in a owl's face" (387).

These descriptions of eyes illustrate the basic distinction emphasized throughout the novel between the outer world of human action and the inner sphere of self-conscious emotion. Jewel's eyes are "pale" and "wooden" to Darl because they express the former's atmosphere of mechanized or frozen violence. Dewey Dell's eyes reveal her burning desire to reach Jefferson and not her expressed loyalty to Addie. Darl's eyes reveal his madness and indicate his insight into family tensions. Like Dewey Dell's "wet seed wild" the eyes of all these characters indicate the dynamism of human existence as opposed to the static human world. The physical milieu which appears in *As I Lay Dying* is largely two-dimensional and functions as a barrier or flat screen which conceals human passion and makes everything seem wooden and lifeless. The physical universe is entirely dehumanized, and existential reality seems lost or hidden behind a "paper screen," as Addie describes it, of word and gesture.

This interpretation is supported by Faulkner's manner of describing important scenes. Jewel's horse against the background of woods resembles "a patchwork quilt hung on a line" (457). He and Gillespie, framed by the "proscenium" of the doorway of a burning barn, are "like two figures in a Greek frieze, isolated out of all reality by the red glare" (500). The monologuists, Darl in particular, seem to visualize a twilight world in which figures of men and objects are cast into strong relief by darkness, by moonlight, or by the catastrophes of flood and fire. In one scene Darl, though several miles away, seems to be watching Cash work by night on Addie's coffin. The lantern casts everything into extreme silhouette against a flat background. The chips of wood resemble "random smears of soft pale paint on a black canvas." The boards are "like long smooth tatters torn from the flat darkness and turned backside out." Even the sounds made by Cash as he moves the planks share in this two-dimensional quality, making "long clattering reverberations in the dead air as though he were lifting and dropping them at the bottom of an invisible well, the sounds ceasing without departing, as if any movement might dislodge them from the immediate air in reverberant repetition." Darl notes the shadows cast by Cash and his father upon the "impalpable plane" of the air, "as though like sound they had not gone very far away in falling but had merely congealed for a moment, immediate and musing." Cash works on, "his face sloped into the light with a rapt, dynamic immobility above his tireless elbow" (391–392). The action described is broken down into a series of flat landscapes or snapshots in which all human reality, in fact all temporal motion, has given way to two-dimensional appearances.

The explanation of this method of description is contained within the imagery itself. Darl describes Cash at Addie Bundren's death bed looking down upon "her peaceful, rigid face fading into the dusk as though darkness were a precursor of the ultimate earth, until at last the face seems to float detached upon it, lightly as the reflection of a dead leaf" (373). In a second passage the flood water seeping through the woods beside the river gives the effect of cane and saplings suspended by invisible wires from the branches overhead. "Above the ceaseless surface they stand—trees, cane, vines—rootless, severed from the earth, spectral above a scene of immense yet circumscribed desolation filled with the voice of the waste and mournful water" (439). Both the darkness and the water represent a milieu that deprives natural objects, in the first case Addie's face and in the second the young trees, of their natural physical dimension. The dynamism of time reduces human life to an abstract "clotting" and assumes dramatic shape only as the secret refuge of self hiding in Dewey Dell's womb.

Humanity and its natural environment are not in harmony with time but exist in futile opposition to its destructive and alienating force. This is best represented dramatically by the scene in which the three brothers and their mother's body flounder helplessly in the wild and uncontrollable river. The external world of flesh and wagons is in fact rendered static and immobile by its conflict with the unleashed forces of nature. These primitive forces are represented in macrocosm and in microcosm by the swollen river and the private feelings of isolated individuals. Everything else partakes of stasis and death.

This is why Darl wants his consciousness to merge and become one with time. Madness has ripped the veil from his eyes and revealed to him and to the reader a universe in which the human self is alienated from its dead world of human flesh. To partake of this outer world of dead flesh is tantamount to immersing one's consciousness in a series of mechanized actions, to become, like Jewel, "a figure carved clumsily from tough wood by a drunken caricaturist" (457). On the other hand, to forsake the world and "ravel out into time" is to surrender all hope of personal identity. Thus Darl is made to view the grim paradox of human life with unsheltered eyes, and the reader is forced to do likewise. At the same time the situation of *As I Lay Dying* is a contrived one in which Darl's obsession, and those of his sister and brothers, are projected onto and made one with the dramatic surface. There is no objective point of view which the reader can isolate from the several distorted accounts and use to evaluate each personal world. This unity of reality and obsession is responsible for the novel's mock-epic power and marks the depth of its psychological exploration.

Chapter Eight

THE PURITAN SINNER:
LIGHT IN AUGUST

*I*N *Light in August* Faulkner continues his exploration of the
South's puritan mentality; at the same time he introduces racial
miscegenation as a central dramatic issue. As a white Southerner
convinced that he has Negro ancestry, Joe Christmas directs his
racial prejudice inward, against himself, and the resulting torment
commits him to a path of lonely violence. He is driven by a strong
sense of guilt and a need for some kind of punishment or moral
expiation. Faulkner fits Joe's pattern of self-destruction into a dramatic context that establishes it as an exploration of the central
moral and social problem of the racially divided South. Joe assumes
unwittingly the role of a sacrificial victim who accepts the white
South's own burden of past sin and present injustice. His characterization brings out into the open issues that lie deep within the

Southern mind, and his death suggests a personal atonement for the racial crime of his region.

Joe Christmas's early life is associated with a number of fanatical Protestant Christians. His grandfather, Eupheus (Doc) Hines, kills Joe's father, a dark-skinned circus man, and allows Joe's unmarried mother to die in childbirth. Hines believes that Joe represents the very "teeth and fangs" (338) of Satan's evil, and he becomes convinced that God wants him to wait for this evil to bear fruit. "I have put the mark on him, and now I am going to put the knowledge" (325). Hines finds a job as the janitor of an orphanage and abandons the infant Joe Christmas at its doorstep. As Joe grows up, the other children respond to the grandfather's malignant influence and begin to call Joe a "nigger," a charge which the boy convinces himself must be true. Hines's religious mania is introduced not only to explain Joe's obsession, but to call the reader's attention to the internal puritan force which oppresses the boy and against which he reacts.

Although Joe escapes the religious fanaticism of his grandfather, he finds a similar figure in McEachern, the Presbyterian farmer who adopts him. Through his relation with the farmer, who is characterized by a Bible or catechism held in one hand and a strap in the other, Joe is given a taste of the expiating punishment for which he unconsciously yearns. He rebels against the grim farmer, but the two are symbolically joined by their mutual "stubbornness" and "rigid abnegation of all compromise" (130). The salient feature of their common puritanism is its abstract or impersonal nature. McEachern's voice is "not unkind," but it is inhuman and impersonal. "It was just cold, implacable, like written or printed words" (130).

The repressed emotions of Faulkner's puritans are usually associated with a masklike facial expression. Such figures are described as looking simultaneously calm and rapturous, and terms like "fury," "outrage," and "implacable urgency" are combined with those implying outward repose or immobility. Doc Hines and his wife are excited at finding their grandson still alive, but to the Reverend Hightower they appear transfixed by "frozen and mechanically moved inertia," as if they were puppets "operated by clumsy springwork" (323). Hines appears oblivious and indifferent to his surroundings, "and yet withal a quality latent and explosive, paradoxically rapt and alert at the same time" (323). When Joe's mistress,

Joanna Burden, tries to shoot him, her eyes are described as "calm and still as all pity and all despair and all conviction" (247). The implication here is not merely that Joanna's eyes appear calm in spite of her emotion, but that such emotions as pity and despair are associated with calm and still facial expressions.

In the narrative world of *Light in August* emotion itself seems to adopt the posture and pose of impersonal rapture and martyrdom. Hearing the sound of church singing, the Reverend Hightower describes the Southern mind and heart as being "expiated by the stern and formal fury" of its Sunday morning service. Whereas the voices of the singers adopt "the shapes and attitudes of crucifixions, ecstatic, solemn, and profound," the music itself is "stern and implacable, deliberate and without passion" (321). That is to say, puritans tend to express their emotions, if at all, within the framework of rigid social conventions.

Puritan emotion occasionally breaks out in unrestrained violence, as in the mass fury of a lynching mob, but such violence is not a spontaneous expression of pent-up emotions. According to Faulkner the puritan mind avoids natural expression of feelings. "Pleasure, ecstasy, they cannot seem to bear: their escape from it is in violence, in drinking and fighting and praying." By forcing human emotions into the service of abstract convictions, these Southerners transform themselves into moral fanatics. Hightower explains that a mob of Southern churchgoers will lynch Joe Christmas in order to stifle their own consciences. They will crucify him gladly, "since to pity him would be to admit selfdoubt and to hope for and need pity themselves" (322). In other words the whole town will resort to a stylized and traditional act of violence rather than admit emotional realities.

This combination of moral conviction and ruthless violence is succinctly characterized by the desire of Calvin Burden, Joanna Burden's grandfather, to "beat the loving God" (213) into his four children. This staunch figure stands for a tradition of New England Puritanism that is related in both spirit and doctrinal roots to the more evangelical Presbyterian sects dominating the American Middle West and Deep South. It is significant that he reads the Bible to his children in Spanish, a language which they cannot understand. What they do understand is a series of impromptu sermons, composed half of "bleak and bloodless" New England logic and "half of immediate hellfire and tangible brimstone of which any country Methodist circuit rider would have been proud" (212). The result is the Protestant blend of emotionalism and abstract morality which Faulkner consistently satirizes.

Faulkner's aim in introducing Calvin Burden and his New England heritage is to show the relation between the attitude of the abolitionist Burdens toward the Southern Negro and the racial hatred of a man like Doc Hines. Whereas Hines sees his grandson's Negro ancestry as a token of the Devil, the Burdens look upon Negroes as the sign and symbol of the white man's moral sin. Joanna Burden sees the curse of slavery as a "black shadow in the shape of a cross" (221) falling upon all white children. The curse of the black race is the irrevocable fate of being held in bondage, "but the curse of the white race is the black man who will be forever God's chosen own because He once cursed him" (222). The Burdens take up social work among the Negroes in the postwar South as a step toward expiating the curse which has fallen upon their own white blood. Their abstract approach to the race problem is comparable to that of Hines, who reacts in hatred to his similar belief that the Negro race is a curse upon the white. Joe Christmas inherits the prejudice of his grandfather, but he is also influenced by Joanna Burden and presumably by the doctrines which her family represents. Faulkner's references to the religious heritages of both New England and the South link social and political issues involving all of America to the racial obsession underlying Joe's violence.

At the heart of Joe Christmas's puritanism is a strong sense of moral guilt. At the orphanage where his grandfather has placed him the five-year-old boy is caught eating toothpaste in the dietician's bathroom and naturally expects extreme punishment. But the frightened woman believes that Joe has witnessed an assignation, and instead of punishing him she tries to bribe his silence with a gleaming silver dollar. The boy associates the money with his memory of guilt and the sensation of being sick from the toothpaste. "He was still with astonishment, shock, outrage. Looking at the dollar, he seemed to see ranked tubes of toothpaste like corded wood, endless and terrifying; his whole being coiled in a rich and passionate revulsion. 'I dont want no more,' he said. 'I dont never want no more,' he thought" (109).

This episode symbolizes the main currents of Joe's adult life. His consciousness of unexpiated guilt becomes involved with the belief that he is part Negro and in need of moral absolution. His experience with the dietician, herself a food symbol, confirms his revulsion against food, money, and women.

Upon leaving the orphanage Joe encounters a series of symbolic repetitions of this same traumatic experience. He does not mind the brutality of McEachern, his stepfather, so much as the "soft kindness" of Mrs. McEachern. When she washes Joe's feet upon his arrival, he keeps waiting for something unpleasant to take place, and he is upset because it never does. Later on he imagines the woman standing between himself and the punishment from McEachern which, "deserved or not, just or unjust, was impersonal, both the man and the boy accepting it as a natural and inescapable fact" (146). When McEachern sends him to bed without any supper, the boy feels "weak and peaceful" (134). But the woman spoils his martyrdom by secretly bringing him a tray of hot steaming food. Joe throws it on the floor, but an hour later he is on his knees devouring the food resentfully, "like a savage, like a dog" (136).

Joe's early hatred of food anticipates a later disgust at his own sexual needs. His first traumatic experience is with a Negro girl, a "womanshenegro," who waits for the boy and his friends in a dark shed where her eyes glint like "dead stars" reflected at the bottom of a "black well" (137). Instead of doing what is expected, Joe kicks the girl and fights with the other boys as they rush in. His resort to violence is an effort to escape a primitive force far stronger than his male puritanism: "it was as if a wind had blown among them, hard and clean" (137). A similar incident takes place when Joe first learns about the menstruation of women. Unable to live with his knowledge, he buys immunity, as Faulkner puts it, by killing a sheep and dipping his hands in its blood. But Old Testament ceremonies cannot help Joe when the information is repeated by Bobbie, his first mistress. "In the notseeing and the hardknowing as though in a cave he seemed to see a diminishing row of suavely shaped urns in moonlight, blanched. And not one was perfect. Each one was cracked and from each crack there issued something liquid, death-colored, and foul" (165).

This blanched and cracked world in which Joe Christmas finds himself trapped is a projection of his own puritan thinking. Joe learns to hate his own body as well as its physical and emotional needs, and to him hunger and desire seem oppressive forces associated with darkness and evil. Food is always something "hot and fierce," prepared by women, which he must eat hurriedly and with a vague feeling of self-betrayal. When Joe steals into Joanna Burden's kitchen in desperate hunger, "he seemed to flow into the dark kitchen: a shadow returning without a sound and without locomotion to the allmother of obscurity and darkness" (200). Since food and sex are closely related in Joe's mind, it is no accident that he rapes Joanna that same night.

Opposed to these dark forces is the power of abstinence, which is associated in Joe's mind with calm certainty and the hard clean air of masculinity. As a boy he feels weak and peaceful because of the lack of food; and once more, before his death, he is able to rise above such human needs. Before surrendering to a society that he knows will crucify him, Joe has a feeling of peace and unhaste and quiet. He wonders why, "until suddenly the true answer comes to him. He feels dry and light. 'I dont have to bother about having to eat any more,' he thinks. 'That's what it is'" (295).

Christmas's guilty hatred of sex is illustrated most strongly in his relations with Joanna Burden, the product of a puritan heritage similar to his own. At first Joe is drawn toward his alter-ego (Joanna) because she acts more like a man than a woman. She combines a woman's body with "the mantrained muscles and the mantrained habit of thinking born of heritage and environment" (205). When Joe attacks her, she seems to resist as a man might, "as if he struggled physically with another man for an object of no actual value to either, and for which they struggled on principle alone" (205). But Joanna soon reveals a split personality, becoming a mannish old maid by day and a nymphomaniac by night. This transformation is explained in terms of her religious heritage as "the abject fury of the New England glacier exposed suddenly to the fire of the New England biblical hell" (225). He watches in passive disgust as his mistress seeks to compensate for the "frustrate and irrevocable years" by "damning herself forever to the hell of her forefathers" (226). Two creatures seem to struggle within her for mastery. "Now it would be that still, cold, contained figure . . . who, even though lost and damned, remained somehow impervious and impregnable; then it would be the other, the second one, who in furious denial of that impregnability strove to drown in the black abyss of its own creating that physical purity which had been preserved too long now ever to be lost" (228).

During this period Joe Christmas discovers in Joanna the epitome of the primitive forces of nature which he has tried to escape. Her nymphomania is described in terms of darkness and lust, her eyes "in the dark glowing like the eyes of cats" and her body caught in the wild throes of passion. "She would be wild then, in the close, breathing halfdark without walls, with her wild hair, each strand of which would seem to come alive like octopus tentacles, and her wild hands and her breathing: 'Negro! Negro! Negro!'" (227). She desperately seeks to drown her long-preserved purity in a morass of corruption. To his own horror Joe finds himself drawn into this quagmire. He imagines himself lying "at the bottom of a pit in the hot wild darkness" (235) and watching his own body "turning slow and lascivious in a whispering of gutter filth like a drowned corpse in a thick still black pool of more than water" (93).

Joe's puritan hatred of women and the physical desire they represent is consistently involved with his hatred of the Negro blood which he seems to hold responsible for the terrifying world in which he must live. He imagines relations with women as a pit or pool of glimmering darkness out of which he cannot extricate his own lost and damned mulatto body. The religious and sexual agony of Joanna Burden reflects, as in a distorted Beardsley drawing (the comparison is Faulkner's), Joe Christmas's own tormented self.

Joanna's late burst of passion comes to a sudden end as she passes through her change of life and resumes her spinster's role. Now she tries to send Joe to a Negro college where he can learn enough law to become her secretary and carry on her social work. When Joe indignantly refuses, she tries to make him kneel down with her and pray. By these twin demands she crystallizes both Joe's racial obsession and his hatred of orthodox Calvinist piety. He recalls the bowed head of McEachern and the latter's ruthless morality. Imagining the print of his own knees beside Joanna's bed, he jerks his eyes away "as if it were death that they had looked at" (244). Joe is bound to his former mistress just as he is bound to his own destiny. Their conflict over his future becomes a stalemate in which neither party can surrender or escape. "They would stand for a while longer in the quiet dusk peopled, as though from their loins, by a myriad ghosts of dead sins and delights, looking at one another's still and fading face, weary, spent, and indomitable" (244).

The main difference between Joe and Joanna lies in their response to comparable racial, religious, and sexual dilemmas. Joanna finds that her old maid's "virginity," which she sought to destroy, is returning with her change of life. Before this happens, she asks God to let her be damned a little longer before having to pray. "She seemed to see her whole past life, the starved years, like a gray tunnel, at the far and irrevocable end of which, as unfading as a reproach, her naked breast of three short years ago ached as though in agony, virgin and crucified; 'Not yet, dear God. Not yet, dear God'" (231). This "crucifixion," which parallels the more serious one of Joe Christmas, is only temporary, and Joanna does return to the religion of her forefathers, accepting its spiritual complacency along with its doctrines.

In her inverted religious feeling, in her obsession with the Negro race, and in her sexual masochism, Joanna Burden mirrors the important features of Joe Christmas's destiny. This is the meaning of Joanna's surname: it suggests Joe's burden as well as her own. However, in submitting to spiritual piety she rejects the demonism, the raging puritanism, that characterizes Joe's life. Her function in the novel's structure is first to reveal to Joe what he is, then to abandon him to his solitary path.

Because of their intractable opposition, the two ex-lovers decide that both of them must die. Joanna tries to kill Joe with her grandfather's antique pistol, but the pistol misses fire. Joe then kills her with his razor. After the crime, he spends a week wandering through the country and preparing himself for death. During this time he makes more "progress," the reader is told, than in all the preceding thirty years of unremitting anguish. This progress is toward a realization of what his sense of guilt means and how it can be expiated. Refusing to identify himself as either white or Negro, and refusing to live any longer in two contradictory worlds, he drives on, knowingly, to his self-created fate.

Throughout *Light in August* the Negro blood that Joe imagines surging within him is associated, along with hunger and sexual desire, with the hot, savage, and dark forces of nature. Between Joe's flight from McEachern and his arrival in Jefferson, a period of at least twelve years, he tries to unite himself with that primitive force by crossing the color line. Living with a Negro woman in a northern city, he lies in bed, sleepless, breathing hard and deep: "trying to expel from himself the white blood and the white thinking and being" (197). But Christmas cannot escape his puritan hatred of nature, and even as he tries to make the "dark odor" of Negroes his own, he writhes and strains "with physical outrage and spiritual denial" (197).

A comparable struggle takes place the night of Joe's crime, when he takes a walk in both the white and Negro sections of Jefferson. In the white man's world he resembles "a phantom, a spirit, strayed out of its own world, and lost" (99). Then he passes down the hill into Freedman Town, the Negro quarter. In sharp contrast to "the cold hard air of white people," it lies "lightless hot wet primogenitive Female" (100) and assumes the shape of a "black pit" about to engulf him. With "drumming heart and glaring lips" (101) Joe races back to the white man's part of town. In symbolic terms he walks both racial streets at once, with "his steady white shirt and pacing dark legs" (101). His primary allegiance is to the white world, even though the dark one, as he conceives it, draws him to his death.

The few actions associated with Joe Christmas between the time of the murder and his surrender at Mottstown represent his violent acknowledgment of the primitive force which he has equated with Negro blood. He bursts into a Negro cabin and gorges himself on the occupants' prepared food. He invades a Negro church during a night service and stands in the pulpit cursing God, while the congregation flees in terror. These actions indicate Joe's realization that his racial guilt can be expiated only through death. He affirms his white nature but accepts the burden which his puritan training has imposed. The climax occurs when Joe exchanges his shoes for those of a Negro woman. The shoes are a symbol of the death which he now accepts: "the black shoes smelling of Negro: that mark on his ankles the gauge definite and ineradicable of the black tide creeping up his legs, moving from his feet upward as death moves" (297).

THE CENTRAL CHAPTERS of *Light in August,* dealing with Joe Christmas's life and death, are preceded and followed by chapters devoted to less important characters. The opening chapter describes the arrival of Lena Grove in Jefferson, and the closing one describes her departure. The other chapters concern the actions and perceptions of such figures as Gail Hightower, Byron Bunch, and Lucas Burch, alias Joe Brown. These characters establish the Yoknapatawpha environment and provide a series of perspectives in which Christmas's violent life and sacrificial death are viewed. The reader is led from Lena's indifference through Byron's absorbed interest into the heart of the story, and back out again by virtually the same route in reverse. The result in many cases is a series of multiple views of the same events. When Joe frightens a Negro congregation or surrenders to the Mottstown authorities, the reader is given in quick succession the incident from Joe's point of view and the same incident as it affects the community.

As the novel opens, Lena Grove unhurriedly searches for the father of her unborn child. Like other Faulkner primitives she takes life as it comes without trying vainly to understand it. The "peaceful corridor" of time in which she lives is opposed symbolically to Joe Christmas's "savage and lonely street." Joe believes that an unshakable fatality is pursuing him, but his narrow destiny is shaped by his own puritan imagination. "He thought that it was loneliness which he was trying to escape and not himself. . . . But the street ran on in its moods and phases, always empty . . . driven by the courage of flagged and spurred despair; by the despair of courage whose opportunities had to be flagged and spurred" (197).

The opposition between the attitudes represented by Lena and by Joe is modified when the latter accepts the certainty of coming death. The day opens peacefully for him, "like a corridor, an arras, into a still chiaroscuro without urgency" (97). As Joe reads a magazine, he permits each separate word, devoid of meaning, to hold his attention as if his entire being were suspended in space: "so that hanging motionless and without physical weight he seemed to watch the slow flowing of time beneath him" (97). Like Lena Grove he is free of the pressure of space, time, and physical needs. "He is not sleepy or hungry or even tired. He is somewhere between and among them, suspended, swaying to the motion of the wagon without thought, without feeling" (296).

For the first time in his life Joe Christmas feels no contradiction between his human emotions and his moral convictions. This fact explains the "progress" which he is described as making during his week of spiritual retreat. His destiny has always been a "flat pattern" (246), but for the first time he stops trying to avoid it; he realizes that with approaching death he has no need to escape the raging paradox within himself.

Although Lena's undeviating faith is non-Christian and obtained at the cost of near-imbecility, her placidity prefigures Joe's "peace and unhaste and quiet" (295) when he is captured at Mottstown and, later on, when he is brutally castrated. The relation between Joe Christmas and Lena Grove may be compared to that between a point on the circumference of a moving wheel and the wheel's center or hub. The outside point moves faster and covers a larger area, but at the end of the trip it has advanced no further than the central point. Joe and Lena travel in the same direction, yet their paths never meet. They are joined only in the confused mind of Joe's grandmother, who believes that Lena is Milly, Joe's mother, and that the baby is Joe. Lena even thinks for a moment that the "Mr Christmas" (359) she hears about is the baby's father.

The lives of Joe Christmas and Lena Grove are both associated with that of the cowardly Lucas Burch, or "Joe Brown" as he is known in Jefferson. After abandoning Lena because she is pregnant, Brown flees to Jefferson, where he becomes the companion and foil of Joe Christmas and sells the latter's bootleg whiskey. Brown's irresponsible behavior emphasizes by contrast Joe's "brooding and savage steadiness" (34). Even though he imitates Christmas's movements, Brown "merely contrived to look scattered and emptily swaggering where the master had looked sullen and quiet and fatal as a snake" (39). He is a fatalist like Joe Christmas, yet of a different kind: "it seemed to him now that they were all just shapes like chessmen—the Negro, the sheriff, the money, all—unpredictable and without reason moved here and there by an Opponent who could read his moves before he made them and who created spontaneous rules which he and not the Opponent, must follow" (383). The key phrase here is "unpredictable and without reason." The force that determines Joe's chessboard moves does not operate according to "spontaneous" rules but rather, in the words applied to Percy Grimm, "with the delicate swiftness of an apparition, the implacable undeviation of Juggernaut or Fate" (403). There is no deviation from purpose, however blind Joe's actions may seem, because the compelling force is within, and the arbitrary "rules" are constant and devised by will.

Whereas Brown is driven here and there by life's unpredictable forces, the Reverend Gail Hightower tries to avoid the complexities of life altogether. He identifies his own life with his grandfather's, and tries to convince himself that since his grandfather is dead he no longer has any responsibility toward the living. As a divinity student, confusing religion with this effort to escape into the past, Hightower imagines "his future, his life, intact and on all sides complete and inviolable, like a classic and serene vase, where the spirit could be born anew sheltered from the harsh gale of living and die so, peacefully, with only the far sound of the circumvented wind, with scarce even a handful of rotting dust to be disposed of" (419). This "serene vase" is an echo of the grecian-urn image associated with Lena Grove, but Lena's rejection of the spatial and temporal world is instinctive rather than deliberate and rational. Moreover Hightower's vision is projected onto an elusive past and bears comparison with the urn of death and not the ideal one of beauty and truth.

Although Hightower represents a serious moral fault, he is treated almost comically. When the minister's wife commits suicide in a Memphis brothel, his congregation becomes enraged. Already angered by Hightower's confusion between the Civil War and the gospel, the elders drive him from the pulpit and expect him to leave town in disgrace. He refuses to do so and accepts with delight a mock "crucifixion" at the hands of a town mob:

He seems to watch himself, alert, patient, skillful, playing his cards well, making it appear that he was being driven, uncomplaining, into that which he did not even then admit had been his desire since before he entered the seminary. . . . allowing himself to be persecuted, to be dragged from his bed at night and carried into the woods and beaten with sticks, he all the while bearing in the town's sight and hearing, without shame, with that patient and voluptuous ego of the martyr, the air, the behavior, the *How long, O Lord* until, inside his house again and the door locked, he lifted the mask with voluptuous and triumphant glee: *Ah. That's done now. That's past now. That's bought and paid for now* (428–429)

In treating Hightower's martyrdom as burlesque, Faulkner contrasts it to Joe Christmas's subsequent death—at the hands, no doubt, of the same Jefferson mob. The minister's gesture is exposed as false and hypocritical because he wants to live to enjoy his sacrifice. Hightower has looked forward to this moment all his life because it provides him with an excuse for rejecting the present world and retreating into the past.

Another figure who has tried to escape reality is the minister's only friend, Byron Bunch. Byron takes refuge from human emotion by working hard during weekdays and preaching in the country over the weekend. As the novel develops he slips away from Hightower's influence and is taken in tow by Lena Grove, whom he is presumably destined to marry. Byron's false sanctuary is symbolically demolished, and he is forced into the mainstream of conventional existence. This is why the minister counsels his friend to escape Lena's orbit, to "leave this place forever, this terrible place, this terrible, terrible place. I can read you. You will tell me that you have just learned love; I will tell you that you have just learned hope. That's all; hope" (275–276).

Hope becomes a terrible thing for Byron because his new personality, anticipating his future role as husband and father, represents a disruptive force. Believing that Lena is returning to her former lover, Byron at first takes Hightower's advice and prepares to flee. He imagines the future—a future without Lena—as a state of nothingness where trees would not be trees, men would not be men, "and Byron Bunch he wouldn't even have to be or not be Byron Bunch" (371). He is about to re-enter his past sanctuary where he was sheltered from ordinary responsibilities. But when Byron sees Joe Brown fleeing town he knows that Lena will now need him. Thinking of their future life together, he is aware of becoming "Byron Bunch" again. For a moment the moving train carrying Brown away seems like a barrier between Byron and the world: "a dyke beyond which the world, time, hope unbelievable and certainly incontrovertible, waited, giving him yet a little more of peace" (386–387).

Hightower is also affected by the life force which Lena Grove's mere presence seems to generate. When her time comes and no doctor is available, he officiates at her delivery and afterwards feels an unaccustomed surge of energy, a "glow of purpose and pride." When he chooses a book from his library, it is not the usual Tennyson, but *Henry IV*, "food for a man" (355). But the minister cannot sustain his new mood, and he surrenders to inertia. "I am not in life any more," he has stated earlier. "That's why there is no use in even trying to meddle, interfere" (263). At one point Byron finds in the sleeping figure of Hightower "a quality of profound and complete surrender," as if his friend "had given over and relinquished completely that grip upon that blending of pride and hope and vanity and fear, that strength to cling to either defeat or victory, which is the I-Am, and the relinquishment of which is usually death" (345). Hightower's absorption in the past is thus defined as a loss of personality, of self, the equivalent of death.

This theme is further emphasized, after the death of Joe Christmas, when Hightower sits at his window reviewing his life's pattern. As sundown approaches, he tries to retreat as usual into his vision of his grandfather galloping with General Forrest's cavalry down what was once the main street of town. This fusion between past and present is concentrated for Hightower upon a moment of "*soonness*," just before dusk, when he can look out and actually see the riders "sweep into sight, borne now upon a cloud of phantom dust" (431).

This moment of fusion, when the past becomes real, is called the *soon* rather than the *now* because once the galloping horses do appear the timeless moment of Hightower's vision will have pushed present reality entirely from his mind.

Prior to the culmination of Hightower's vision the old man's "wheel of thinking" is described as turning "with the slow implacability of a mediaeval torture instrument, beneath the wrenched and broken sockets of his spirit, his life" (429–430). This remarkable image indicates Hightower's realization that he has failed to avoid responsibility for present events. Projecting the face of an accusing

God before him, Hightower hears himself blamed for his wife's death. The argument is strange: "And if I am my dead grandfather on the instant of his death, then my wife, his grandson's wife—the debaucher and murderer of my grandson's wife, since I could neither let my grandson live or die—" (430). Even though he identifies himself with his own grandfather, the minister cannot avoid self-accusation. Hightower is defeated by his own sophistry, and in this sense his wheel of thought makes a destructive cycle as it rushes on, "going fast and smooth now, because it is freed now of burden, of vehicle, axle, all" (430).

AFTER HIGHTOWER'S WHEEL of thought or destiny has been released, "it seems to engender and surround itself with a faint glow like a halo" (430). This halo is filled with faces, "peaceful, as though they have escaped into an apotheosis" (430), his own among them. Among the faces seen by the minister is that of Joe Christmas, whose features appear superimposed upon those of the mob leader who pursues and castrates him. The two "seem to strive (but not of themselves striving or desiring it: he knows that, but because of the motion and desire of the wheel itself) in turn to free themselves one from the other, then fade and blend again" (430–431).

The fusion of the faces of Joe Christmas and Percy Grimm helps to define for the reader the meaning of Joe's sacrificial role. The two characters are driven by the same excess of puritan zeal even though the one figure is consistently self-righteous and the other marks himself as a deserving victim. Grimm becomes an unwitting instrument of Christmas's yearning for self-expiation in blood. At the same time the castration scene reveals dramatically the guilt and self-hatred that are locked within Grimm's intolerant fury. Together they act out the drama of the Southern puritan mind and its tragic dilemma. Because they both represent a South divided against itself, they are pursued by the same sense of guilt. Thus Joe Christmas becomes his own pursuer and Percy Grimm his own victim.

Faulkner's effort to create for Joe Christmas this highly complex and symbolic role is responsible for the lavish use of Christian imagery. Joe gets his last name because he is found on the steps of the orphanage on Christmas Eve. The name follows him, as Byron Bunch puts it, like an augur or sign, as if "he carried with him his own inescapable warning, like a flower its scent or a rattlesnake its rattle" (29). He has the mark of God or Satan upon him, according to Doc Hines, and his name suggests the nature of this mark. Throughout the novel Joe is treated in terms which combine Old Testament moral severity with references to the life of Christ. Upon arriving in Jefferson, Joe is thirty-three years old. In one passage his feet are ceremoniously washed; he is betrayed for a thousand-dollar reward by a disciple, Joe Brown, and so on. He commits his crime on a Friday and surrenders a week later, having spent the intervening time in retreat and mental preparation. In this respect the symbolism is at odds with the chronology, for Joe is described as surrendering on "Friday" to a "Saturday" crowd of farmers.

Other less detailed references to Christianity or to religious ceremony and ritual may be found. Faulkner's typical manner of describing puritan qualities is to compare the faces of his characters to the rapt and inscrutable ones of monks or hermits. When Joe is whipped by his stepfather, his body seems "a post or a tower upon which the sentient part of him mused like a hermit, contemplative and remote with ecstasy and selfcrucifixion" (140). Such language is sometimes extended to the physical scene, as when countrymen in overalls move "with almost the air of monks in a cloister" (364). Faulkner often describes Southern puritans as if they always wore a stylized mask, expressive of moral certitude, in confronting the complex and shifting facts of human experience. Such a mind will insist upon formalized behavior, ranging from group worship to mob violence. Racial intolerance or any other kind of moral prejudice is a natural outlet for this attitude just as a Christ-like expression is a natural posture. The Christian imagery of *Light in August* dramatizes puritan intensity of mind and also defines the central meaning of Joe's sacrifice.

Faulkner's effective use of religious imagery may be illustrated by the several references to the glint of handcuffs above Joe Christmas's head as he runs before his pursuers. Joe's "bright and glittering hands" (406) are compared to "the flash of a heliograph" (404), to the glint of fire, and finally to "lightning bolts" (406). Although Joe's face has "that serene, unearthly luminousness of angels in church windows" (404–405), his "raised and armed and manacled hands" give him the appearance, as he strikes the Reverend Hightower down, of a "vengeful and furious god pronouncing a doom" (406). The symbolic meanings are almost too numerous for expression. In Christian terms the handcuffs function as a combined halo and crown of thorns. In terms of the tragic action of the novel they represent Joe's manacled destiny and the inevitability of his death. The images by which the cuffs are described suggest punishment or judgment. As a "vengeful god," Christmas pronounces judgment upon Hightower and by implication upon the society whose divided conscience he embodies.

The religious imagery as well as the temporal mysticism associated with Joe Christmas prepare the reader for an understanding of his death and its significance. In his flight from the mob Joe seeks refuge in the Reverend Hightower's home and is there shot down and castrated by Grimm:

But the man on the floor had not moved. He just lay there, with his eyes open and empty of everything save consciousness, and with something, a shadow, about his mouth. For a long moment he looked up at them with peaceful and unfathomable and unbearable eyes. Then his face, body, all, seemed to collapse, to fall in upon itself, and from out the slashed garments about his hips and loins the pent black blood seemed to rush like a released breath. It seemed to rush out of his pale body like the rush of sparks from a rising rocket; upon that black blast the man seemed to rise soaring into their memories forever and ever. They are not to lose it, in whatever peaceful valleys, beside whatever placid and reassuring streams of old age, in the mirroring faces of whatever children they will contemplate old disasters and newer hopes. It will be there, musing, quiet, steadfast, not fading and not particularly threatful, but of itself alone serene, of itself alone triumphant. Again from the town, deadened a little by the walls, the scream of the siren mounted toward its unbelievable crescendo, passing out of the realm of hearing. (407)

The symbolism of this passage is emphasized by the narrative point of view which soars, like Joe's pent blood, to a transcendent theme. The dark blood which leaves his white body stands both for mortality and for the final expiation of guilt. Joe's eyes are "peaceful and unfathomable" because he is free at last from his own divided nature. Yet his eyes are "unbearable" to others, just as the "black blast" which leaves his body becomes a part of their conscience. The burden of guilt, no longer tormenting Joe, becomes public property.

147

The crucifixion image which dominates this climactic scene derives its meaning less from Joe's martyrdom than from the violence of society's retribution. The men who watch the scene are confronted with their own need for violent expiation. They see Joe's death as a mirror of the "old disasters and newer hopes" from which their victim is now absolved. Joe's martyrdom, like its Christian counterpart, is a deliberate self-sacrifice. Yet Faulkner's hero is barely aware, if at all, of society's existence. Among the townspeople he alone, the crucified, is the one that is saved.

Chapter Nine

A PURITAN TRAGEDY:
ABSALOM, ABSALOM!

THE FAILURE of Thomas Sutpen to establish the roots of a family dynasty in the South's fertile soil assumes the status of personal tragedy as well as social allegory. But the sense of tragic action that pervades *Absalom, Absalom!* is in ironic contrast to the narrowness of Sutpen's ambition and the ignominy of his defeat. The moral inflexibility that frustrates his life's design also makes self-understanding impossible for him. In spite of his tragic role, Sutpen lacks the status of a tragic hero able to recognize the source of destruction. Sutpen seems to diminish rather than increase in stature, and at the time of his death he seems only a caricature of his wasted ambition. In his consistent demonism he is comparable to Melville's Captain Ahab, even though Sutpen is in search not of metaphysical truth but of social respectability.

149

Sutpen's stylized characterization and his allegorical function render difficult the introduction of dramatic action and moral development into a novel based upon his personality. But Faulkner solves this problem by concealing as long as possible the motivation for Sutpen's behavior and by filtering his actions through the speculations of a number of witness-narrators, who impose their own obsessive social and moral concerns upon the events they narrate. The reader is forced to take at face value the conflicting interpretations of these witness-figures, who belong to the Southern aristocracy (with the exception of Quentin Compson's Harvard roommate) and read the tragedy of their region into the Sutpen events. The reader's understanding of the social allegory thus passes through a series of metamorphoses which may be said to correspond, however imperfectly, with the psychological transformations of the traditional hero. The novel is an extraordinary study in conflicting points of view, in which the reader joins Quentin Compson in coming to understand not only the course of Sutpen's failure but also, as Miss Rosa Coldfield puts it, "why God let us lose the War" (11).

The witness-figures that dominate the first half of the novel are Miss Rosa and Jason Lycurgus Compson III, Quentin's father. Both narrators distort or misinterpret the facts at their disposal, the one through childish romanticism and the other through an obsessive fatalism. Yet they provide the reader with an adequate outline of the important events between Thomas Sutpen's arrival in Jefferson and the crime committed by his son Henry. During this period Sutpen becomes a wealthy planter, marries Ellen Coldfield, the daughter of a respectable shopkeeper, and begets two promising children, Henry and Judith. But his plantation is ruined by war and his hope for descendants is thwarted by the arrival of Charles Bon, Sutpen's part-Negro son by a former marriage. Bon becomes engaged to Judith and is murdered at the gate of Sutpen's Hundred by Henry, his own half-brother. Miss Rosa Coldfield and Mr. Compson narrate only what is public knowledge, the betrothal and the murder, without understanding Bon's relationship to Henry and the significance of the crime. Their limited knowledge is nevertheless supplemented by rhetorical flourishes and personal interpretations that contribute to the reader's eventual understanding of why Sutpen can neither acknowledge Bon as a long-lost son nor drive him away as a Negro interloper. The collapse of his ambition is traceable both to racial prejudice and to his willingness to let his son Henry bear the full burden of unacknowledged guilt.

Through the eyes of Miss Rosa Coldfield, Thomas Sutpen is seen as a "demon" who bursts into Jefferson from "out of nowhere and without warning" (9) and violently tears a plantation from virgin Mississippi land. Miss Rosa's interpretation is colored by her undying hatred, her "air of impotent and static rage" (7), but her image of Sutpen as a mysterious and demonic stranger establishes the importance of his origin and raises the vital question of his motivation. Sitting in an oversized chair, like a "crucified child" (8), she invokes for Quentin the "garrulous outraged baffled ghosts" (9) of the Southern past. Events and personalities take on the dimensions of her childish fantasy, "as though by outraged recapitulation evoked, quiet [and] inattentive and harmless, out of the biding and dreamy and victorious dust" (8).

As a narrator Miss Rosa invests the melodramatic events of the past with a Gothic atmosphere of social sin and moral damnation. But as Ellen's young sister, younger even than Ellen's daughter, she is an important actor in the story she narrates. Both roles are dominated by a triumphant emotionalism that distorts human values as well as historical fact. In the novel's structure she stands for traditional Southern romanticism and is a foil to Sutpen's equally obsessive moral rationalism. Miss Rosa inherits her emotionalism from her shopkeeper father, Goodhue Coldfield, who expresses it only through the repressive channels of hatred and renunciation. Coldfield is a pillar of Presbyterian respectability, but he is persuaded by Sutpen to enter a glamorous though shady business deal. In spite of the success of the scheme, he rejects his share of the profits and even allows Sutpen to marry his daughter Ellen, presumably as an act of expiation. Coldfield's puritan hatred of self and region is also expressed in his repudiation of the Southern cause. He calls the war a just retribution for the South's "having erected its economic edifice not on the rock of stern morality but on the shifting sands of opportunism and moral brigandage" (260). His grotesque expression of this attitude is to shut himself in his attic—never to see his country or family again.

Miss Rosa combines the Coldfield habit of renunciation with the emotional abstractions traceable to her youthful frustrations. Faulkner allows full rein to her verbalizations of experience, but in doing so he encourages the reader to accept her narration, at least in part, as a satire directed against the vapid romanticism which she embodies. As a young girl Rosa never meets Charles Bon in the flesh, but she falls in love with his picture and spends her visits to Sutpen's Hundred gazing at his two-dimensional image or searching for his footprints in the garden. "What suspiration of the twinning souls," she exclaims, "have the murmurous myriad ears of this secluded vine or shrub listened to? what vow, what promise, what rapt biding fire has the lilac rain of this wistaria, this heavy rose's dissolution, crowned?" Faulkner also makes fun of Rosa's eulogy of the "nooky seat" which held invisible imprint of Charles Bon's absent thighs, and of her reverence for the footprints which would have been his "save for this obliterating rake" (148). The weird comedy of her monologue reaches its climax when Miss Rosa learns from Wash Jones of Bon's death. She takes out her frustration on the old man as he drives her to the scene—her urgency of mind and body in strong contrast to his exasperating slowness. Sutpen's poor-white retainer is seen as an animal who is capable of bellowing the scandal to the neighborhood but who cannot force his mule beyond a walk because "hit warn't none of mine nor hisn neither and besides hit aint had a decent bait of vittles since the corn give out in February," and who "turning into the actual gate at last, must stop the mule and, pointing with the whip and spitting first, say 'Hit was right yonder.'—'What was right there, fool?' I cried, and he: 'Hit was' until I took the whip from him into my own hand and struck the mule" (135). The humor stems from the introduction of a change of pace into Miss Rosa's frenzied rhetoric. Faulkner tells the story from her point of view, yet indicates the clash of two alien personalities by contrasting Wash's torpid realism to the narrator's verbal fantasies.

Miss Rosa's vicarious love for Charles Bon prepares the reader for her romantic attachment to Sutpen after the death of her sister Ellen, Sutpen's wife. Their relationship indicates an equation of sorts between Miss Rosa's romanticism and Sutpen's ambition. This implicit equation is supported by her frequent references to Sutpen's "wild braggart dream" (165) and by their brief betrothal: "O furious mad old man, I hold no substance that will fit your dream but I can give you airy space and scope for your delirium" (168). Miss Rosa believes at the time that only Sutpen's dream is insane, "and not his methods" (166). But Sutpen's puritan narrowness has corrupted every aspect of his personality, including his judgment. In a desperate wish for male descendants he takes back his marriage proposal by suggesting to Rosa that they marry only if she bears him a son. It is Sutpen's impersonality that drives her into unremitting hatred: "as if he were consulting with Jones or with some other man about a bitch dog or a cow or mare" (168).

William R. Poirier [1] has pointed out some important ways in which Sutpen and Miss Rosa are similar. Sutpen's lack of human sentiment is a counterpart of his "braggart dream" and corresponds to her romantic pride and abstract unforgiving. The characterization of her as "cold, implacable, and even ruthless" (10) is similar to the description of Sutpen's eyes as "at once visionary and alert, ruthless and reposed" (33). When Quentin Compson comes with her to exorcise the ghost at Sutpen's Hundred he feels something "fierce and implacable and dynamic" (367) which he realizes is not fear but hatred. Like Sutpen, Miss Rosa sacrifices natural human emotions for abstract substitutes. Her devotion to emotional abstractions is a counterpart of his consuming ambition.

Mr. Compson is just as unreliable a witness-narrator as Miss Rosa, but he is blinded by misdirected rationality and not emotionalism. He possesses all the Sutpen facts made known to the reader—though these facts are only gradually revealed—but he does not understand their significance. Past events are filtered through his own philosophical despair; so that Sutpen appears as the victim of "folly and mischance" (87) or "the illogical machinations of a fatality" (102). In a significant passage Mr. Compson admits his inability to understand the members of Sutpen's family:

They are like a chemical formula exhumed along with the letters from that forgotten chest . . . the writing faded, almost indecipherable, yet meaningful, familiar in shape and sense . . . you bring them together in the proportions called for, but nothing happens . . . just the words, the

[1] William R. Poirier, " 'Strange Gods' in Jefferson, Mississippi: Analysis of *Absalom, Absalom!*" in *Two Decades*, pp. 217–243.

symbols, the shapes themselves, shadowy inscrutable and serene, against that turgid background of a horrible and bloody mischancing of human affairs. (101)

Like Miss Rosa Coldfield, he poses the question of moral and social significance without providing an adequate answer. Mr. Compson's narration also provides the reader with a perspective by which an aspect of Sutpen's moral and dramatic role can be understood. But the reader cannot use Mr. Compson's insights, just as he cannot make the Coldfield-Sutpen sociological equation, until all the chapters of the novel are in place.

One consequence of the poverty of narrative events in the opening narrations is an absence of the kind of imagery found in such novels as *The Sound and the Fury* and *Light in August*. In these two works the narrative point of view follows directly the dramatic activity of major characters, whether the narration is first-person or not. The result is that patterns of significant imagery tend to be associated with material objects or distinct actions: for example, references to actual clocks or shadows permeate Quentin Compson's monologue and the actions of Joe Christmas are associated with Christian parallels. The opening chapters of *Absalom, Absalom!* are dominated instead by rhetorical abstractions, and there is almost no imagery related to specific objects or events. Nevertheless the metaphorical patterns associated with each *Absalom, Absalom!* narrator function in a comparable manner. Miss Rosa's frequent references to a divine curse upon Sutpen and upon the South provide a *leitmotiv* that associates her narration with Old Testament religious concerns. In a similar way Mr. Compson's narration is larded with references to Greek mythology and to the notion of fate or destiny associated with the themes of Greek tragedy. Such language is appropriate to his fatalistic philosophy and to his effete classicism, just as the language of sin and damnation is appropriate to Miss Rosa's Christian romanticism. In each case the narrator's language becomes indistinguishable from the events and personalities of the Sutpen story. Sutpen appears through Miss Rosa's narration as a "demon" or "ogre" figure, whereas Charles Bon is described as an "indolent fatalist" (105) willing to accept the blind decrees of a malevolent destiny. Both points of view are appropriate to an understanding of the Sutpen tragedy, although they must be adjusted and set into proper balance by the reader.

This rhetorical technique has an important effect upon the novel's characterization. Figures about whom very little is known are often loosely identified with characters of Greek tragedy or with the moral concerns of the Old Testament or mediaeval romance ("the bombast of a madman who creates within his very coffin walls his fabulous immeasurable Camelots and Carcassonnes" [160]). In some instances, notably passages narrated by Mr. Compson, characters are described by reference to elaborate conceits that are related to the novel's general themes. The frequent mention of Miss Rosa's doll-like size or her general resemblance to a child refers satirically to her lack of emotional maturity. The imagery of a helpless butterfly is used by Mr. Compson to explain Ellen's willingness to assume a passive role in the unfolding of Sutpen's fate. Giving birth to two children, she subsequently rises "like the swamp-hatched butterfly, unimpeded by weight of stomach and all the heavy organs of suffering and experience, into a perennial bright vacuum of arrested sun" (69–70). In a similar way Judith is described by Miss Rosa as passing through cocoon stages, "bud, served prolific queen, then potent and soft-handed matriarch of old age's serene and well-lived content" (156). These descriptions are occasionally inept, like this one of Judith, but such narration keeps the characters before the reader's attention, and at the same time tells the reader very little about them. The reader's interest is maintained even as he is encouraged to view Sutpen and his family as a collection of lifeless abstractions: the five faces "with a sort of lifeless and perennial bloom like painted portraits hung in a vacuum, each taken at its forewarned peak and smoothed of all thought and experience" (75).

A pattern of imagery that dominates the entire novel is the use of banking and mercantile terms to describe human emotions and motivations. References to "prices" and "notes of hand" enable Faulkner to expose the excessive puritanism of his characters and yet establish important facts and dramatic relationships. Thus Ellen's marriage to Sutpen is tantamount to her signing "notes of hand on pride and contentment and peace" (18). Goodhue Coldfield is said to invest sacrifice and self-denial in Protestant Christianity for the sake of "a demand balance of spiritual solvency." His church is used by the puritan merchant "as he would have used a cotton gin in which he considered himself to have incurred either interest or responsibility" (50). The fate of Charles Bon is symbolized by a ledger kept by his mother's lawyer: "where he had just finished adding in the last past year's interest compounded between the intrinsic and the love and pride at two hundred percent" (337). On the last page of the novel Shreve McCannon compares the Sutpen story to complicated ledger entries finally cleared by death and destruction. "You can tear all the pages out and burn them," he tells Quentin, except for the haunting figure of the last living Sutpen, a part-Negro idiot (378).

The numerous bookkeeping references support Faulkner's condemnation of Thomas Sutpen's moral code as inhumanly logical and brutally abstract. Sutpen frequently is described as reducing human relations to the level of a calculating business deal; for example he chooses women slaves "with the same care and shrewdness with which he chose the other livestock—the horses and mules and cattle—which he bought later on" (61). Sutpen accepts liquor offered by his hunting friends but only with sparing calculation as though mentally keeping "a sort of balance of spiritual solvency between the amount of whiskey he accepted and the amount of running meat which he supplied to the guns" (40). His failure is characterized as moral bankruptcy, or the ultimate worthlessness of his elaborate "sight drafts on self-denial and fortitude" (84). "His code of logic and morality" vanquishes Sutpen, "his formula and recipe of fact and deduction whose balanced sum and product declined, refused to swim or even float" (275). In characterizing Goodhue Coldfield and Thomas Sutpen by the same self-defeating moral temperament, Faulkner joins symbolically religious and secular expressions of Southern puritanism.

THE RELATION between the Sutpen tragedy and the South's moral failure is worked out explicitly in two narrations, one by Mr. Compson and one by General Compson, Quentin's grandfather. Mr. Compson analyzes the destructive puritanism that he believes is responsible for Henry Sutpen's decision to murder Charles Bon.

Though Mr. Compson's historical reconstruction is shown later to be nonsensical, his description of Southern puritanism is validated when the real source of conflict between Henry and Charles, the issue of miscegenation, is revealed. The importance of this issue is made evident through Grandfather Compson's factual account of Sutpen's youth in West Virginia and his first marriage, in the West Indies. Relayed to Quentin by his father, this account exposes Sutpen's desperate effort to understand his own experiences and to fit them into inadequate moral categories.

According to Mr. Compson's sociological fantasy, Henry Sutpen refuses to allow Charles Bon to marry Judith unless Charles will renounce an octoroon mistress he maintains in New Orleans. Henry's opposition to the marriage is rooted in the puritan conviction that an acknowledged part-Negro mistress cannot be compatible with a respectable marriage. In the scene imagined by Mr. Compson, Charles hopes to break down Henry's opposition by introducing him to the values associated with the city's French culture. Mr. Compson imagines Henry, "with his puritan heritage—that heritage peculiarly Anglo-Saxon—of fierce proud mysticism and that ability to be ashamed of ignorance and inexperience, in that city foreign and paradoxical, with its atmosphere at once fatal and languorous, at once feminine and steel-hard" (108–109). Charles brings the young man to New Orleans in order to develop gradually "the innocent and negative plate of Henry's provincial soul and intellect" (110). In a similar passage Henry's "puritan mind" is compared to "a cramped and rocky field" (109) that Charles must prepare for ideological planting. According to Mr. Compson's imaginary account, young Sutpen has the "innocent" and dogmatic faith that simple moral principles can be applied to any perceived facts, however complex they may be. Even when confronting facts beyond his comprehension, the Mississippian will never admit that his rational categories are inadequate.

Charles hopes to take advantage of Henry's moral pride and capacity for self-deception by persuading his provincial friend to accept the New Orleans way of life rather than admit the inability to understand it. Bon believes he can rely upon Henry's tendency to disregard any facts not lending themselves to immediate judgment. He can trust "that puritan heritage which must show disapproval

instead of surprise or even despair and nothing at all rather than
have the disapprobation construed as surprise or despair" (111). In
other words, Charles hopes that Henry's moral consciousness, in its
primitive "undeveloped" state, will avoid all moral reactions altogether rather than be trapped into a disapproval which could be
construed as naive.

Bon plans his strategy with care. First he takes Henry to a market
where octoroons are sold. In this way he hopes to bypass Henry's
moral code and appeal solely to the youth's imagination. "Without
his knowing what he saw it was as though to Henry the blank and
scaling barrier in dissolving produced and revealed not comprehension to the mind, the intellect which weighs and discards, but
striking instead straight and true to some primary blind and mindless foundation of all young male living dream and hope" (112). As
a typical puritan, Henry has what Mr. Compson calls the "puritan's
humility toward anything which is a matter of sense rather than
logic, fact" (111). Yet Henry will instinctively try to conceal this
humility by acts of moral judgment. Bon's task is consequently to
persuade Henry to accept what he cannot understand without
taking refuge in moral decision. Mr. Compson represents Henry
struggling to accept Bon's arguments without having to judge and
consequently to reject them. *"I will believe! I will! I will!"* he cries,
"Whether it is true or not, I will believe!" (111).

According to Mr. Compson's hypothesis, Henry is able to accept
what are called Bon's "old-world" values as long as the beliefs of the
Mississippi puritan, though emotionally undermined, are not explicitly contradicted. Henry can tolerate the presence of Charles's
Negro mistress, but he balks at the formal contract by which Bon
has pledged his honor as a Southern gentleman to support the
octoroon as long as they both live. "It would be the fact of the
ceremony, regardless of what kind, that Henry would balk at: Bon
knew this" (109). The fact of a formal ceremony and the presence of
a written contract disturbs the provincial's "simple and erstwhile
untroubled code in which females were ladies or whores or slaves"
(114). Bon's well-educated and loyal octoroon is not quite a
prostitute, nor, being part-Negro, is she a lady. The conditions of
purchase recognize her inferior status as a Negro, but the presence
of a contract raises her from the category of mere slave.

Charles is unable to break through Henry's formal logic and is forced to reverse his tactics and appeal solely to the friendship between himself and Henry—a friendship that symbolizes the brotherhood actually uniting them. Henry's capacity for self-deception has proven inadequate and Charles must rely, as Mr. Compson phrases it, "on the corruption itself, the love" (115). Love is spoken of as a corruption of puritanism because it implies forgiveness and the relaxation of moral judgment. Love is the only force which can liberate the Southern puritan from the self-imposed bondage of his rational categories. But, in spite of Henry's love for Charles, his puritan mind balks at his friend's formal obligation to support and maintain "a bought woman. A whore" (115). In desperation Bon tries first to defend the octoroon system as less inhuman than absolute slavery, and then to protest that a contract with a Negro woman is not after all legally binding. But Henry remains adamant: "Yes. I know. I know that. But it's still there. It's not right. Not even you doing it makes it right. Not even you" (118).

Though Mr. Compson's account has no basis in narrative fact, it does help to explain the reaction of both Sutpens, father and son, to the fact that Charles is part-Negro. Thomas Sutpen is given a quality of puritan "innocence," like the innocence that Mr. Compson ascribes to Henry, and is described as "fog-bound by his own private embattlement of personal morality: that picayune splitting of abstract hairs" (271). He is unable to adapt his moral categories to complex experiences, even when his personal ambition and the lives of his family are at stake. Sutpen finds his democratic principles at odds with a social structure founded upon racial injustice. Instead of recognizing a Negro as a son, and admitting the possibility of injustice, he is forced by moral pride and inflexible logic to deny Bon's right to address him as father.

The conflict in Sutpen's life between democratic principles and social realities is directly revealed through Grandfather Compson's account of Sutpen's family background. When Sutpen's family moves from hill country to the rich Virginia coast, the young backwoodsman becomes envious of the Tidewater aristocracy and resolves to emulate the wealthy planters of the region. He migrates to the West Indies, where by great loyalty and courage he marries a planter's daughter and obtains sufficient wealth to satisfy his wishes.

But racial prejudice has become associated with Sutpen's ambitious design, and he repudiates his wife and infant son upon discovering that they are part-Negro. In a second effort to achieve respectability he purchases a large tract of land from Mississippi Indians and with the help of a French architect—suggesting the New Orleans influence upon the culture of the Deep South—he builds a mansion and assumes a patriarchal role. But his hopes for the future are threatened by the arrival of Charles Bon, his first son. Sutpen cannot recognize a Negro as a son, yet he cannot stop the marriage peacefully without doing so. He tries to avoid the dilemma by telling Henry the truth about Bon, but his expedient only leads to disaster.

Faulkner traces the source of Thomas Sutpen's failure to the aristocrat's confusion between ambition and racial prejudice. Although the young Sutpen spends his childhood in a classless white society, he is forced to recognize his "poor-white" status when his family migrates to the coast. The ante-bellum poor-white, as has been long recognized, tended to identify himself racially with the white aristocracy even though his economic status was often inferior to that of Negro slaves. Sutpen is consequently outraged when a well-dressed Negro butler refuses to let him enter the front door of a Tidewater mansion. The immediate object of the boy's hatred is the Negro butler and not Pettibone, the aristocrat. Sutpen seems to blame Pettibone less for social injustice than for placing slaves in a position where they can intimidate himself and his family. Standing at the door which he cannot enter, the youth remembers incidents in the past involving Negroes. Once a coachman drives his proud sister off the road with a scornful "Hoo dar, gal! Git outen de way dar!" The boy retaliates by throwing clods of dirt at the disappearing coach. He sees himself throwing dirt not at a hated superior, but at "the actual dust raised by the proud delicate wheels, and just that vain" (231). Sutpen employs the scapegoat mechanism of his class, whereby hatred and persecution of Negroes are escape valves for economic unrest. The exploited white man can express an envy of his rich brother without sacrificing his feeling of social equality. One night Sutpen's father describes how he and his friends have whipped one of Pettibone's slaves. The boy asks what the man has done, and receives the simple but eloquent reply: "Hell fire, that goddam son of a bitch Pettibone's nigger" (231). The boy accepts this denial of a

Negro's individuality and imagines the slave's balloon face poised above the men, "levitative and slick with paper-thin distension." When someone tries to strike the balloon face, it seems to escape and "overwhelm" them with "roaring waves of mellow laughter meaningless and terrifying and loud" (232).

This scapegoat image is metamorphosed in the boy's mind into the "monkey nigger" who bars Pettibone's door. As young Sutpen's hatred and jealousy come to a focus, he sees himself "looking out from within the balloon face" (234) as if he were the aristocrat. He discovers for what seems the first time the squalid poverty of his family. He imagines its members as cattle, "creatures heavy and without grace, brutely evacuated into a world without hope or purpose for them." Their only future is "a succession of cut-down and patched and made-over garments bought on exorbitant credit because they were white people, from stores where niggers were given the garments free, with for sole heritage that expression on a balloon face bursting with laughter" (235). Negro laughter is a "barricade" which guards Pettibone and his riches from poor-white ambitions.

As an adult, Sutpen translates his humiliation into a morally glamorous "boy-symbol:"

Now he would take that boy in where he would never again need to stand on the outside of a white door and knock at it: and not at all for mere shelter but so that that boy, that whatever nameless stranger, could shut that door himself forever behind him on all that he had ever known, and look ahead along the still undivulged light rays in which his descendants who might not even ever hear his (the boy's) name, waited to be born without even having to know that they had once been riven forever free from brutehood just as his own (Sutpen's) children were—(261)

But unfortunately for the planter's peace of mind, the boy-symbol who seeks admittance at Sutpen's "white door" is Charles Bon. In refusing to acknowledge a part-Negro son, Sutpen reveals that resentment at being insulted by a Negro is far stronger than his social idealism. In denying recognition to Bon, Sutpen rejects the best part of himself and reveals the selfishness of his moral design.

Thomas Sutpen's confused reaction to Tidewater splendor is

parallel to Henry Sutpen's hypothetical reaction to the Old World sophistication of New Orleans. Sutpen also retains his faith in *a priori* rules and principles regardless of the changed circumstances. Like Henry he is unwilling to admit his bewilderment at an incomprehensible social world, and he insists upon moral simplification. The boy is hurt and confused when a hated Negro closes a door in his face, but he will not admit his naïveté. He compares the aristocrat's action in permitting such an insult by a Negro to the injustice of a man who owns a fine rifle but allows no one else, not even someone who brings bullets for the rifle, to handle it. Pursuing this moral analogy, young Sutpen decides that to combat such a man he has to get himself a rifle. But as the boy phrases it, "this aint a question of rifles. So to combat them you have got to have what they have that made them do what the man did. You got to have land and niggers and a fine house to combat them with" (238). Through his use of the rifle analogy, Sutpen is able to express his social ambition in moral terms. The boy convinces himself that his conflict with the aristocrat is a personal matter and not a reaction to impersonal social forces. More significantly, he ignores the fact that the rifle analogy supports the extension of democratic rights not only to poor whites but to Negroes, as those who also supply "bullets" for the rich man's rifle.

Sutpen is blinded by the same kind of mental rigidity that is said to provide Henry Sutpen with only the sharply defined categories of lady, whore, and slave by which to consider Charles Bon's octoroon mistress. On the other hand Bon represents the conviction that moral categories should not be rigidly applied to human situations. He is willing to accept a situation that he recognizes to be evil, but that he knows he cannot change. By signing a document pledging himself not to sell his mistress, Bon places her midway between the categories of slave and wife. He accepts the fact of social inequality without seeking to conceal it by the myth of ownership. To Henry's objection, "But a bought woman. A whore," Bon answers that he and the thousand other white men like him have made the laws decreeing "that one eighth of a specified kind of blood shall outweigh seven eight[h]s of another kind" (115). But some of these men have at least preserved their mistresses from abject slavery. The white man who enters into a formal agreement with an octoroon may not free her from servitude, but he does acknowledge her human dignity. "We do save that one, who but for us would have been sold to any brute who had the price, not sold to him for the night like a white prostitute, but body and soul for life to him who could have used her with more impunity than he would dare to use an animal, heifer or mare, and then discarded or sold or even murdered when worn out or when her keep and her price no longer balanced" (116).

Bon implies that the Southerner's greatest sin is not so much the original degradation of the primitive Negro, as the refusal to accept moral responsibility for that degradation, once slavery had become an established fact. In a similar way Thomas Sutpen is condemned for his failure to recognize the Negro's right to human dignity, as symbolized by Charles Bon's right to call Sutpen his father. *Absalom, Absalom!* is an implicit analysis and criticism of the South's pretensions to moral righteousness and democratic status in the face of obvious injustice. Ante-bellum Southerners closed their eyes to the moral degradation of slavery, both to white and Negro, and tried to protect the South's moral frontier by the doctrine of Negro inferiority. In this way they justified the denial to Negroes, whether slaves or not, of the human and legal rights guaranteed by the Bill of Rights. In the famous Dred Scott fugitive-slave decision by the Supreme Court, a pro-South verdict was based upon the argument, in the words of the Chief Justice, that the Constitutional words, "people of the United States," do not refer to slaves.[2] The distinction is between the free man and the slave, but the implication is that the Negro's legal status becomes his human status as well.

THE REVELATION of Sutpen as an allegorical representative of the South's puritan aristocracy is accompanied, as the novel progresses, by an increased emphasis upon the true relationship between Henry Sutpen and Charles Bon, victims of their father's inhuman ambition. Faulkner very cleverly associates this aspect of the novel with the narration of Quentin Compson and Shreve McCannon. These two witnesses are the furthest removed in both space and time from the original events, but they represent the deepest understanding and the closest identification with the tragic participants. Their emo-

[2] Chief Justice Taney, "Opinion of the Court" in *Report of the Dred Scott Case*, Washington, 1857, p. 10.

tional involvement in the Sutpen tragedy gives Faulkner a narrative excuse to penetrate the barrier between past and present, between actor and witness, and narrate directly Henry Sutpen's struggle to overcome social prejudice in the name of brotherly love. The Sutpen drama becomes intensely realistic in this latter part of the novel, but the realism centers upon the tragic consequence of Sutpen's demonism and not the demonism itself. In this way Quentin Compson, the modern Southerner, is no less involved in Sutpen's fate than Henry Sutpen, his historical counterpart.

Faulkner's effort to postpone the reader's understanding of Henry Sutpen's murder of Charles Bon involves a major narrative problem. Mr. Compson is forced to confess that he finds no connection between Sutpen's life in the West Indies and the murder of Judith's suitor. Mr. Compson's incredible lack of understanding is a necessary defect in the novel's factual scheme. Yet Faulkner takes advantage of his narrator's ignorance in order to introduce the latter's speculation concerning Henry Sutpen's reason for killing Charles Bon. In addition, Quentin Compson, who represents modern sensibility, can be effectively described as the witness who discovers the real explanation of the murder. During his first trip with Miss Rosa to the decayed Sutpen mansion, Quentin suddenly realizes that Bon must be Sutpen's discarded Negro son. The young narrator's trip to Sutpen's Hundred, and his brief conversation with the aging Henry Sutpen, constitute a bridge between the past and the present, between the South's tragic past and its significance for present and future generations of Southerners.

The novel opens with Miss Rosa's request of Quentin that they visit Sutpen's Hundred to see who or what is there; and it ends with their final visit, when Clytie sets the mansion on fire to save Henry from being arrested for the old crime. The first few chapters consist of interlaced interpretations by the first two narrators: the old maid, who is blinded by sentimentality and hatred, and Mr. Compson, who has all the facts at his disposal but does not understand them. When Quentin returns from his first visit to Sutpen's Hundred he and his father work out more adequate, though still imperfect, interpretations. Finally Quentin and Shreve McCannon, his Harvard roommate, summarize what has been learned from Quentin's grandfather, and through an emotional identification with Henry and Charles they grasp the ultimate significance of the Sutpen tragedy. Shreve's name indicates his function as a means by which Quentin can bring into focus his awareness of the South's moral guilt. Both removal in space and time, and the help of his Canadian friend, are necessary before Quentin can understand his own social heritage.

A parallel exists between Mr. Compson's helplessness before events that defy his rational analysis and Faulkner's method of narration. The available details gradually become known to the reader, just as they are always known to Mr. Compson, but they cannot be properly understood until the reader has identified himself with the various Southern points of view relevant to the tragedy. Mr. Compson's ineffectuality prefigures Thomas Sutpen's helpless confrontation of experiences that cannot be understood or controlled by moral categories alone. Mr. Compson is able to diagnose destructive puritanism in others, but his ineffectuality suggests a similar sterility of mind. True understanding of Sutpen's tragedy can only come through Quentin Compson, who is represented as suffering an emotional identification with the Sutpen phantom-shapes of his own Southern past. It is only by parodying such identification that Shreve McCannon, who does not profess to understand the South, can help Quentin achieve his desperate recognition: "not two of them there and then either but four of them riding the two horses through the iron darkness" (295). Shreve and the reader cross the barriers of time and space with Quentin, but they are spared Quentin's nightmare encounters with Jim Bond, the surviving Negro idiot.

UNDERLYING *Absalom, Absalom!* is a conflict between two conceptions of human dignity, one based upon social abstractions and involving the effort to control nature by rational means, and the other based on the isolated human element, on what Bon calls "the old mindless sentient undreaming meat that doesn't even know any difference between despair and victory" (349). In his role as a rejected part-Negro son, Charles is the chief representative of an antipuritan philosophy, the categorical rejection of abstract rules and ideals as a basis for human endeavor. Before his death he tries to teach Henry that this is the South's lesson of defeat, that human abstractions are less important than human flesh. Yet Bon finds a source of dignity in this perverse philosophy and in forcing Henry to shoot him he seems, paradoxically, to martyr himself to it. In writing to Judith, announcing his determination to go ahead with the wedding, Bon uses language which anticipates Faulkner's Nobel Prize vision of the aboriginal spirit of man rising triumphant from the destruction of his cities. "Only there is something in you that doesn't care about honor and pride yet that lives," Bon writes, "that even walks backward for a whole year just to live; that probably even when this is over and there is not even defeat left, will still decline to sit still in the sun and die, but will be out in the woods, moving and seeking where just will and endurance could not move it, grubbing for roots and such" (349).

Judith is imagined by Quentin as partially accepting Bon's radical humanism, in spite of her Mississippi heritage. "I believed that there were things which still mattered just because they had mattered once. But I was wrong. Nothing matters but breath, breathing, to know and to be alive" (207). Her intermediary position is shown by her disastrous effort, following Sutpen's death, to raise as her own child Charles Etienne Saint-Valery Bon, the son of her fiancé and his octoroon mistress. She tries to break down the abstract barrier between Negro and white by insisting that the boy call her "Aunt Judith" and sleep in a trundle bed in her room. But the youth responds more to her "cold implacable antipathy" (198) than to her mask of kindness. He rejects the moral compromise and tries to assert his Negro blood by marrying "a coal black and ape-like woman" (205) and by living as a Negro in one of the old slave cabins. Like Joe Christmas he treads "the thorny and flintpaved path toward the Gethsemane which he had decreed and created for himself, where he had crucified himself" (209). Valery Bon's suicidal gesture is compared by the narrator to the "demon" Sutpen's own furious rage "when his own fate which he had dared in his turn struck back at him" (202–203). Both Sutpen and his part-Negro descendants live by principles of honor and abstract decorum; however, Charles Bon is at least aware of the superior forces of nature, and of the destruction that awaits anyone who tries to force nature into abstract molds.

Sutpen's self-destructive endeavor is illustrated by his refusal to modify the terms of his original social scheme upon discovering that his first wife, the daughter of a Haiti planter, has Negro blood. He immediately abandons her, convinced by his puritan "innocence" that leaving her money absolves him of further responsibility. Sutpen is thus dismayed to discover his tainted son in the person of Henry's new friend at the State University. In the words of Quentin's grandfather, he recognizes Charles Bon as the symbolic boy knocking at the "white door" that the young Sutpen was not allowed to enter. At this point, General Compson surmises, Sutpen "must have felt and heard the design—house, position, posterity and all—come down like it had been built out of smoke" (267).

Sutpen bares his problem to General Compson, not for advice or self-justification, but simply in the hope that the "legal mind" might pick out his "mistake," so that it could be corrected. Sutpen is convinced that he has only two alternatives. "Either I destroy my design with my own hand, which will happen if I am forced to play my last trump card, or do nothing, let matters take the course which I know they will take and see my design complete itself quite normally and naturally and successfully to the public eye, yet to my own in such fashion as to be a mockery and a betrayal of that little boy who approached that door fifty years ago and was turned away, for whose vindication the whole plan was conceived and carried forward to the moment of this choice" (274). Sutpen has already told Henry that Charles Bon is his half-brother, so the "trump card" can only refer to the further revelation to Henry that Bon has Negro blood, a course of action that Sutpen finally adopts. The other choice is that of allowing Bon to marry his daughter, which would be a mockery and betrayal of Sutpen's ambition. The key word used by Sutpen is "vindication." In spite of the moral glamour attached to it, the plan is based upon vindication of a personal insult given by means of a Negro butler to a white boy. Sutpen believes that to associate the "boy-symbol" with a person having Negro blood—even if that person is his own son—would mean a confusion of the clear pattern of moral vindication.

Sutpen must either humanize his abstract design or save the boy-symbol at the expense of the boy. He chooses the latter course and reveals to Henry that the marriage of Charles and Judith would mean miscegenation. Sutpen does not realize that Henry will fail to

persuade Bon to break off the engagement, or that he will murder
Bon rather than allow him to enter Sutpen's Hundred. This act of
murder transforms Henry into an exiled murderer and Judith into an
embittered "widow." All Sutpen has left of his ambition is its dehumanized shell—a desperate lust to beget a man child upon the
future.

The artificiality of Sutpen's dilemma is revealed by Charles Bon's
reason for refusing to give up Judith in the face of Henry's violent
opposition. His motive is neither Old World fatalism, as Mr. Compson believes, nor even a desire for revenge, but primarily his loneliness and deep emotional need. He craves at least an informal recognition from his father. "That's all I want. He need not even
acknowledge me; I will let him understand just as quickly that he
need not do that, that I do not expect that, will not be hurt by that,
just as he will let me know that quickly that I am his son" (319).
Like primitive figures in other novels, Bon stands for values of love
and forgiveness that are opposed to puritan inflexibility. Yet by
refusing to give up his marriage to Judith, he betrays a moral ob-
stinacy comparable to Sutpen's. In this respect Bon is Sutpen's true
son, and his acceptance of death at the hands of his half-brother is
roughly comparable, although with different implications, to Sutpen's own death a few years later.

Throughout the latter part of the novel Charles Bon and Thomas
Sutpen engage in a struggle for influence over Henry. The imaginary
New Orleans scene involving the two brothers foreshadows Henry's
moral dilemma as he fights the Civil War by Bon's side. Henry is
willing to accept Charles's marriage to Judith as long as the difficulty is only that of incest. When his father calls Henry to a family
conference, the latter parrots Bon's argument rejecting social abstractions in favor of the basic human principle: "Nothing matters
except that there is the old mindless meat that dont even care if it
was defeat or victory, that wont even die, that will be out in the
woods and fields, grubbing up roots and weeds" (354). But Henry's
discipleship to Bon collapses before the irreconcilable fact, which
Sutpen then reveals, that Bon is part-Negro.

The rejected son's search for recognition now breaks itself against
the staunch rock of Southern Calvinist racial prejudice. During the
four years of war Charles Bon waits for a sign from his father,

hoping that the suffering will have changed him. But Sutpen's mind is inflexible on this point, as is Henry's. "So it's the miscegenation, not the incest, which you cant bear" (356) Charles asks his half brother. When Henry cannot deny this, the doom of both is sealed. Henry kills his brother and flees Mississippi, not to return until shortly before his death. Charles Bon's last gesture is to place a picture of his octoroon mistress in the metal case which Judith, along with her own picture, has given him. If Henry fails to kill him, it will not matter. If he succeeds, then the picture will be a message to her: "*I was no good; do not grieve for me*" (359).

It is significant that Charles Bon yearns for social leadership from Sutpen as well as personal recognition. "All right," he thinks, "I am trying to make myself into what I think he wants me to be; he can do anything he wants to with me; he has only to tell me what to do and I will do it; even though what he asked me to do looked to me like dishonor, I would still do it" (330). Bon is thus allied with Wash Jones, who seeks the same kind of leadership. Wash thinks of how Sutpen has touched and ennobled his life: "Maybe I am not as big as he is and maybe I did not do any of the galloping. But at least I was drug along where he went. And me and him can still do hit and will ever so, if so be he will show me what he aims for me to do" (287–288). Sutpen's ruthless treatment of both figures represents his refusal, as an architect of Southern society, to include the Negro and the poor-white in his ambitious design.

It is appropriate that Wash Jones, whose poor-white status suggests Sutpen's family background, should be the agent of retribution. Wash hears Sutpen tell the retainer's granddaughter, "Well, Milly; too bad you're not a mare too. Then I could give you a decent stall in the stable" (286). Sutpen's mania exceeds the bounds of common sense as well as common decency. He forces even Wash Jones to realize that courage and determination are empty virtues if they destroy human dignity and self-respect. "Better if his kind and mine too," Wash thinks, "had never drawn the breath of life on this earth. Better that all who remain of us be blasted from the face of it than that another Wash Jones should see his whole life shredded from him and shrivel away like a dried shuck thrown onto the fire" (290–291).

After killing Sutpen, Wash refuses to flee, knowing that he cannot escape "beyond the boundaries of earth where such men lived, set the order and the rule of living" (290). He also realizes that the South's aristocratic society, represented by Sutpen, has no place for him. Perhaps he understood, Mr. Compson suggests, "how it had been possible for Yankees or any other army to have whipped them —the gallant, the proud, the brave; the acknowledged and chosen best among them all to bear the courage and honor and pride" (290). For Miss Rosa Coldfield, too, Sutpen's story explains why God had to let the South lose the war, "that only through the blood of our men and the tears of our women could He stay this demon and efface his name and lineage from the earth" (11).

In tragic drama the hero's general development is from a social to an individual status, as from Lear the proud king to Lear the penitent father, or from a regal Oedipus to an old blind man led off the stage. In *Absalom, Absalom!* the process is reversed; Sutpen the stranger to Jefferson becomes Sutpen the Civil War colonel and archetypal aristocrat. A comparable shift takes place in the narrative point of view as the romantic account of Miss Rosa Coldfield gives way to the fatalistic speculations of Mr. Compson and finally to the search by Quentin Compson and his Harvard roommate for both truth and symbol in the Sutpen legend. The force of Sutpen's ambition, which Miss Rosa explains as demonism, is traced finally to a bloodless denial of human emotion.

As this process of analysis and redefinition takes place, Sutpen's aura of tragedy becomes increasingly depersonalized. His life is made to symbolize the failure of Southern society, but the man himself is denied self-understanding. The rigid dimensions of his rational puritanism prevent him from perceiving the evil which his actions have brought into the world. If such a moral awareness does exist in *Absalom, Absalom!*, it can only be in Wash Jones's discovery of Sutpen's treachery or in the tormented consciousness of Quentin Compson, the final narrator.

PART THREE

Later Works

Chapter Ten

❧

FROM GO DOWN, MOSES TO A FABLE

*I*N HIS NOBEL PRIZE SPEECH Faulkner declares that man's "puny inexhaustible voice" will do more than survive society's downfall. "I believe that man will not merely endure: he will prevail. He is immortal, not because he alone among creatures has an inexhaustible voice but because he has a soul, a spirit capable of compassion and sacrifice and endurance." It is the task of the writer both to proclaim man's immortality and to help him achieve it, "to help him endure and prevail." [1] These words express the theme of such recent Faulkner works as *Requiem for a Nun, A Fable,* and to some extent *The Town* and *The Mansion,* but they also point to a weakness or contradiction within that theme.

Faulkner clearly associates human value with the qualities of endurance and suffering. This is why he speaks of man's puny voice

[1] "The Stockholm Address" in *Three Decades,* p. 348.

173

triumphing beyond "the last ding-dong of doom." Yet if man's spirit will triumph when civilization lies in ruins, what can be the worth of such a victory? How can that worth be demonstrated and proclaimed by a novelist concerned, as any novelist must be, with the relation of individual characters to some kind of social world? Faulkner's description of human "immortality" implies the existence of values that can be revealed only in isolation from society or by negative or passive responses to social influences. The fact that such a triumph or assertion of immortality could never take place undermines the spirit of Faulkner's optimism and deprives his faith in mankind of any coherent meaning.

In works written prior to *Go Down, Moses* (1942) Faulkner's negative affirmation of human value proves neither disturbing nor paradoxical. The author's social pessimism dominates both characterization and narrative structure, in that figures who represent an uncorrupted humanity play only a passive dramatic role. When Lena Grove in *Light in August* and Eula Varner in *The Hamlet* influence the behavior of others, they do so by their mere presence or by what their presence symbolizes. Such figures can be vehicles for revelation of moral value, but they cannot function as moral agents. Their task is to stand in dramatic opposition to archetypal Southern puritans, and to represent the antithesis of the South's egotistical puritan will.

After *Go Down, Moses* Faulkner continues to associate moral awareness with a character's isolation from society. But social activity is less corrupting, and primitive characters play a more dynamic social role. In *Requiem for a Nun* and *A Fable* Nancy Mannigoe and the Corporal are able to bridge the gap between understanding and action. But inasmuch as their moral awareness is socially effective, they function as agents of destruction. Instead of modifying his definition of social action as demonic, Faulkner tries to justify the destructive actions of both characters by emphasizing their moral aims and their Christ-like suffering. The self-martyrdom of Joe Christmas, which both explains and partially atones for his path of violence, anticipates this technique. Faulkner also creates spokesman-characters, for example Gavin Stevens of *Requiem* and the old Marshal of *A Fable*, who are unable to work for social salvation, but can assist and interpret the redeeming gestures of others.

Ike McCaslin in *Go Down, Moses* is not quite an uncorrupted primitive, but through his experience as a hunter he learns to submit his will to the mysterious and fructifying power of nature. Ike saves his moral categories from the corruption of a rational puritanism, and is able to apply them in opposition to the values accepted by his social world. Believing that human truth and the needs of organized society are incompatible, Ike surrenders his patrimony, the McCaslin plantation, and takes up Christ's profession of carpentry. But in return for his redeeming vision he pays the price of social ineffectuality. A forlorn seer with no disciples, he is fated to witness the destruction of the primitive wilderness which he loves.

Special objects of Ike's religious concern are the descendants of the McCaslin plantation slaves. Because the plantation system symbolizes human injustice, the Negro victims of that system are alone free of its corrupting influence. According to Ike's personal mythology the white man's pride and intolerance has brought a divine curse to the entire region:

He created man to be His overseer on the earth and to hold suzerainty over the earth and the animals on it in His name, not to hold for himself and his descendants inviolable title forever, generation after generation, to the oblongs and squares of the earth, but to hold the earth mutual and intact in the communal anonymity of brotherhood, and all the fee He asked was pity and humility and sufferance and endurance and the sweat of his face for bread. (257)

The sin of holding false title to the land is inherited from the Chickasaw tribe that created the fiction of ownership in order to sell the land to white man. But the sin of slavery, violating the "communal anonymity of brotherhood," is the white man's own.

It is a truism that no evil can be eradicated or redeemed by rational means unless its nature and its cause are known. Before Ike can expiate his inheritance of guilt he must come to some understanding of its cause. By creating a private mythology he establishes slavery and the South's plantation system as sources of corruption, and in this manner clears the way for personal atonement. As a white man Ike cannot escape his heritage of guilt, but he can "repudiate the wrong and shame, at least in principle" (351). He takes no definite steps to surrender his grandfather's plantation; for

175

he believes that the land is not really his to surrender. But he repudiates it in principle by allowing his patrimony to fall into the hands of a cousin.

The longest and most successful of the *Go Down, Moses* stories, "The Bear," concerns the basis for Ike's decision to repudiate his McCaslin inheritance. He learns the extent of his family's racial guilt by studying plantation records; but before he can make his redeeming gesture he must learn to appreciate primitive nature. Ike's moral lesson is provided by the aged Sam Fathers, who knows when to shoot and when not to shoot, and by an old bear, the object of a yearly hunt by a party of Jefferson aristocrats. "Solitary, indomitable, and alone; widowered childless and absolved of mortality" (194), the bear is given the status of a forest deity, and the yearly hunt the function of ritual worship. Ike's development as a man and as a hunter is coterminous with his gradual understanding of what the bear signifies. In a climactic scene he deliberately loses himself in the forest, having "relinquished" his watch and compass, in order to encourage the bear to appear. When he finds the bear's tracks, they lead him back to his compass: "Then he saw the bear. It did not emerge, appear: it was just there, immobile, fixed in the green and windless noon's hot dappling, not as big as he had dreamed it but as big as he had expected, bigger, dimensionless against the dappled obscurity . . . Then it was gone. It didn't walk into the woods. It faded, sank back into the wilderness without motion as he had watched a fish, a huge old bass, sink back into the dark depths of its pool and vanish without even any movement of its fins" (209).

This semidivine creature cannot be subject to a conventional death. He is killed with a knife, rather than a rifle, and through the agency of a man and a dog who are associated with the untamed forest. The dog, Lion, is trained especially for this task and dies with its accomplishment. The man, Boon Hogganbeck, is not an accomplished woodsman, like Sam Fathers or Ike McCaslin, but is a primitive white man more crippled by the vices of civilization than redeemed by the virtues of the wilderness. His participation in the old bear's death indicates that although the skilled hunters can pursue the bear and be responsible for his death, they have no power to touch him. Just as the bear dies, Sam Fathers is struck down, as if by a sudden illness, and is subsequently killed at his own request, or so it is implied, by the faithful Boon. These deaths indicate the end not only of the hunt but of hunting itself, as Sam Fathers and his Indian ancestors have known it. Shortly afterward Major de Spain sells the timber in the hunting-camp area.

In "Delta Autumn" a much older Ike McCaslin describes his refusal to claim the family plantation as a protest against what is called "progress," against the division of land into abstract squares to be owned and exploited. He compares his own life to that of the wilderness: "the two spans running out together, not toward oblivion, nothingness, but into a dimension free of both time and space where once more the untreed land warped and wrung to mathematical squares of rank cotton for the frantic old-world people to turn into shells to shoot at one another, would find ample room for both" (354). His memories of the past coalesce into a single vision of all the faces he has known and loved, "moving again among the shades of tall unaxed trees and sightless brakes where the wild strong immortal game ran forever before the tireless belling immortal hounds, falling and rising phoenix-like to the soundless guns" (354). This vision is the old man's refuge from a world where even the act of destruction has no recognized significance and no ritual value. According to Ike the "ruined woods" require no retribution, since "the people who have destroyed it will accomplish its revenge" (364). The significance of the wilderness for humanity lies in the symbolism of its destruction. Thus Ike is redeemed not so much by his devotion to the wilderness as by his awareness of the alienation between social man and primitive nature.

The fourth section of "The Bear" is devoted to a dialogue between the youthful Ike McCaslin and his older cousin, McCaslin Edmonds, in which Ike explains his renunciation. The section includes Ike's discovery that his grandfather, Carothers McCaslin, had committed incest with his own mulatto daughter. The product of this incest, Tomey's Turl, has more of Carothers' blood in him than his white half-brothers, Uncle Buck and Uncle Buddy, who are nominally Turl's masters. Carothers never recognizes his Negro children while he lives, but he bequeaths a thousand dollars to Tomey's Turl. "So I reckon that was cheaper than saying My son to a nigger," Ike comments, "even if My son wasn't but just two words." But there must have been love. "Some sort of love. Even what he would have

177

called love: not just an afternoon's or a night's spittoon" (269–270).

Ike's father and uncle try ineffectually to cope with their unwelcome heritage. But all they do is triple Turl's legacy for the benefit of his three surviving children, James, Fonsiba, and Lucas. Ike sees the money, or the debt it acknowledges, as an indication of the South's guilty conscience. He also sees it as a sign that uncorrupted Negro blood will eventually inherit the South. Ike assumes the responsibility of delivering the money to his Negro cousins, in spite of the fact that James and Fonsiba have left Mississippi. When the boy finds Fonsiba and her husband on a small farm in Arkansas he cries out that the South is cursed by slavery. "Granted that my people brought the curse onto the land: maybe for that reason their descendants alone can—not resist it, not combat it—maybe just endure and outlast it until the curse is lifted. Then your peoples' turn will come because we have forfeited ours. But not now. Not yet. Dont you see?" (278).

This hysterical prophecy is repeated in "Delta Autumn," where Ike meets a young mulatto girl, descended from James, who has borne an illegitimate child to Roth Edmonds, Ike's white cousin. Ike gives her an old hunting horn, a gift from General Compson and a symbol of the old South. He touches the girl's hand, "the gnarled bloodless, bone-light bone-dry old man's fingers touching for a second the smooth young flesh where the strong old blood ran after its long lost journey back to home" (362). Torn between his insight and his traditions, Ike predicts the triumph of the Negro race, but only in the distant future: "Maybe in a thousand or two thousand years in America . . . But not now! Not now!" (361).

Faulkner's successful handling of difficult social problems in "The Bear" is traceable to his reluctance to let characterization be subordinated to abstract theme. When Ike McCaslin seems to be speaking directly to the reader, as in this passage, his personality weaknesses are readily apparent. Faulkner permits him to echo, at least in principle, the Southern bugbear that desegregation will lead to intermarriage and the eventual subordination of Anglo-Saxon to Negro stock or to some combination of the two. Ike seems to feel that the South must belong to either the white or the mulatto race; it cannot belong to both. He is willing to acknowledge the white man's guilt and even the Negro's moral superiority. But as a typical

Southerner he is unwilling to view social issues realistically. The reader is asked to accept Ike both as Faulkner's spokesman on the race question, and as an hysterical and self-deceiving old man.

A related point concerns the extraordinary ending of "The Bear." Ike McCaslin pays a final visit to the hunting-camp area before a lumber company moves in. Having arranged to meet Boon Hoggan-beck near a gum tree in the middle of a clearing, he finds his drunken friend breaking his gun into pieces, "with the frantic abandon of a madman," while equally frantic squirrels rush from limb to limb of the tree. Without recognizing Ike, Boon shouts to him "Get out of here! Dont touch them! Dont touch a one of them! They're mine!" (331). Boon's statement recalls his earlier words to McCaslin Edmonds, "By God, you wont touch him" (252), when the latter is approaching Sam Fathers' body; and they point to the general theme in "The Bear" of man's desecration of the wilderness and its inhabitants. The destruction of the gun symbolizes Boon's rejection of the civilized world that constructed it. But Boon is "protecting" only squirrels; his gun has always proven ineffectual in a hunt, and he is clearly inadequate as a practicing conservationist. In addition, his words parody the concept of private ownership, which Ike McCaslin associates with the moral and spiritual failure of social man. Perhaps Boon's hysteria is related to the fact that he has been the instrument of Old Ben's death and of Sam Fathers' suicide. Like the ritual hunt, Boon simultaneously represents primitive value and its corruption. He is a white man surrounded by symbols of impotence and failure, a diminished forest and a broken gun; he cannot bear the burden of what Sam Fathers and the wilderness have taught him, and what he has had to do.

In *Intruder in the Dust* and *Requiem for a Nun* Faulkner makes an even stronger effort to give characters representing moral awareness a positive social role. In the former novel he establishes Lucas Beauchamp, a son of Tomey's Turl and therefore Ike McCaslin's cousin, as a symbol for the blood union of the two races. To this extent Lucas is comparable to Joe Christmas in *Light in August* and to Charles and Valery Bon in *Absalom, Absalom!* But unlike these figures, who are raised in white society, he can accept his divided status with equanimity. Lucas first appears in *Go Down, Moses* as a comic Negro who nevertheless has sufficient shrewdness and composure to get the better of Roth Edmonds, his white cousin. In *Intruder in the Dust* he is described as inheriting the best features of both the white and the Negro race. The pride and dignity of Carothers McCaslin, his grandfather, is combined with Negro patience and capacity for endurance. He is free of both curses described by Joanna Burden in *Light in August*—that of enslaving and that of being enslaved—and he has no need to strive with or to deny, as Faulkner puts it, his Negro blood. "He resisted it simply by being the composite of the two races which made him, simply by possessing it" (*Go Down, Moses*, 104). Whereas Joe Christmas destroys himself in the effort to expiate his past, Lucas Beauchamp accepts both past and future. In his characterization the South's racial conflict is for a moment resolved.

Lucas signifies the end of the old order as well as a means by which the South can come to terms with the new. Like Sam Fathers, who also has Negro blood, Lucas acts as a spiritual guide to a white boy-witness. But he carries out his role passively, by what he represents and not by what he does or says. In fact Chick Mallison is an unwilling disciple and joins the rest of the town in trying to fit Lucas's behavior into the traditional pattern associated with "niggers." But when Lucas is falsely accused of murdering a white man and asks Chick to help demonstrate his innocence, the boy cannot refuse. Lucas has done Chick a prior service for which he scornfully refused monetary payment. The boy's sense of a debt unpaid emphasizes the theme of Southern society's debt to the descendants of its Negro slaves.

The result is a sociological detective novel, cleverly constructed but too long-winded to be very successful. Lucas Beauchamp's innocence of the murder is revealed through the efforts of Chick and Miss Habersham, an aged white spinster also aware of the debt owed the Negro race. She was nursed by the mother of Molly Beauchamp, Lucas's wife, and grew up with Molly, "almost inextricably like sisters, like twins, sleeping in the same room, the white girl in the bed, the Negro girl on a cot at the foot of it" (87). The ability of Chick, Miss Habersham, and a Negro boy to confound logic and set Lucas free illustrates Faulkner's stylized distinction between Southern male adults and figures uncorrupted by puritan rationality. Even Gavin Stevens, a spokesman for Faulkner's social ideas, assumes without question that since Lucas was found standing by the body with a fired pistol, he is guilty of the crime. Miss Habersham explains why Lucas did not ask Gavin Stevens, or even the sheriff, for help: "Lucas knew it would take a child—or an old woman like me: someone not concerned with probability, with evidence" (89).

The action of Chick and Miss Habersham in digging up the murdered man's grave sets up a chain of events that ultimately reveals the victim's brother as the real murderer. The anger and potential violence of the would-be lynchers, led by the murderer, symbolizes the mob's hidden sense of guilt. The proof of Lucas's innocence brings "into the light and glare of day something shocking and shameful out of the whole white foundation of the county which he himself must partake of too since he too was bred of it, which otherwise might have flared and blazed merely . . . and then vanished back into its darkness or at least invisibility with the fading embers of Lucas's crucifixion" (138). A dramatic reversal takes place; "Lucas Beauchamp, once the slave of any white man within range of whose notice he happened to come, now tyrant over the whole county's white conscience" (199).

The themes of *Intruder in the Dust* recur in *Requiem for a Nun*, although in a grotesque form. The main part of the work, written in dramatic dialogue, concerns Nancy Mannigoe's success in preserving the marriage of her white employers, Temple and Gowan Stevens. These two characters are bowdlerized versions of Temple Drake and her dipsomaniac boy friend in *Sanctuary*. The plot of the sequel hinges upon Nancy's discovery that Temple is about to elope with a blackmailer. Rather than confess to her husband what he already suspects about her past, she is prepared to desert her family and go away with Pete, the ruffian brother of Red, her *Sanctuary* lover. Nancy can frustrate this plan only by murdering the small baby, the younger of two children, that Temple intends to take with her. Her action is presented as a redeeming gesture. She knows that the salvation of the world lies in human suffering, and out of this dubious knowledge comes her determination to destroy the child.

Nancy's sacrifice is a virtual parody of Dilsey's devotion to the Compson family in *The Sound and the Fury*. In both works the stock literary image of the Negro mammy devoted to her "white folks" is transformed into a symbol for moral understanding. But Dilsey's role is fortunately a static one; the significance of her patience and understanding is evident only to the reader. Nancy's role, on the other hand, is carefully elucidated by herself and by Gavin Stevens. The reader is expected to reconcile her philosophy of passive suffering with the fact that she intends her sacrifice to accomplish a definite social end. "So good can come out of evil," Temple says, and Gavin adds, "It not only can, it must" (208). Faulkner suggests a comparison between Nancy's suffering and the Crucifixion. But the Negro is deprived of the divine status that would make her sacrifice bearable to others, or even assure its success. She is an inadequate moral agent because she so ruthlessly places ends over means, an error that Faulkner ordinarily condemns. She surrenders a concrete value, her responsibility as the child's nurse and guardian, for an intangible moral lesson.

Temple Drake's experiences in *Sanctuary* are described as the sins which as Temple Stevens in *Requiem for a Nun* she must recognize and accept. But a curious thing happens. The events and characters that are heavily stylized in *Sanctuary* are treated in *Requiem for a Nun* as if they were entirely realistic. The shift from the tragicomic atmosphere of *Sanctuary* is exemplified by Gavin Stevens's solemn commentary on Popeye:

You underrate this *precieux*, this flower, this jewel. Vitelli. What a name for him. A hybrid, impotent. He was hanged the next year, to be sure. But even that was wrong: his very effacement debasing, flouting, even what dignity man has been able to lend to necessary human abolishment. He should have been crushed somehow under a vast and mindless boot, like a spider. (145)

Perhaps Stevens is unaware of the valuable irony, in *Sanctuary*, of Popeye's being hanged for a crime that he did not commit. By giving Popeye a surname, even a symbolic one, and by making him into a realistic demon, Faulkner implies that Temple Drake was not necessarily responsible for her own corruption. Once Temple is transformed from an eager sinner into an innocent victim, she becomes eligible for salvation. Temple must cease to represent the corrupt Southern aristocracy, and become an ordinary sinner, before her past sins can be effectively redeemed.

A similar movement from myth to reality characterizes the prose sections which precede the three acts of the drama. Each of these prefaces discusses the origin and significance of a public building associated with the dramatic action. First, the Jefferson courthouse represents Yoknapatawpha history, and discussion of this building enables Faulkner to summarize the characters and major events of his mythological world. The section devoted to the Jackson State Capitol permits a combination of private myth with public history, including a composite roster of real and fanciful Mississippi names, "Claiborne. Humphries. Dickson. McLaurin. Barksdale. Lamar. Prentiss. Davis. Sartoris. Compson" (110). In the last preface the narrator returns to Jefferson and gives the story of the town jail, which is older than the courthouse and a more faithful record of human passion and suffering.

What is unfortunately missing in this fusion of Yoknapatawpha mythology with Southern history is the moral analysis usually present in Faulkner's novels. The Civil War is described neither as a symbol of the South's moral sin nor as the consequence of its refusal to accept responsibility, but as the destiny of the land "whirling into the plunge of its precipice." The plunge is not recognized at first "because the first seconds of fall always seem like soar: a weightless deliberation preliminary to a rush not downward but upward, the falling body reversed during that second by transubstantiation into the upward rush of earth; a soar, an apex, the South's own apotheosis of its destiny and its pride" (229–230). The extravagant rhetoric of this passage is a curious echo of the *Sartoris* passage, previously quoted, where a similar description of the Civil War is intended as an ironical comment upon the romanticism of Miss Jenny, the speaker. In his apparent effort to communicate directly to the reader, Faulkner deprives his rhetoric of its customary significance. Yoknapatawpha County history is ordinarily an effective means by which the bizarre action of particular novels can be made symbolic of moral and social themes. But when the mythology is treated as if it were history, and made the focus of dramatic interest, such a function is no longer possible. The admission of Yoknapatawpha County to the state of Mississippi is accomplished at the expense of

Faulkner's success in reconciling stylized characterization and realistic social themes.

In *A Fable,* as in *Requiem for a Nun,* Faulkner concentrates upon a character's effort to translate moral awareness into effective social action. The novel concerns the reincarnation of Christ as a World War I soldier, and a subsequent revolt against war by the enlisted men of both the Allied and the German armies. This long work suffers from poor organization and rhetorical excess, but it represents the author's most impressive dramatization of moral and philosophical themes that dominate his later fiction.

The theme of a returned Christ is associated with the eulogy of universal human brotherhood and man's capacity for triumphant endurance. In complementary opposition to the idealistic Christ-figure is the French commander of the Allied armies, who understands and appreciates the Corporal's humanistic message, but nevertheless feels compelled to crucify him. Like Captain Vere in Melville's "Billy Budd," the old Marshal is saddened by his awareness of incompatibility between personal human values and a corrupt human society. However, Faulkner's character acts not out of a sense of duty but out of his author's paradoxical conviction that the two forces are only superficially opposed, that the Corporal's crucifixion is the best way of securing his martyrdom and thus confirming the value of his mission.

This reconciliation of opposed visions, of innate good and intrinsic evil, is indicated by the fact that the old Marshal is the Corporal's father. Like Faulkner's other primitive characters, the Corporal represents values that are in conflict with social organization, but he also represents the blind faith that social evil can be conquered. His sophisticated father, on the contrary, knows that mankind can never put an end to warfare and bloodshed. The problem is verbally resolved by the Marshal, who perversely describes his own pessimism as an idealism far more substantial than the Corporal's naive faith. As Faulkner's primary spokesman-figure, the old man substitutes a faith in human "rapacity" for the vague notion of moral salvation proclaimed by the Corporal. Human immortality is made possible neither through divine grace nor human goodness, but through man's "deathless folly," or his infinite ability to endure the consequences of his own evil and tomfoolery. "I am ten times prouder of that immortality which he does possess," cries the old man, "than ever he of that heavenly one of his delusion" (354).

In contrast to the Corporal, a stranger to civilization, the Marshal symbolizes the wealth of French society and the glamour of its tradition. As a young officer he is inspired by a belief, similar to his son's, in man's perfectibility. Yet he finds himself in a situation where in order to save a garrison—and perhaps the French empire—he betrays his personal word and sends a soldier to certain death. Understanding the corruption basic to social leadership, the Marshal abandons his commission and disappears beyond the borders of the known world. Acting through neither passion nor folly, as Faulkner puts it, he begets a son upon a mountain woman and causes her disgrace and death. His life is thus dedicated to a self-redeeming evil: "I mean Evil, as if there was a purity in it, a severity, a jealousy like in God—a strictness of untruth incapable of compromise or second-best or substitute" (286).

The Marshal's acceptance of man's evil nature is contrasted to the Corporal's faith, even though the latter, in a sense, is the consequence of the old man's sacramental evil. The Marshal declares to his son that they are two "articulations": "I champion of this mundane earth . . . you champion of an esoteric realm of man's baseless hopes and his infinite capacity—no: passion—for unfact" (348). He advises the Corporal to "close that window fast; lock it forever on that aberrant and futile dream" (345). The Corporal replies that his father must be afraid of man's dream of immortality. But the Marshal answers that he and not his son has the most faith in humanity: "Afraid? No no, it's not I but you who are afraid of man; not I but you who believe that nothing but a death can save him" (352). The Corporal's naïveté is revealed, and the Marshal's faith in man's divided nature, in his being evil as well as good, is shown to be stronger. The son cannot defend himself against his father's charge and must take refuge through silence into what the Marshal calls man's "passion for unfact."

The ideological conflict between the Marshal and the Corporal is reflected in both the situation and the dramatic action of the novel.

For example, an absolute division is said to exist between the attitudes of enlisted men and those of their officers. The Corporal's scheme to end the war infiltrates the noncommissioned ranks of four armies, including the German one, without a single leak. One consequence of the extreme stylization is that an ineffectual Pauline figure, known simply as the Runner, discovers that he must repudiate his commission in order to achieve self-respect. Even so, he is the last man below the rank of sergeant in the entire Allied front to learn about the Corporal and his twelve soldier disciples (66). Other figures associated with the Corporal's plan are an aged Negro minister, the Reverend Sutterfield, and a self-tormenting character known in separate episodes as the Sentry and the Groom. Although Sutterfield supports the Corporal's idealism, he also echoes the Marshal's view that good and evil cannot be separated. Like the Marshal, he respects man's need to believe—even if there is nothing completely worthy of belief. Echoing this paradoxical position, the Runner just wants to believe, as he puts it, "not in anything: just to believe" (203).

The ugly and dwarflike Sentry or Groom is one of Faulkner's strangest and most unsuccessful characters. As a soldier he is described as a member of the Masonic Order, freely initiating enlisted men into its rites. He also lends them sums of money to be paid back piecemeal at exorbitant rates. The men gamble on the chance of their being killed and not having to pay. They become Masons partly because they are attracted to the Sentry and partly because interest rates are thereby lower. The Masonic sign is treated as a symbol for human brotherhood, and much of the novel's action involves the Runner's effort to persuade the Sentry to use the sign as a means of leading the soldiers out of the trenches where they can fraternize with the Germans. Several times the Runner tries to persuade the Sentry to do this and fails. At last, with Sutterfield's help, he forces the Sentry with them out of the trenches and through the barbed-wire entanglements. The entire regiment follows. A great deal is made of the symbolic gesture which the Sentry never seems to make; it is the soldiers' own concerted impulse rather than the Sentry's direct influence that brings them out into the open.

A similar ambiguity pervades the long flashback scene in which the Sentry appears as the groom of a world-famous horse which is sold to a Southern millionaire. When the horse breaks his leg in a railroad accident the Groom and a Negro helper (Sutterfield) steal him. They enter the racehorse—who runs on three legs—in a series of local races in isolated communities. Their aim is not financial profit, but prevention of the horse's being exploited at stud. "We had to save it until it could die still not knowing nothing and not wanting nothing but just to run out in front of everything else" (198). In this curious way Sutterfield and the "misshapen, savage and foul" Groom achieve a sense of dedication to a universal cause (190). By joining both the Baptist Church and the Masonic Order, the Groom gains "truth, love, sacrifice, and something else even more important than they: some bond between or from man to his brother man stronger than even the golden shackles which coopered precariously his ramshackle earth" (165).

It is because of the Groom's search for brotherhood that his self-contained story finds a place in *A Fable*. But only grotesque features and a love for obscene language connect the characterization of the Groom to that of the Sentry. When the Sentry is dragged by Sutterfield and the Runner into No Man's Land, he seems to experience a moral initiation that duplicates the earlier one. The narrator makes a point of the Sentry's using the plural instead of the singular pronoun upon crying out "Not to us!" (321) when the English and German regiments are shelled. If the Sentry achieves his sense of brotherhood only at this climactic moment, his experiences as a Mason and Baptist, as well as horsethief, are deprived of structural significance.

The Sentry and the Groom may be described as two different characters with parallel histories. Like the Runner and a friend of the Marshal known as the Quartermaster General, they are given abstract ideals as substitutes for realistic drives. These four characters are all compelled to action by what Faulkner at one point calls their "hungry and passionate hope" (282), their desperate wish to believe in a faith in man that is only vaguely understood. To them are contrasted Sutterfield and the Marshal, who have presumably graduated to a wise and more stable faith in man's divided moral nature. The Runner's attachment to Sutterfield and the Corporal is

thus comparable to the Quartermaster General's life-long hope that
the Marshal will finally do something to save mankind. The Quartermaster General is shocked by his idol's part in the slaughter of two
regiments of soldiers. But like the Corporal he is silent before the
Marshal's assertions of faith in human rapacity.

The Runner and the Quartermaster General are symbolically
joined when they both appear at the Marshal's funeral following the
end of the war; however, the one appears out of hatred and the
other out of love. The Runner, now "a mobile and upright scar, on
crutches" (435) lurches to the scene and throws his French medal of
honor at the coffin: "This is yours: take it!" he shouts. "You too
helped carry the torch of man into that twilight where he shall be no
more; these are his epitaphs: They shall not pass. My country right
or wrong. Here is a spot which is forever England—" (436). These
bitter words are a clear indictment not only of nationalism but also
of the Marshal's belief that man's evil is a guarantee of his immortality. As the Runner lies in a gutter, knocked down by the angry
French crowd, he is helped by a stranger, who is recognizable by his
giant size and his "vast worn sick face with hungry and passionate
eyes" as the Quartermaster General.

The novel ends with the Runner's statement of defiance:

"That's right," he said: "Tremble. I'm not going to die. Never."
"I am not laughing," the old man bending over him said. "What you
see are tears." (437)

What will never die is presumably man's spirit of optimistic faith,
which the author seems to equate with human indestructibility.
Faulkner's sympathy at this point is clearly with the Runner and not
with the Marshal. Yet the final scene is an affirmation of the
Marshal's belief that man's puny but inexhaustible voice will never
cease talking and planning. The meeting between the Runner and
the Quartermaster General suggests the fusion of the two contrary
views. Nevertheless the fusion is unsatisfactory. The Runner proclaims that the marshals of the world will lead humanity to destruction; but practically in the same breath he adds that he, as a symbol
for human faith, will never die. The author's social pessimism is in
effect answered only by the rhetorical vision of man's immortal
struggle to achieve unattainable goals. The Marshal may have a

greater faith in humanity than the Corporal, but he is nevertheless responsible for the Corporal's death and the failure of the latter's social aim.

The Marshal's philosophy is partially embodied in a short tale which he relates to the Corporal. A condemned man has confessed to his crime and made his peace with God. In his last moment of life he hears the song of a bird:

Whereupon he who less than a second before had his very foot lifted to step from earth's grief and anguish into eternal peace, cast away heaven, salvation, immortal soul and all, struggling to free his bound hands in order to snatch away the noose, crying "Innocent! Innocent! I didn't do it!" even as the trap earth, world and all, fell from under him. (351)

This story illustrates what the old man calls the wisdom of age, the knowledge that nothing is as valuable as simple breathing, "simply being alive even with all the regret of having to remember and the anguish of an irreparable worn-out body" (350). Throughout *A Fable* the call of a bird is simultaneously an affirmation of life and a harbinger of death. Levine, a chauvinistic flyer upset by the false armistice and its suppression by the combined general staffs, hears a lark's cry just before committing suicide. So does the disgraced general in charge of the French regiment that refuses to make an advance: "And sure enough, there was the lark again, incredible and serene, and then again the unbearable golden silence, so that he wanted to clap his hands to his ears, bury his head, until at last the lark once more relieved it" (37).

Of equal significance is the aura of silence which, as in the above passage, almost always accompanies the call of a bird. The murmur of a suffering crowd of people rises "into the incredible silence like a chirping of lost birds, forlorn and defenseless" (321). Such references to moments of silence suggest the stilled guns of the armistice as well as the spirit of man that remains uncorrupted by war. Having known warfare since he can remember, Levine believes that during the false armistice he hears silence for the first time in his life. To the men in the trenches the silence of the guns is synonymous with hope for a better world; they wait with "dawning and incredulous hope" (320). The silence of war may be said to represent both Faulkner's affirmation of the human spirit, and his pessimistic view of the conditions that must be satisfied before this spirit can manifest itself. The false armistice is after all unrealistic, and the silence which men hear for the first time is not ordinarily audible. Even when man's last engine is destroyed, the reader of *A Fable* is told, "the silence must be conquered too: the silence in which man had space to think and in consequence act on what he believed he thought or thought he believed" (187).

It is significant that passages in which "silence" is heard usually involve death as well as life. Even the silence of the false armistice is the direct cause of a fraternization which results in the destruction of the German and British regiments that take part. Faulkner seems to be saying that only when man confronts death does he become fully aware of human indestructibility. This paradoxical theme may be compared to the insistence of Charles Bon, in *Absalom, Absalom!*, that human breath is far more important than social abstractions. But Charles Bon goes to meet his death for the sake of what amounts to an abstract value, his refusal to be denied recognition as Thomas Sutpen's part-Negro son. Nancy Mannigoe's redeeming action in *Requiem for a Nun* may also be interpreted as an assertion of values greater than that of simple breathing. In all these works Faulkner affirms a humanistic philosophy which is in part undermined by the dramatic action. The Marshal tries to reconcile the contradiction in *A Fable* by implying that it is man's willingness to die for the sake of moral abstractions that best characterizes the immortality of his spirit. But it is doubtful if this view is a genuine reconciliation, since the conviction that man cannot reach his moral and social goals is not a very substantial basis for optimism. It may well be that Faulkner's confused thinking on this crucial issue is responsible for the excessive wordiness of his recent work. In the effort to raise a pessimistic moral psychology into a source of hope rather than despair, he is forced to rely too heavily upon naked rhetoric, upon meaningless tone and gesture.

This point is supported, in *A Fable*, by the degree to which important patterns of imagery are seldom associated with the acts and obsessions of particular characters, except in a very general sense. The sexual and religious references of *Light in August*, the time symbols of *The Sound and the Fury* and *As I Lay Dying*, and the dark wind of *The Wild Palms* are closely related to specific attitudes and specific characters. In *A Fable* the patterns of imagery and symbolism usually involve underlying situations or themes rather than individual patterns of behavior. The entire novel can be considered a dramatization of a single symbol, the articulate silence of the false armistice. But establishing a theme as abstract as the triumphant spirit of humanity is tantamount to having no theme at all; this fact helps to explain why the action of the novel never seems dramatically real.

Another recurrent image in *A Fable* is that of men "rising erect" and walking without fear. This image occurs several times in the speeches of the Runner and the Quartermaster General before it is expressed dramatically in the ill-fated fraternization of the English and German regiments. In symbolic terms this manifestation of man's idealism is made possible by the period of silence represented by the false armistice. The weakness of this image lies in the fact that even when illustrated by the novel's action it never ceases to be primarily rhetorical, a way of talking about abstract humanity. *A Fable*'s rhetoric, like its symbolism, blends into the dramatic situation too easily and lacks a functional relation to it. Instead of making his language appropriate to individual characters, as in *Absalom, Absalom!* and *Go Down, Moses*, Faulkner seems to be speaking directly to the reader.

The result is a tendency for the various spokesman-characters to fuse with one another, creating the impression of an homogeneous linguistic whole. This is especially evident in the speeches of the Runner, the Marshal, and the Quartermaster General. The Marshal in particular defines human endurance in a language virtually identical not only with the Nobel Prize speech but also with the author's 1930 "Folklore of Speed" review, discussed in Chapter Three. In the *American Mercury* review Faulkner states that man will unite himself with the blind mechanical forces he has created or disappear entirely from the cosmos. This vision of doom persists in *A Fable* with the difference that man will survive—if only as a witness of his self-destruction. Like the Marshal, Faulkner seems to be saying that man will be saved from ultimate disaster by the force of evil propelling him toward it.

Symbolism and rhetoric are essentially literary devices by which characters and events can be equated with general concepts. To be successful, such identifications must remain incomplete. Otherwise there can be no dramatic surface, no living picture of experience, to hold the reader's imagination and only then to be translated into abstract statement. Before Wash Jones in *Absalom, Absalom!* can represent indestructible humanity, he must first be presented as an ineffectual poor-white laborer. If Quentin Compson's rage against time is to be involved with Southern puritanism, it must also express Quentin's personal despair. Ike McCaslin's rhetoric in *Go Down, Moses* is all the more meaningful as a revelation of the Southerner's divided feelings concerning the role of the Negro in the South. As narrative devices, both symbolism and rhetoric must mean something concrete within the magic circle of fiction before suggesting anything beyond. Otherwise they disintegrate into mere words. In this respect the opposition between the Marshal and the Corporal may be contrasted to the conflict between Thomas Sutpen and Charles Bon in *Absalom, Absalom!* Both Sutpen and the Marshal find their hierarchical society threatened by a democratic idealist, who also functions as a rejected son, begotten in the distant past. The two situations differ in that Sutpen's world collapses at this intrusion; the Marshal's is preserved. The latter protects his corrupt society by acknowledging his son and by crushing the reform movement that his son represents. In both novels Faulkner's sympathy is clearly with the underdog. But in *A Fable* the author's admiration for the Corporal's futile dream is at odds with his endorsement of the Marshal's philosophy.

In *Absalom, Absalom!* the moral corruption of Thomas Sutpen illustrates that of Southern society. In *A Fable* the Marshal proclaims the fact of man's innate rapacity, but his own life does not illustrate or embody moral evil except through the author's mechanical account of the character's early sins. The witness-narrators of the earlier novel discuss the South as a whole only in trying to explain Sutpen's behavior. In *A Fable* the Marshal and the other characters discuss the behavior of universal humanity, but seldom that of individual characters. The symbolical connections which in earlier novels are left to the reader's perception are stated and re-stated at great length.

There are many similarities of language and symbolism between the two novels. In *A Fable* there are frequent comparisons between extreme age and extreme youth, or descriptions of old men and women as childlike in appearance. In *Absalom, Absalom!* Miss Rosa Coldfield is frequently described in this way, as when Quentin sees her short legs dangling from a chair like those of a "crucified child" (8). By limiting this manner of description to Miss Rosa, Faulkner heightens its force and establishes a definition of her unique personality. In the later work the description is applied without apparent restriction or control.

There is also a close similarity between Marthe, the Corporal's older sister, and Miss Rosa in their use of such terms as "fatality" and "doom." Marthe takes her infant brother to Beirut and marries a French soldier for the evident purpose of obtaining passage to France, where her brother may fulfill his destiny. "The doom was his," as she puts it, "but at least I was its handmaiden" (292). Miss Rosa attaches herself to Sutpen's fate in a similar way. "O furious mad old man," she imagines herself crying out, "I hold no substance that will fit your dream but I can give you airy space and scope for your delirium" (168). Faulkner is satirical in his portrayal of Miss Rosa's obsession, but he makes no implicit qualification in describing Marthe's. The reader is expected to accept her motivation at its face value: that she is the willing instrument of inescapable destiny.

The Christian imagery of *Light in August* bears close comparison with that of *A Fable*. In both novels Faulkner is concerned with the concept of personal sacrifice. But Joe Christmas, unlike the Corporal, is an inverted or demonic Christ-figure and has no intention of saving any soul, including his own. The imagery which haunts his life and death reflects his Presbyterian upbringing and is not merely the author's comment upon his sacrificial role. Joe comes to accept his personal destiny, in so far as he understands it, but he is never aware of any larger significance. On the contrary, a supernatural background is hinted for the Corporal, and the events of his life parallel Christ's much more closely. He is born in a stable and has a last supper with his twelve disciples. He is betrayed and denied, is given a barbed-wire crown, and so on. Yet the Corporal preaches no doctrine of spiritual salvation. He is not even a rhetorician; his message is his simple faith in the ability of the masses, acting as individuals, to halt wars. It is this faith, and not the Corporal's personality or his ideas, that inspires the enlisted men of four armies to concerted revolt.

The social pessimism of Faulkner's early work is not basically changed in *A Fable;* but it is expressed as a positive, though loosely defined, moral faith. This paradoxical quality of Faulkner's optimism is suggested by his ascribing elements of faith in humanity both to a figure removed from normal social involvement and a character symbolizing social corruption. The Corporal represents the best in each isolated human individual, and the Marshal indicates the reconciliation with evil necessary before human goodness can justify moral and social optimism. The unresolved conflict of the novel is not so much between the son's idealism and the father's cynicism, as between Faulkner's social despair and his use of that despair as a basis for humanistic faith. Associated with this conflict of tone is a separation between the dramatic action and the language by which it is described and interpreted. As a character the Marshal is made the deliberate agent of the Corporal's failure to stop the war. But as the author's spokesman he tries to employ that failure as proof of the interrelationship of good and evil and of man's ability to endure his own "deathless folly." He steals the Corporal's moral thunder, and relegates the latter to social ineffectuality. Like *A Fable* itself, the Corporal's mission turns out to be a splendid failure.

Chapter Eleven

❦

THE SNOPES TRILOGY

*W*ITH THE DEATH of Flem Snopes in *The Mansion,* Faulkner brings to an end the cycle of events set in motion by *The Hamlet* (1940) and continued in *The Town* (1957). Yet it is misleading to think of the three novels as an artistic unit. *The Hamlet* is based upon a number of short stories published originally in the early thirties. *The Town* incorporates two stories published at this time, and both it and *The Mansion* contain widespread references to earlier novels and stories. But the extent of these references suggests a conscious effort on Faulkner's part to write social history, or at least to give a realistic picture of the modern South. The frequent result is that stylized elements retained from *The Hamlet* seem out of place in this new city of Jefferson, Mississippi. In *The Hamlet* the Snopes family is an antisocial force destined paradoxically to fill the social vacuum created by the decline of the local aristocracy. In *The Town* and *The Mansion* Faulkner is true to his prediction that Flem Snopes will become president of the Sartoris bank. But the author's new realism has intervened, and the clan as a whole fails to take over Jefferson as it did the village of Frenchman's Bend. At the end of *The Town* only two important Snopeses are left in the city, Flem and Wall (Street Panic) Snopes. Flem is a respectable figure, and Wall has turned his back on Snopesism, becoming a wealthy and public-spirited merchant. The Snopes menace entirely evaporates in *The Mansion,* and society is again controlled by men of good will. Snopesism is brought more in line with actuality, but at the expense of its fictional *raison d'etre.*

The first criticism that treated Faulkner's work with understanding emphasized the social mythology which it seemed to contain. It is likely that Faulkner was influenced by this criticism or found that it supported the increased self-consciousness of his Yoknapatawpha County work. But a distinction must be drawn between a social mythology which is merely added to a fictional narrative, and a mythology which is part and parcel of a stylized text. What is missing in *The Town* and *The Mansion* is the sense of a special imaginative world of which the reader, abandoning realistic standards, can make himself an integral part. In *The Mansion* the detailed County references distract the reader from any such special awareness; they intrude upon the elements of stylization rather than compensate for them. Thus the reader is led past Joanna Burden's mailbox (*Light in August*) and told that Chick Mallison (*Intruder in the Dust*) goes hunting with Benbow Sartoris (*Sartoris*). He learns that Jason Compson escapes his financial doldrums (*The Sound and the Fury*), only to lose his money again to Flem Snopes. Benjy Compson is returned from the state asylum to the Compson mansion and, like Henry Sutpen in *Absalom, Absalom!,* burns to death within it. And so on.

In a prefatory note to *The Mansion,* Faulkner anticipates the reader's discovery of "discrepancies and contradictions" and explains that he has "learned, he believes, more about the human heart and its dilemma than he knew thirty-four years ago; and is sure that, having lived with them that long time, he knows the characters in this chronicle better than he did then." It is significant that Faulkner wants to defend his discrepancies and contradictions, but it is even more significant that *The Mansion,* in contrast to *The Town,* is re-

markably tidy in its County references. It may be compared to a
new work of history, in that incontrovertible facts and details are
put into a context of new facts and subjected to new explanations
and interpretations. The historical tidiness of *The Mansion* may be
ironically contrasted to the appendix added to *The Sound and
the Fury* years after the novel's original publication. In this appendix Faulkner permits himself numerous errors of fact, but he is
faithful to his original characterization. However, in completing the
Snopes trilogy he makes radical changes in characterization, as well
as in style and theme.

This change is illustrated by what happens to Flem Snopes and
Eula Varner. In *The Hamlet* Flem Snopes is devoid of human personality, and his thoughts, if he has any, are inscrutable. "Flem
Snopes dont even tell himself what he is up to. Not if he was laying
in bed with himself in a empty house in the dark of the moon"
(284). In *The Town* and *The Mansion* there is little comedy in his
misdeeds, and he is given normal powers of introspection as well as
conventional doubts and fears. The transformation of Eula Varner
is even more striking. As Flem's wife she sheds both her obesity and
her role as earth-mother or sexual matrix. It is scarcely less astonish-
ing to see her smoking cigarettes and attending church functions
than to find her inspiring a constant and strangely platonic devotion
in a young Gavin Stevens, fresh from Harvard. Her husband's impotence, an inheritance from *The Hamlet,* has the principal function
of explaining Eula's new role as the faithful mistress of Mayor Man-
fred de Spain, the son of Major de Spain in *Go Down, Moses.*

The fact that much of the action of *The Town* is predetermined
by the predictions as well as the characterizations of *The Hamlet*
and to some extent of *Sartoris* creates for the author many structural
problems. Chief among them is the necessity of explaining the rise
to financial power in Jefferson of a man as unpopular with his fellow citizens as Flem Snopes. Faulkner solves this problem by having
Flem become vice-president of the Sartoris bank, not under old
Bayard as stated in *Sartoris,* but under young de Spain, who is not
mentioned in the earlier novel. The introduction of de Spain as
Eula's lover is an obvious means of explaining Flem's rise to power.
He gets political help from the new bank president and financial
support from Will Varner, Eula's father. Another source of assistance

is Gavin Stevens, who wants to make sure that Eula is formally accepted by Jefferson society.

Years later, the lawyer carries out a soda-fountain romance with Linda, Eula's daughter. This affair is concluded by Gavin's convincing Linda that Flem really is her father—how this untruth could save anyone's soul is not made clear—and by his shipping her off to Greenwich Village to get an education. This gesture symbolizes hope for the South as well as for Linda's future. But the lie that buys that freedom only tightens Flem's grip on Jefferson respectability. And it is never clear whether it is Flem or Southern society, or both, that Linda escapes.

The characterization of Gavin Stevens represents the most serious weakness of the novel. In his other Yoknapatawpha County appearances he is sometimes an ineffectual witness and sometimes a behind-the-scenes moral agent, like the psychiatrist of T. S. Eliot's *The Cocktail Party*. In *The Town* Stevens is still primarily a detached witness, but he has an important role in the action. His involvement with Eula and her daughter is emphasized even though he has almost no influence upon the lives of the other characters. A significant comparison can be made between Gavin Stevens of this novel and Horace Benbow of *Sartoris* and *Sanctuary*. Both are idealistic Jefferson lawyers, and both lack a full understanding of the evil they seek to combat. Gavin is almost the last person in the novel to realize that "respectability" and not social chaos is Flem Snopes's aim. However, the differences between the two characters cover the full range of Faulkner's work. Horace is a futile aesthete, consumed by despair, who imposes his moral impotence upon everything he does. Gavin Stevens is also blinded by his abstract intelligence, but his characterization indicates Faulkner's effort to modify his customary treatment of human reason as self-destructive, and moral idealism as ineffectual.

A significant detail involving Gavin Stevens in *The Town* is identical to an event concerning Horace Benbow in *Sartoris*. Like Horace, Gavin experiences the first World War not as a soldier, nor even for long as a stretcher bearer, but as a YMCA official—a position of which the author of *Sartoris* is clearly scornful. Horace takes with him Montgomery Ward Snopes, whom he wishes to reform. When asked about this Snopes, his face clouds over "with a fine cold distaste"; "I was very much disappointed in him. I don't even care to talk about it" (173). Gavin Stevens has the same companion and makes the same comment. "Don't mention that name to me again. I wont discuss it. I will not" (107). In borrowing from his earlier work, Faulkner apparently wants to introduce this obnoxious Snopes figure to the action of *The Town*. But the result is the fusion of two characters who represent opposed points of view.

The relationship between Horace Benbow and Gavin Stevens is not the only way in which *Sartoris*, the author's first Yoknapatawpha novel, is linked to *The Town*. The Sartoris bank is a dominant symbol in both works, and *Sartoris* events are retold in *The Town*. Faulkner continues the tale of Byron Snopes, the bank clerk who writes scandalous letters to Narcissa Benbow and who absconds in both novels with a small percentage of the bank's funds. The Narcissa Benbow episode is ignored, but the last few pages describe the appearance of Byron's half-Indian children in Jefferson. This event parallels in structure the arrival of Flem Snopes at the novel's beginning. The Snopes children symbolize, through outward savagery, the destructive force of the antisocial Snopes principle. But Flem has become a church deacon, and Byron's children are quickly expelled. The world in which Sartoris males are consumed by a self-destructive social puritanism changes to a world in which Sartorises and Snopeses join forces in maintaining respectability. Jefferson, Mississippi, has no outside force, only itself, to fear.

One of the incidents of *The Hamlet* involves Mink Snopes, who ambushes and murders Jack Houston after a court judgment in which he is required to pay Houston three dollars for pasturage of Mink's strayed yearling bull. In *The Town* Mink is described as "the only mean Snopes" because of the absence of a profit motive in the crime: Mink does not try to rob his victim until another Snopes reminds him of the possibility. When Mink is brought to trial to be sentenced to life imprisonment he expects his cousin Flem to help him, but Flem fails to appear. In writing *The Mansion* Faulkner uses this incident, the details of which are slightly changed, in order to round out Flem's life history. Thus Mink believes that Flem has violated the obligations of kinship and resolves to kill him.

The manner of Flem's death in *The Mansion* is similar to that of

Thomas Sutpen in *Absalom, Absalom!* Wash Jones's feeling of kinship with Sutpen stems from the poor-white's faith that he and his wealthy landlord belong to the same social class and that Sutpen will at least respect his dignity as a free human being. He murders Sutpen when the latter denies that fundamental dignity and by implication contradicts the social idealism which he, Sutpen, had originally proclaimed. The rags-to-riches career of Flem Snopes parallels that of Sutpen, with the important exception that Flem has no admirable qualities, and his success represents the downfall and not the apotheosis of the Southern aristocracy. Consequently the theme of self-destruction implicit within the manner of Flem's death has the effect of negating the theme, introduced in *The Hamlet,* of a Snopes triumph over Jefferson society. At the end of *The Mansion,* as at the end of *The Town,* there are virtually no Snopeses left in Jefferson and certainly none of any importance. Even Clarence Snopes, of the State Legislature, is defeated for Congress by means of a practical joke for which Ratliff is partially responsible—a reversal of Flem Snopes's defeat of Ratliff in *The Hamlet.*

The alteration in the presentation of Snopesism reflects in part a modification of Faulkner's own social pessimism. But more important is the change in Faulkner's manner of expressing or dramatizing his social concerns. In *The Hamlet* the social theme is initially embedded in the personalities of such characters as Flem Snopes and Eula Varner. The dramatic action in which they appear is more a stylized revelation of what these characters represent than the author's effort to create a realistic social scene. To some extent the Yoknapatawpha environment of *The Hamlet* and earlier novels is a device for modifying the gap between these stylized characters and the reader's social experience. Although Yoknapatawpha references may give the reader the impression of a realistic environment, they are often tailored to harmonize with Faulkner's bizarre characterization. In *The Town* and *The Mansion* the protective covering is not present and the reader discovers Flem and Eula Snopes confronting what is meant to approximate twentieth-century society: the world of Greenwich Village, of Loyalist Spain, and of Mississippi television sets. Instead of dominating their new environment, the important characters, drawn largely from earlier works, are radically transformed. The author can still claim that Eula has only one hair permanent in her life, and that one just before her suicide. But this is a rather small victory for the genius that created *The Hamlet* to wrest from an encroaching realism.

As in other recent Faulkner novels, the scenes involving Gavin Stevens are sources of structural weakness. In *The Town* Gavin's effort to free Linda Snopes from Snopesism culminates in his convincing her that Flem really is her father: "now that I know he is my father, it's all right. I'm glad. I want her to have loved, to have been happy.—I can cry now" (346). In *The Mansion* Linda has presumably outgrown this sentimental attitude and the focus of her relation to Stevens is more complex. Her escape to Greenwich Village leads to her cohabitation with and eventual marriage to a sculptor, a Communist, who takes her with him to fight in Spain. After her husband's death and the complete loss of her hearing, she returns to Jefferson.

The narrators of *The Mansion* devote much attention to an explanation of why Gavin and Linda never marry, in spite of their love and close relationship. Probably the true reason lies outside the novel, in the fact that the Gavin Stevens of *Knight's Gambit* is described as marrying Melisandre Backus, the mother of two children. In writing *The Mansion* Faulkner was careful to incorporate already-published Yoknapatawpha County details, even though in some cases there were conflicting ones to choose from.

Faulkner creates the impression, unusual for his work, of a Yoknapatawpha County world no different in kind and not much in degree from historical and geographical reality. The result is that the elements of stylization traceable to Faulkner's earlier techniques appear contrived and occasionally distasteful in the new Jefferson, Mississippi. Conversely, narrative elements that could be justified upon the grounds of social realism appear at odds in a milieu still haunted by the Sartorises and the Compsons.

At best the passages of *The Mansion* involving Mink Snopes act to redeem the novel's weaknesses. For example, Faulkner cleverly contrasts the Jefferson (Oxford), Mississippi of 1908, which Mink visits before going to prison, with the Memphis, Tennessee, of 1946, where he goes after his term is over. However, the elaborate discussion of Mink's reasons for killing Houston is far less convincing than the bizarre description of Mink's fighting off Houston's dog in *The*

Hamlet or his effort to force Houston's body into its hiding place, in a hollow tree, by jumping up and down on it. Mink's characterization is typical of *The Mansion* in that he loses most of his "rattlesnake" quality and, by implication, the essential Snopesism that underlies his earlier role.

The style of *The Town* and *The Mansion,* much less pretentious than that of *A Fable,* is no disgrace to the author of *The Sound and the Fury* and *Light in August.* But passages expressing the full quality and scope of Faulkner's narrative genius are relatively scarce, and when they do appear they seem to lack the close relationship to structure and theme that characterizes his great novels. Toward the end of *The Mansion* Mink Snopes experiences the enduring power of the primitive earth, a force that opposes his rational will and its murderous design. Mink avoids sleeping too close to the ground because, as he imagines it, "once you laid flat on the ground, right away the earth started in to draw you back down into it. The very moment you were born out of your mother's body, the power and drag of the earth was already at work on you" (402). After shooting Flem Snopes, Mink has no desire to resist this primitive force, and he even invites the rest and peace which it affords.

The passages describing this power of the land have little to do with other aspects of Mink's characterization, or with the rest of the novel. But it is a typical Faulkner theme in the extreme contrast indicated between the male world of rational or at least wilful endeavor and what is called, in this context, "the old patient biding unhurried ground" (403). The strength of this theme is so great in Faulkner's work that where it is present, in *The Mansion* as in earlier novels, the conventional boundaries of narrative realism are often ignored. The novel ends with a rhetorical eulogy of the panorama of human joy and suffering, "the passions and hopes and skeers, the justice and the injustice and the griefs, leaving the folks themselves easy now, all mixed and jumbled up comfortable and easy so wouldn't nobody even know or even care who was which any more" (435). Mink Snopes, in flight from the law, literally loses himself in the author's humanistic vision.

To SAY that the entirety of human experience can be a novelist's theme is to voice an absurdity. But Faulkner's work can be viewed as an extraordinary attempt to transform the panorama of man's social experience into thematic material. His two-dimensional characters, his rhetorical circumlocutions, and his technical experiments are efforts to achieve a dramatic focus upon material too unwieldy, at least in principle, for any kind of fictional condensation. Faulkner makes use of devices of stylization that apply to virtually every aspect of his successful novels. For example, the complex facts of Southern history and culture are reduced to the scale of a simplified and yet grandiose social mythology: the degeneration of the white aristocracy, the rise of Snopesism, and the white Southerner's gradual recognition of his latent sense of racial guilt. Within Faulkner's fictional universe human psychology takes the form of absolute distinctions between puritan and nonpuritan characters, between individuals corrupted by moral rationality and those who are simultaneously free of moral corruption and social involvement. Faulkner does not hesitate to place his characters in absurd situations and have them behave unrealistically. He often manipulates the point of view of narration with little regard for chronological sequence and even less concern for the reader's effort to follow the action. In fact important narrative details are often withheld or obscured in order to sharpen the reader's attention and increase his sense of involvement in the fictional situation.

In this way Faulkner is able to create the impression of a comprehensive treatment of important social concerns and universal moral issues. The world of a Faulkner novel can be understood in its entirety in a way that the complex and ambiguous details of ordinary experience cannot be grasped. Once having created a stylized world, with its simplification of realistic issues and concerns, Faulkner describes this world as if it embodied the full complexity of human experience. He generates an atmosphere of mystery and importance about his characters, and reveals only gradually the stylized obsessions which dominate their actions. Like Henry James, he makes as much as he can of clearly defined dramatic events, until they seem to echo the potential complexity and depth of situations outside the realm of fiction. When this technique is successful the reader is left with the impression that he knows a Faulkner character far better than he could know an actual person. At the same time the character retains the atmosphere of complexity and mystery imposed upon it by Faulkner's handling of style and structure. This method of characterization reflects Faulkner's simplifications of experience and yet suggests the inadequacy of any rigid interpretation of actual human behavior. The reader is supplied with special eyeglasses by which the tragedy of the South, as well as man's general inhumanity to man, can be viewed in a perspective of simultaneous mystery and symbolic clarity.

In generating an atmosphere of universal truth the novelist must solve the paradox of symbolic representation, the fact that qualities which make a character comprehensible as a symbol tend to deprive that character of dramatic uniqueness. The novelist is caught between the need to create a transparent symbol and the equally urgent need to make the symbol sufficiently opaque to embody what is being symbolized. Faulkner solves this artistic problem by simultaneously accentuating and concealing the elements of arbitrary stylization. The behavior of significant characters is revealed to the reader in full dramatic vividness, but the underlying thoughts and motivations, which are keys to the characters' universality, remain elusive—at least until the novel approaches its conclusion.

The situation of "Old Man" illustrates this technique. Although the convict's actions, and even his thoughts and feelings, are directly reported, the reader can obtain at first only a confused notion of the convict's personality. Only when the nature and extent of the hero's stylization are fully grasped can his actions be understood. And such a comprehension is difficult, if not impossible, unless the reader knows other Faulkner works, in particular the companion work, "Wild Palms." Nevertheless, the reader immediately senses the consistency of Faulkner's technique and is persuaded by the brilliance of isolated passages to seek a total comprehension.

In a striking passage the convict is forced into anguished recognition of his inability to control rationally the natural world around him. Having been told that he must evacuate an area where dynamiting is scheduled, he refuses to admit that his plans must be changed. The following morning he boards his skiff and starts off toward the region where he and his partner have been hunting alligators. Not only is he unwilling to quit the place he has been warned against, "he must establish and affirm the irrevocable finality of his refusal by penetrating even further and deeper into it."

But then and without warning "the high fierce drowsing of his solitude gathered itself and struck at him . . . the sudden cessation of
the paddle, the skiff shooting on for a moment yet while he thought,
What? What? Then, *No. No. No,* as the silence and solitude and
emptiness roared down upon him in a jeering bellow" (269). Although the convict's moment of extreme loneliness is intensely personal, it is closely related to his stylized puritanism, to his helpless
rage at natural facts that cannot be ignored. In this manner the
"high fierce drowsing" of the convict's solitude is given archetypal
or universal status. Faulkner creates a symbol for human loneliness
by first creating a believable, though unrealistic, dramatic situation
and a character who in spite of his stylization is capable of strong
personal feeling.

Throughout his work Faulkner demonstrates this ability to create
characters whose loneliness functions both as a dramatic fact and
as a psychological theme. In *The Sound and the Fury* Quentin
Compson's personal despair, or sense of irrevocable isolation, is related to his puritan meddling with the lives of others. In *As I Lay
Dying* the individual members of the Bundren family are motivated
by secret and lonely desires that are in strong contrast to the apparent solidarity of the family venture. Darl Bundren's madness is
the price he pays for a full understanding of human loneliness, of
how "the clotting which is you" (458) struggles to preserve its
identity in the relentless flux of time. The moral themes of *Light in
August* are directly related to Joe Christmas's puritan loneliness. But
his loneliness is only a product of his desperate search for moral
absolution. Human isolation is implicitly identified in such novels
with the search for selfhood in a dynamic and time-ridden world.
An individual's sense of isolation is never a quality imposed upon
him by circumstances; it is rooted in human nature, and circumstances only bring to light its destructive consequences. Loneliness
has its particular origin at the heart of puritan self-consciousness,
when man tries to create a bulwark of morality and reason against
the fear that nothing in this world really matters. Only Faulkner's
nonrational characters are free of the destructive fluctuation between moral pride and amoral despair. His primitive characters are
never lonely; they never see themselves as isolated human agents.

Faulkner's success in portraying human loneliness lies in the fact that only individuals can be lonely—and the characters of his early novels are always individuals. But in Faulkner's later novels a character's sense of isolation is treated primarily as an abstract or universal theme. The opposition between man and his social world becomes a question of philosophy and not of dramatic organization.

In the jail section of *Requiem for a Nun* the narrator discusses a girl's name and a Civil War date scratched in a glass window. This forlorn gesture, this signature by a "frail and workless" hand (229), annihilates time and space to affirm the indestructible human dream: *"Listen, stranger; this was myself: this was I"* (262). In *A Fable*, during the silence which falls upon war, a single gun is heard, directed at some vast but immune target: "at cosmos, space, infinity, lifting its voice against the Absolute, the ultimate I-Am, harmless: the iron maw of Dis, toothless, unwearyable, incapable, bellowing" (57).

In such passages, loneliness is associated rhetorically with abstract humanity. Simultaneously it becomes a cause less for despair than for transcendental affirmation, a theme related in *A Fable* to the Marshal's faith in irrevocable human evil. The loneliest experience of all, the reader is told in this novel, is just breathing. But in its identification with the human condition, the concept of loneliness loses all personal meaning. Only by declining to state such identifications can the novelist successfully establish them. In his best work Faulkner demonstrates that loneliness is a particular, never a universal state of mind. Loneliness is not an abstract concept of human experience but the world in which each individual must live.

A NOTE ON *THE REIVERS*

PUBLISHED SHORTLY BEFORE Faulkner's death, *The Reivers* is a satisfactory work in many respects. It contains a minimum of disturbing rhetoric and illustrates its author's command of narrative craft and his power as a comic writer. Like *The Town* and *The Mansion*, this work echoes many aspects of previously published novels and stories. But *The Reivers* is better organized than its two predecessors, and is relatively free of the excessive moralizing and the inappropriate stylization that mar their dramatic surface.

The action of *The Reivers* takes place in 1905, although it is narrated in 1961, and describes the escapades of three characters associated in various ways with the McCaslin family. The events take place when the narrator, Lucius Priest, is an eleven-year-old boy very much in awe of his grandfather, who has married into the McCaslin family and is president of the oldest Jefferson bank. The boy's adult friend, Boon Hogganbeck, is imported from *Go Down, Moses* and given a job in the livery stable kept by Lucius's father. The third major figure is a Negro farm servant, who calls himself "Ned William McCaslin Jefferson Mississippi" and is just as proud of his white McCaslin ancestry as is Lucas Beauchamp of *Intruder in the Dust*. Although Ned often plays the buffoon before white adults, his influence over the boy at times suggests the moral discipline which Sam Fathers exacts from young Ike McCaslin in "The Bear." The trip which Boon and Lucius make to Memphis also recalls the trip taken to that city by Ike and Boon in the *Go Down, Moses* story. However, Boon passes through a metamorphosis which is the reverse of his drunken collapse in "The Bear." He begins *The Reivers* in a wild rage and concludes its action by marrying a reformed prostitute and fathering a male child, named Lucius Priest Hogganbeck.

Several barely related plot situations or actions dominate the comic structure of *The Reivers.* The three reivers (or petty thieves) take advantage of the absence of the boy's grandfather and borrow his new automobile, one of the first in Jefferson. Driving to Memphis, they stay in Miss Reba's brothel, made famous in Faulkner's *Sanctuary.* Once the reivers are in Memphis, they find their automobile exchanged for a thoroughbred horse, which according to Ned must be raced in a neighboring Tennessee town as an indirect means of getting the automobile back. Like the theft of a racehorse in *A Fable,* where the motive is to prevent putting the best horse in the world to stud, the events leading up to and culminating in the horse's victory are given a transcendental significance. The boy describes the climactic race as what "all the finagling and dodging and manipulating and scrabbling around" (213) had been leading up to, and he defines his own responsibility in riding the horse as "a mystical condition which a boy of only eleven should not really be called to shoulder" (224).

The result is a serio-comic saga in which ridiculous and unbelievable events are filtered through the boy's serious narration and his retrospective view of the total adventure as an initiation rite into manhood. Much of the novel's humor, like that of *As I Lay Dying,* stems from the disparity between solemn characters and their absurd behavior. But the narrator occasionally contributes an ironic commentary or encourages the reader in other ways to take the action as comic. While the reivers are still in Jefferson the primary source of comedy is the white man's social world. The patterns of behavior thus exposed range from Boon Hogganbeck's murderous rage at being ridiculed by a Negro ("I never said he was norrerasted," the Negro insists, "I said he was norrer-headed" [15]) to Grandfather Priest's buying an automobile, which he does not intend to use, merely because the president of the younger town bank has had a law passed keeping automobiles off Jefferson streets. Reference is made to Grandmother Priest's way of expressing anger at her husband. Instead of calling him "Mr. Priest," as is usual, she calls him by his given name, "as though she were no kin to him" (38). Her annoyance, in this instance, stems from a slapstick scene in which Grandfather Priest, unaccustomed to the speed of automobiles, spits tobacco juice into his wife's face. On future trips the riders in the back seat use a screen which they immediately raise into position every time the old man turns his head.

Perhaps the best single episode of the novel involves the failure of the three reivers to push their automobile past Hell Creek bottom, where the road to Memphis resembles "a big receptacle of milk-infused coffee from which protruded here and there a few forlorn impotent hopeless odds and ends of sticks and brush and logs and an occasional hump of actual earth which looked startlingly like it had been deliberately thrown up by a plow" (84). The road has in fact been plowed by a Charon-surrogate figure, described as a "mudfarmer," who waits until travelers are thoroughly bogged down before helping them out at an exorbitant price. He charges extra for each passenger, in spite of Boon's objection that when Ned gets his mud washed off "he aint even white!" "The man looked at distance awhile. Then he looked at Boon. 'Son,' he said, 'both these mules is color-blind'" (91).

Another source of comedy is the visit of Boon and his young companion to the brothel. Miss Reba has not yet picked up the voluminous folds of fat described in *Sanctuary*, or the two desperate dogs that console her for the loss of Mr. Binford. In fact the real Mr. Binford, the "landlord" who pays bills and talks to the police, is happily introduced to the reader. The Memphis scenes of *The Reivers* seem flat and dull only by comparison to richer scenes in *Sanctuary*, where situations are saved from slapstick only by underworld grotesquerie and the tough precision of the narrator's language. This is especially true of Miss Reba's reference to "Us poor girls" (*Sanot.* 173) or her continuous lament over Mr. Binford's death: "'We was happy as two doves . . . As two doves,' she roared in a harsh, choking voice" (189). Just returned from church, she waves in one hand a tankard of beer, the dogs furiously licking at it, and in the other a wooden rosary: "She drank beer, breathing thickly into the tankard, the other hand, ringed with yellow diamonds as large as gravel, lost among the lush billows of her breast" (171). The young Miss Reba of *The Reivers* also wears diamonds, but the effect is not the same. To Lucius she has a "kind hard handsome face and hair that was too red, with two of the biggest yellowish-colored diamonds I ever saw in her ears" (98–99).

Faulkner exploits in *The Reivers*, as in *Sanctuary*, the comic situation in which innocent young males are introduced to a brothel. But the plight of the two young men in the earlier novel, who believe they are staying in a boarding house, is more stylized and much more amusing. The *Sanctuary* hayseeds associate the strong aroma of sexual desire with the city itself and not with their respectable landlady and her daughters: "They could hear the city, evocative and strange, imminent and remote; threat and promise both—a deep steady sound upon which invisible lights glittered and wavered: colored coiling shapes of splendor in which already women were beginning to move in suave attitudes of new delights and strange nostalgic promises" (233). But the eleven-year-old Lucius smells the significance of the place from the moment he steps inside: "I didn't dislike it; I was just surprised. I mean, as soon as I smelled it, it was like a smell I had been waiting all my life to smell" (99). Finally, one may compare the mudfarmer's "color-blind" joke in *The Reivers* to its equivalent in *Sanctuary*. When Clarence Snopes takes his country cousins to a brothel much cheaper than Miss Reba's, one of them objects that the girls are Negroes. " 'Course they're niggers,' Clarence said. 'But see this?' he waved a banknote in his cousin's face. 'This stuff is color-blind' " (239).

The relative weakness of the brothel humor in *The Reivers*, when compared to that of *Sanctuary*, stems from Faulkner's commitment to the boy's point of view and the consequent difficulty of contrasting reality and innocent illusion. Moreover, the boy is incapable of making such a mistake as the country boys' belief that the lattice vestibule before the front door is a privy; to Lucius it only resembles a well house. In striving for comedy Faulkner is forced to emphasize the boy's naive and rather cute remarks ("Maybe they've all gone to early prayer meeting") and Boon's ironical replies ("No . . . I dont think so. Likely they're just resting" [97]). Effective comedy is created when Lucius asks if any men live there and Boon answers "Dont no men actively live here except Mr Binford" (106). But such passages conceal sordid realities that in *Sanctuary* are fully evident, even though slop jars are dressed in "fluted rose-colored paper" (*Sanct.* 186).

In *Sanctuary* reference is made to a beer-snitching boy of five or six, Uncle Bud, who belongs to one of the prostitutes and is on vacation from an Arkansas farm. The reader of *The Reivers* is introduced to a similar although older figure, a stunted youth named Otis, who steals Minnie's gold tooth while the Negro maid is sleeping. Both in his physical deformity and in his view of the world, Otis resembles the adolescent that Popeye of *Sanctuary* might have been. Faulkner's humor is at its broadest in Otis's conversations with Lucius, especially in the creature's description of his making a peephole and selling tickets to watch his aunt's business life. The reader may be reminded of Popeye's sexual perversion in *Sanctuary* and of the similar ticket sale in *The Hamlet,* where the attraction is Ike Snopes and his cow. But Faulkner's art has radically changed and the outraged narrator of *The Reivers* drains the scene of any grotesque humor it might contain: "I was hitting, clawing, kicking not at one wizened ten-year-old boy, but at . . . all who had participated in her debasement: not only the two panders, but the insensitive blackguard children and the brutal and shameless men who paid their pennies to watch her defenseless and undefended and unavenged degradation" (157).

There are numerous references in early chapters to the conflict between Lucius's desire to go to Memphis and his need, if he does go, to tell lies to his family. The embrace of "non-virtue" entailed in the theft of the automobile, as well as the brothel visit, suggests a pattern of values that is the antithesis of conventional Jefferson morality. This aspect of the novel is supported by the narrator's ironic view of Southern social traditions and his sentimental treatment both of Miss Reba's establishment and of the human weakness by which it flourishes. At the same time the boy's flight from home is transformed into an indirect expression of traditional courage and honor (he is not even punished) and the prostitutes are deprived of the legitimate reality of the evil which they represent. In the episodes involving the three reivers and their borrowed horse, Lightning, this reconciliation of opposed attitudes and values becomes increasingly evident. It is suggested by the appearance of Miss Reba and Otis's aunt, Everbe Corinthia alias Miss Corrie, in the guise of respectable white women on a country visit. Everbe has an innocent heart, as well as the proverbial golden one, and her Pamela-like decision to be virtuous brings about the transformation of Boon's lust into a love sufficient for marriage

However, the reconciliation is achieved more by the unrealistic softening of opposed extremes than by any effort to hold extremes in dramatic tension. Grandfather Priest is not disturbed by Miss Reba's association with his grandson and even gives her a public ride in his automobile.

Throughout the novel sentimentality pervades also the humorous descriptions of aristocratic manners and implicit social differences between white and Negro. In earlier novels Faulkner often condemns the moral rigidity of the Deep South aristocracy, and upon occasion he satirizes its values, as in the burlesque rhetoric attributed to Rosa Coldfield in *Absalom, Absalom!* and in the *Go Down, Moses* passage describing the inability of Uncle Buck and Uncle Buddy McCaslin to free the slaves they do not wish to have. But prior to *The Reivers* Faulkner hardly ever laughs at his own social heritage, as he laughs at the poor-white farmers of the country regions around Jefferson. The relative weakness of *The Town* and *The Mansion* can be partially explained in terms of the absence of laughter directed at Snopesism, once it has become respectable. In *The Reivers* the narrator is alive to the comedy of aristocratic manners, but he nevertheless accepts its underlying values. The result is a humor that remains superficial—sometimes the absence of humor when the situation would appear to warrant it. Toward the end of the novel the description of three aristocrats sipping their inevitable toddies and deciding the fate of Negro and white retainers seems tinged with a faint irony, as if Faulkner were deliberately stylizing the scene for comic purposes. Yet the three figures represent genuine *dei ex machina* and the potential satire never breaks the dramatic surface.

Throughout *The Reivers* Faulkner maintains a running joke about the inability of any self-respecting Negro to refer to Boon as "Mister" Boon Hogganbeck. But there is no hint in the novel of Negro restiveness under a social system which requires such absurdities. In fact Ned McCaslin thinks and acts in a manner consistent with the aristocratic image of how Negroes should behave. He conceals both his intelligence and his pride, and indicates not only that he accepts his social position, but that he prefers it. "If you could just be a nigger one Saturday night," he tells the boy's grandfather, "you wouldn't never want to be a white man again as long

as you live" (291). When the aristocrats condescend to drink
whiskey with Ned, he obliges with proper embarrassment and
gulps the first drink down, leaving the second untouched. Ned's
proud behavior is comparable to that of Lucas Beauchamp, in
Intruder in the Dust, who insists that Gavin Stevens give him a
receipt for payment of a two-dollar legal fee, for helping to save
Lucas's life. But in the earlier novel Lucas deliberately refuses to act
like a "nigger," whereas Ned seems pleased enough with the term
and only wants to stretch out its meaning. In this respect he
resembles Miss Reba, who openly calls herself and Everbe "whores,"
as if she were more anxious to change what the term implies than
to avoid its application.

Contradictions and weaknesses of tone of this sort are associated
with contradictions between the moral importance given the
horse-race episodes and what is implied by the rest of the novel.
In spite of Lightning's victory, the elaborate scheme to recover
the automobile is technically a failure. The auto is evidently recovered prior to the race by police action instigated by Grandfather Priest. The boy's worst fears are realized, in that winning
the race proves to be of relatively little importance, except as an
existentialist assertion of human dignity. Yet this aspect of the
race is undermined by elements of pure farce for which the reader
is paradoxically grateful. For example, the horse has the annoying
habit of refusing to run in front of any other horse, and only its
strange love for sardines enables Ned to persuade it to win. Moreover, the adventurers must look to external aid at several crucial
points. First of all, they must pay the "mudfarmer" in order to
get their car past Hell Creek bottom. This necessity is comparable
to Lucius's need to strike the opposition horse illegally in order to
keep from losing the crucial middle heat of the race. The other
horse still passes the finish line first, but only by running outside the
rail. In both cases the result is marvelous comedy, but less funny
passages, which depend for impact upon integrity of theme, are
thereby weakened.

The reivers are also forced to rely excessively upon help provided
by Sam Caldwell, who is introduced for this sole purpose. If you
want something done quietly and efficiently, Ned tells Lucius and
the reader, "you hunt around until you finds somebody like Mr Sam

Caldwell, and turn it over to him. You member that. Folks around Jefferson could use some of him. They could use a heap of Sam Caldwells" (167). In previous Faulkner novels it is always primitive figures undoctrinated into the ways of society that do what the quiet world needs to have done.

Another weakness is the fact that Everbe breaks her solemn promise to Lucius that she will never prostitute herself again. She drives Boon to distraction by her unexpected virtue but surrenders to an obnoxious deputy policeman named Butch. Her purpose is to free the reivers from jail, so they can continue with plans to race Lightning, but it is a surrender all the same. Although Butch is the novel's closest approximation to a villain, excluding the ineffectual Otis, he is the one character to achieve an immediate and unambiguous goal. Even more comically puzzling is the reaction of Boon, who strikes wildly at the policeman not out of jealousy, or so he claims, but because Butch has called his "wife" a whore.

Such structural flaws are no less prevalent in earlier works in which Faulkner tries to dramatize his faith in the ability of human endurance and suffering to conquer evil. But in *The Reivers* the success of individual comic passages more than compensates for the weaknesses. *The Reivers* is by no means comparable to Faulkner's best work, but it does exhibit a satisfactory solution to the problem of conflicting themes and techniques in the later novels. If Faulkner had lived, it is likely that *The Reivers* would have proved the model for similar triumphs of craft and heart over difficulties of characterization and theme.

SELECTED FAULKNER WORKS

Soldiers' Pay. New York: Boni and Liveright, 1926.

Mosquitoes. New York: Boni and Liveright, 1927.

Sartoris. New York: Harcourt, Brace, 1929.

The Sound and the Fury. New York: Jonathan Cape and Harrison Smith, 1929. Modern Library Edition (with *As I Lay Dying*), 1946.

As I Lay Dying. New York: Cape and Smith, 1930. Modern Library Edition (with *The Sound and the Fury*), 1946.

Sanctuary. New York: Cape and Smith, 1931. Modern Library Edition, 1932.

Light in August. New York: Harrison Smith and Robert Haas, 1932. Modern Library Edition, 1950.

Pylon. New York: Smith and Haas, 1935.

Absalom, Absalom! New York: Random House, 1936. Modern Library Edition, 1951.

The Unvanquished. New York: Random House, 1938.

The Wild Palms. New York: Random House, 1939.

The Hamlet. New York: Random House, 1940. Modern Library Edition, 1956.

Go Down, Moses and Other Stories. New York: Random House, 1942. Modern Library Edition, 1955.

Intruder in the Dust. New York: Random House, 1948.

Knight's Gambit. New York: Random House, 1949.

Collected Stories of William Faulkner. New York: Random House, 1950.

Requiem for a Nun. New York: Random House, 1951.

A Fable. New York: Random House, 1954.

The Town. New York: Random House, 1957.

The Mansion. New York: Random House, 1959.

The Reivers. New York: Random House, 1962.

NOTE: Page references in this critical study are to first editions where Modern Library editions are not available.

INDEX

Absalom, Absalom!: general discussion of, 37–38, 149–170; narration of, 12, 76, 77, 81–82, 83, 150, 163–165, 170; narrative technique in, 37–38, 76, 77, 149–151, 153–156, 163–165, 192, 193; social theme in, 17, 37–38, 40, 81–82, 149–170 *passim,* 212; narrative structure of, 20, 37–38, 149–150, 156–157, 163–165, 170; compared to *The House of the Seven Gables,* 25; compared to *Sartoris,* 40; fusion of past and present in, 76; witness narrators in, 76, 82; language of, 77, 82–83, 154; as tragedy, 149, 154–155, 170; and the reader, 150; Gothic atmosphere of, 151; Goodhue Coldfield in, 151; Christian imagery in, 154, 166; mercantile imagery in, 155–156; Jim Bond in, 156, 165; Charles Bon's octoroon mistress in, 157–158, 162–163, 169; puritanism analyzed in, 157–159, 162–163; Thomas Sutpen's youth in, 160–162; Shreve McCannon in, 164–165; "mindless meat" passage in, 165–166; identity theme in, 165–166, 168; Valery Bon in, 166; compared to *A Fable,* 190–193; mentioned, 5, 6, 10, 11, 14, 15, 21, 56, 58, 59, 77, 78, 93, 99, 180, 196, 199–200, 212. SEE ALSO Bon, Charles; Coldfield, Rosa; Compson, Jason (Mr. Compson); Compson, Quentin; Jones, Wash; Sutpen, Henry; Sutpen, Thomas

Addie Bundren. SEE Bundren, Addie

allegory: and Yoknapatawpha County, 11, 14. SEE ALSO characterization; social theme

"All the Dead Pilots": compared to *Soldiers' Pay,* 31

American Mercury review in: 28, 191

Anderson, Sherwood: 23, 32

Anse Bundren. SEE Bundren, Anse

aristocracy, Southern. SEE puritanism; social theme; Yoknapatawpha County

As I Lay Dying: general discussion of, 57–59, 71–74, 108–130; narrative technique of, 6, 24, 71–74, 113–116, 123–130, 205; lack of social theme in, 11, 58, 109–110, 122; comic structure of, 17, 57–58, 60, 110–111, 115–116, 130; compared to *The Wild Palms,* 57, 58–59; puritan characters in, 59; witness figures in, 73–74; language of, 75–76, 123–130; flood and time imagery in, 77, 79, 109, 122–126, 129–130; compared to *The Sound and the Fury,* 108–115 *passim;* existence theme in, 114, 119–122, 123–126, 128–130; and the reader, 115–116; Addie Bundren's monologue in, 116–118, 126; significance of burial in, 117–118, 121; Jewel's horse in, 119–120, 125–126; Vardaman's fish in, 119–120, 127; rain-and-wagon scene in, 121; "wet seed wild" passage in, 125, 128, 129; Dewey Dell's dream in, 127; loneliness theme in, 205; mentioned, 10, 11, 12, 17, 61–64 *passim,* 69, 75, 76,

217

119–120; and Darl, 119–120, 121–
122; and Jewel's horse, 125–126;
and eye imagery, 127. SEE ALSO *As
I Lay Dying*
—family: personal tragedies of, 17;
general, 109–110, 115–116; contrasted to Compson family, 115.
SEE ALSO Bundren, Addie; Bundren, Anse; Bundren, Darl; Bundren, Dewey Dell; Bundren, Jewel;
Bundren, Vardaman; *As I Lay Dying*
Burden, Joanna: and Joe Christmas,
134, 136–139; symbolism of name,
138. SEE ALSO *Light in August*
—family: 133–134, 135–138. SEE
ALSO Burden, Joanna; *Light in August*
Byron Bunch. SEE Bunch, Byron

Caddy Compson. SEE Compson, Candace (Caddy)
Caroline Compson. SEE Compson,
Caroline (Mrs. Compson)
Cash Bundren. SEE Bundren, Cash
characterization: general discussion
of, 14–22, 41–60 *passim;* in the
novel and romance, 3–5; and social
theme, 4, 78; and Yoknapatawpha
County, 12–13; and puritanism, 14–
22, 45, 59, 60; and moral statement,
19; of primitive figures, 20–21; and
narrative structure, 21–22; and
symbolism, 23, 47; in later novels,
78–79. SEE ALSO narration, technique of; primitive figures; puritanism
Charles Bon. SEE Bon, Charles
Charlotte Rittenmeyer. SEE Rittenmeyer, Charlotte
Chase, Richard: 42
Chick Mallison. SEE Mallison, Chick
Christian imagery: and puritan characterization, 23–24; in *The Sound
and the Fury*, 24, 39–40; in *Light in
August*, 24, 43, 75, 135–136, 138,
142–143, 145–148, 193; in *Go

Down, Moses*, 24, 175; in *A Fable*,
24, 193; in *Absalom, Absalom!*, 154,
166; in *Requiem for a Nun*, 182.
SEE ALSO imagery (and symbolism); language; puritanism; social
theme
Christmas, Joe: general description
of, 41–47, 131–148; and social
theme, 14, 131–132, 145, 147–148;
puritan guilt of, 14–15, 41–44, 131–
139, 145–148; and Lena Grove, 20,
41–44, 47, 140–141; Negro blood
of, 41, 137, 139–140; and street
imagery, 41, 140; sense of destiny
of, 41–45; harmony with nature of,
43; and the McEacherns, 43–44,
132, 135; and wind imagery, 44–
45; stylization of, 47; and Christian
imagery, 75, 145–147; and Doc
Hines, 132; early life of, 132, 134–
135; puritan hatreds of, 134–136;
and Negro girl, 135; and Old Testament sacrifice, 135–136; and Joanna
Burden, 136–138; significance of
death of, 139–140, 141, 145, 147–
148; contrasted to Joe Brown, 141–
142; contrasted to Gail Hightower,
143; and Percy Grimm, 145, 147;
and loneliness theme, 205. SEE ALSO
Light in August
—compared to: Thomas Sutpen, 17;
Nancy Mannigoe, 19; Valery Bon,
166; the Corporal, 193
chronology, contradiction in: 146
Civil War, the: and Yoknapatawpha
County, 10, 13; in *Sartoris*, 35, 183;
in *The Unvanquished*, 36–37; in
Absalom, Absalom!, 37–38, 150,
151, 168, 169–170; in *Light in August*, 142, 144; in *Requiem for a
Nun*, 183
Clarence Snopes. SEE Snopes, Clarence
Cocktail Party, The: 198
Coldfield, Rosa: as narrator, 77, 150–
152, 154–155; and Thomas Sutpen,
77, 152–153, 193; puritan emotionalism of, 151–153; loves Charles
Bon, 152; and Wash Jones, 152;

goes to Sutpen's Hundred, 153, 164; language of, 154–155; compared to Marthe (*A Fable*), 193. SEE ALSO *Absalom, Absalom!*

Collins, Carvel: 88

comic structure: and social theme, 11; in *The Hamlet*, 16, 49–51; in *The Wild Palms*, 16, 56–57, 59, 60; in *As I Lay Dying*, 17, 57–58, 60, 110–111, 115–116, 130; in *The Reivers*, 207–211, 214. SEE ALSO characterization; narration, technique of

Compson, Benjamin (Benjy): general discussion of, 64–65, 88–91, 98, 107; as social outsider, 20; as Christ symbol, 24; and Dilsey, 39; 89, 105–106; narrates monologue, 64–65, 70, 88–90; loves Caddy, 65, 88–89; compared to id, 88–89; and mother, 89; moral role of, 88, 89; contrasted to Quentin Compson, 90, 98, 101; smells death, 101; description of, 107; compared to Vardaman Bundren, 114; death of (*The Mansion*), 196. SEE ALSO *Sound and the Fury, The*

—, Candace (Caddy): general discussion of, 89–93; as victim of puritanism, 20–21; and Quentin Compson, 39, 90–93, 94, 98; loves Benjy, 89–91; promiscuity of, 90–91, 92; moral role of, 91; marriage of, 92, 93, 98; and Jason Compson, 101–102; compared to Dewey Dell Bundren, 113, 127. SEE ALSO Compson, Quentin; *Sound and the Fury, The*

—, Caroline (Mrs. Compson): general discussion of, 104–105; lacks social function, 38; moral failure of, 97, 99, 105; and Benjy Compson, 89; and Jason Compson, 104–105; and Dilsey, 105. SEE ALSO *Sound and the Fury, The*

—, Jason: general discussion of, 101–104; as decadent aristocrat, 13, 16; repudiates heritage, 38–39; narrates monologue, 70; cruelty of, 89; exploits Caddy, 101, 102; and time

imagery, 102; contrasted to Flem Snopes, 103; persecutes niece, 103–104; and mother, 104–105; is universalized, 107; and Flem Snopes (*The Mansion*), 196. SEE ALSO *Sound and the Fury, The*

—, Jason (Mr. Compson): corruption of, 38; fatalism of, 94; and Quentin Compson, 94–95, 99–101; sense of irony of, 99; decayed gentility of, 99–100; in *Absalom, Absalom!*, 99, 150, 153–155, 164; analyzes puritanism (*Absalom, Absalom!*), 156–159, 162–163. SEE ALSO *Sound and the Fury, The*

—, Quentin: general discussion of, 65–69, 90–101; as narrator of *Absalom, Absalom!*, 12, 38, 76, 153, 164–165, 170; as decadent aristocrat, 16; as Hamlet figure, 18; puritanism of, 21, 88, 92–93, 96; and the South, 38, 165; suicide of, 39, 40, 94–96, 100–101; and Caddy Compson, 39, 90–93, 94, 98; as own historian, 67; and Henry Sutpen, 76, 93, 165; contrasted to Benjy Compson, 90, 98, 101; incest claim of, 93–94; and grandfather's watch, 94, 95; and despair theme, 100–101; compared to Darl Bundren, 109, 114, 122, 124; compared to Addie Bundren, 118; and Rosa Coldfield, 153. SEE ALSO *Absalom, Absalom!*; *Sound and the Fury, The*

—family: as narrators of *Absalom, Absalom!*, 10, 150–154, 156–159 passim; in *The Sound and the Fury*, 38–39, 97, 99–100. SEE ALSO Compson, Benjy; Compson, Candace (Caddy); Compson, Caroline (Mrs. Compson); Compson, Jason; Compson, Jason (Mr. Compson); Compson, Quentin

Convict, the (*The Wild Palms*): general discussion of, 54–57; puritanism of, 15–16, 51–52, 54–55, 59; and Harry Wilbourne, 51–52, 54, 56; as hero and fool, 57; compared to

Index

Index

125–126; death, 127; eyes, 127–128; immobility, 128–129

—in *A Fable:* Christian, 24, 193; bird, 189; silence, 189–191

—in *Go Down, Moses:* Christian, 24, 175

—in *The Hamlet:* time, 50

—in *Light in August:* Christian, 24, 43, 75, 135–136, 138, 142–143, 145–148, 193; urn, 41, 135, 142; geometrical shape, 42–43, 77; time, 42–43, 140–141; immobility, 43, 44, 132–133, 140–141; wind, 44–45, 77

—in *Sanctuary:* 75

—in *The Sound and the Fury:* Christian, 24, 39–40; time, 40, 77, 88, 94–97, 100–102, 105–106, 109, 129–130, 122–126 *passim;* shadow, 77, 92, 97–98; water, 91–92, 97, 98; death, 92–93, 100–101; honeysuckle, 97; mirror, 98

—in *The Wild Palms:* time and flood, 55–56; wind, 190

immobility imagery: and puritanism, 132–133; in *Light in August,* 43–44, 132–133, 140–141; in *As I Lay Dying,* 128–130. SEE ALSO imagery (and symbolism); language; puritanism; time, imagery of

Intruder in the Dust: general discussion of, 179–181; conflict of tone in, 18; primitive figures in, 18–19; social and moral theme in 78, 179–180; mentioned, 7, 10, 11, 46, 76, 196, 207, 213. SEE ALSO Beauchamp, Lucas; Mallison, Chick; Stevens, Gavin

intuition. SEE primitive figures

Isaac (Ike) McCaslin. SEE McCaslin, Ike

James, Henry: on novel and romance, 3, 7; compared to Faulkner, 25, 61, 203; sentences of, 82

Jason Compson. SEE Compson, Jason

Jewel Bundren. SEE Bundren, Jewel

Joanna Burden. SEE Burden, Joanna

Joe Christmas. SEE Christmas, Joe

John Sartoris. SEE Sartoris, John

Jones, Wash: and Rosa Coldfield, 152: compared to Charles Bon, 169; kills Thomas Sutpen, 169–170, 200; and moral and social theme, 170, 192. SEE ALSO *Absalom, Absalom!*

Joyce, James: compared to Faulkner, 12; interior monologues of, 22, 61–64, 69, 74, 81; and use of symbolism, 24; *Ulysses* of, 22, 62–63, 65, 69; *Finnegan's Wake* of, 63. SEE ALSO narration, technique of

Judith Sutpen. SEE Sutpen, Judith

Keats, John: 41

King Lear: 170

Knight's Gambit: 7, 10, 201. SEE ALSO Stevens, Gavin

language: general discussion of, 75–79, 82–83; and primitive figures, 47–48; and symbolism, 48; and characterization, 48, 76–79; and witness figures, 76; and human truth, 81; and psychological analysis, 81; and saturated sentences, 82–83. SEE ALSO imagery (and symbolism); narration, technique of

—in individual novels: *A Fable,* 19, 188, 190–194; *Mosquitoes,* 33; *Light in August,* 42–44, 75, 145–148; *Sanctuary,* 75, 210–211; *The Sound and the Fury,* 75–76, 97–98; 106–107; *As I Lay Dying,* 75–76, 123–130; *Absalom, Absalom!,* 77, 82–83, 153–156; *Requiem for a Nun,* 78–79, 183; *The Mansion,* 202; *The Reivers,* 209–213

Lena Grove. SEE Grove, Lena

Light in August: general discussion of, 41–47, 131–148; and puritanism, 14, 15, 17, 20, 41–47, 131–148 *passim;* and social theme, 14, 15, 131–132, 134, 137, 139–140, 145, 147; narrative technique in, 17, 20, 41–47, 74–75, 140–142, 145–148, 193, 205; Percy Grimm in, 21, 145, 147; Christian imagery in, 24, 43, 75, 135–136, 138, 142–143, 145–

223

Index

154; and mercantile imagery, 156; inhuman moral code of, 156, 162; early life of, 159, 162, 167; dilemma of, 160, 167–168; hates Negroes, 160–161; "boy-symbol" of, 161, 167; rifle analogy of, 162; and Valery Bon, 166; and Henry Sutpen, 167; and Charles Bon, 167–169; dehumanization of, 169–170; and Wash Jones, 169–170. SEE ALSO *Absalom, Absalom!*

symbolism: and European novel, 22; and moral theme, 40; and stylized characters, 47; and narrative point of view, 75–77; and witness figures, 77; and psychological analysis, 81–82. SEE ALSO imagery (and symbolism); language

Temple Drake (Stevens). SEE Drake, Temple (Stevens)

Thomas Sutpen. SEE Sutpen, Thomas

Thompson, Lawrance: 98

time, imagery of: and puritanism, 50, 58, 77; and nature (*The Hamlet*), 50; in *Light in August*, 42–43, 140–141; in *The Wild Palms*, 56; in *The Sound and the Fury*, 40, 77, 88, 94–97, 100–102, 105–106, 109, 129–130, 122–126 *passim;* in *As I Lay Dying*, 109, 122–126, 129–130; in *As I Lay Dying* and *The Sound and the Fury* compared, 124. SEE ALSO despair, theme of; identity, theme of; imagery (and symbolism); immobility, imagery of; language; primitive figures; puritanism

Town, The: and *The Mansion*, 195–202; Linda Snopes in, 198, 201; Byron Snopes in, 199; realism of, 200; and *The Hamlet*, 195–197, 199–202; and *Sartoris*, 197, 199; and *The Reivers*, 207; mentioned, 2, 10, 12, 13, 49, 76, 173, 212. SEE ALSO Snopes, Flem; Stevens, Gavin; Varner, Eula (Snopes)

Trilling, Lionel: 23

Ulysses: 22, 62–63, 65, 69

Unvanquished, The: compared to *Sartoris*, 36–37; mentioned, 10

Valery Bon. SEE Bon, Valery

Vardaman Bundren. SEE Bundren, Vardaman

Varner, Eula (Snopes): primitivism of, 16, 49–50; description of, 48; in *The Hamlet*, 48–51; and the schoolmaster, 48, 50; and Flem Snopes, 49–50, 197; moral role of, 174; characterization of, 197; in *The Town* and *The Mansion*, 197, 200–201. SEE ALSO *Hamlet, The*

Wash Jones. SEE Jones, Wash

Waves, The: 62

Wilbourne, Harry: puritan guilt of, 15–16, 20, 51–54, 60; compared to the Convict, 51–52, 54, 56; and Charlotte Rittenmeyer, 52–54. SEE ALSO *Wild Palms, The*

"Wild Palms." SEE *The Wild Palms*

Wild Palms, The: general discussion of, 51–57; and puritanism, 15–16, 51–53, 59; narrative structure of, 20; as tragicomedy, 52; time and flood imagery in, 55–56; compared to *As I Lay Dying*, 57, 59; lacks primitive figures, 60; wind imagery in, 190; and loneliness theme, 204–205; mentioned, 11. SEE ALSO Convict, the; Rittenmeyer, Charlotte; Wilbourne, Harry

wind, imagery of: and puritanism, 44–45; in *Light in August*, 44–45, 77; in *Sanctuary*, 75; in *As I Lay Dying*, 125–126. SEE ALSO identity, theme of; imagery (and symbolism); language; puritanism

Wolfe, Thomas: 22

Woolf, Virginia: 22, 61, 62, 81

Yoknapatawpha County: general discussion of, 9–14; and comic works

229

11; and psychological analysis, 11, 81; and the reader, 12–13; and character stylization, 12–13; and symbolism, 81–82. SEE ALSO puritanism; social theme

—in individual novels: *Sanctuary*, 30–31; *Sartoris*, 34–36, 37, 40; *The Unvanquished*, 36; *Absalom, Absalom!*, 37–38, 40; *The Sound and the Fury*, 38–39, 40; *Requiem for a Nun*, 183–184; *The Town* and *The Mansion*, 195–202 *passim*